Frank Worrall is a journalist who writes regularly for *The Sunday Times* and *The Sun*. He is also the author of the No 1 bestseller *Roy Keane: Red Man Walking*, *Rooney: Wayne's World* and *Lewis Hamilton – The Biography*.

THE
MAGNIFICENT
SEVENS

**THEY ALL WORE THE NO 7 SHIRT.
THIS IS THE STORY OF THE FINEST HEROES FROM
THE GREATEST CLUB IN THE WORLD.**

FRANK WORRALL

JOHN BLAKE

Published by John Blake Publishing Ltd,
3 Bramber Court, 2 Bramber Road,
London W14 9PB, England

www.blake.co.uk

First published in paperback in 2008

ISBN: 978-1-84454-609-1

British Library Cataloguing-in-Publication Data:

A catalogue record for this book is available from the British Library.

Design by www.envydesign.co.uk

Printed and bound in Great Britain by Creative Print & Design, Blaina, Wales

1 3 5 7 9 10 8 6 4 2

Papers used by John Blake Publishing are natural, recyclable products made
from wood grown in sustainable forests. The manufacturing processes
conform to the environmental regulations of the country of origin.

This book is dedicated to my mother, Barbara

Acknowledgements

My sincere thanks go to:
Director of Football – John Blake
General Manager – Michelle Signore
Manager – Andy Bucklow of the *Mail on Sunday*
Assistant Managers – Nick Chapman of the *Sun*, Alex Butler
of the *Sunday Times*, Lee Clayton of the *Daily Mail*
First-Teamers – Angela, Natty, Bob, Gill, Alex and Lucy,
Stephen, Suzanne, Michael and William, Frank Sr and
Barbara, Roz Hoskinson
Backroom Staff – Alan Feltham of the *Sun*, Martin Creasy,
Dave Morgan, Paul Hazeldine and Mike Tuck
Supporters – Tim Smith, Derek Whitfield, Nic Petkovic, David
Michael, Collin Forshaw, Russell Forgham
Adrian Baker, Pravina Patel, Alan Tovey, Duncan Craig,
Ian Rondeau, Mike O'Brien, Hugh Sleight, Steven Gordon,
David Burgess, Roy and Pat Stone, Tom Henderson-Smith,
Lee Hassall, Bill, Sharon and Grace, Chase, Debbie and Miles,
Emma Lloyd, Sam Wostear, Natasha Harding of the *Sun*,
Chris Godfrey, Liz Burcher, Paul Collett and Darren O'Driscoll.

Contents

Preface

Manchester United – much to the joy of their followers and dismay of their bitterest opponents – remain the biggest club in the world. From Old Trafford to the Far East, no other football club can match their popularity and unrivalled support. And just as the Red Devils themselves are the stuff of legend, so is the coveted number 7 shirt at the club. It all started when Georgie Best decided it was his favourite number in the late Sixties and early Seventies. Yes, I know he also in his time wore 8 and 11, but it was the 7 shirt that will forever be associated with his greatest triumphs and memories.

Georgie-boy started off a trend that would encompass the greatest players of the next four decades – Bryan Robson in the Eighties, Eric Cantona in the early Nineties, and then David Beckham in the late Nineties and into the millennium. They were all eager to make their mark and earn a place in history as one of United's fabled Magnificent Sevens.

Now Cristiano Ronaldo – who is as much loved by United fans and as reviled by rivals as the club itself after his exploits in the World Cup of 2006 – is the latest to pull on the iconic number 7 shirt and claim he is worthy of it.

All five men have something else in common – they have another side to them, not so much bad as mischievous and controversial. Indeed, it is this darker side that elevated them into the world-beaters they all became, that fuelled their very tunnel-visioned obsession to succeed. They were giants on the field, but human beings struggling with the enormity of a fame few of us can imagine off it. George Best reacted by frequently going AWOL to escape the pressure; Robson liked a drink or two; Beckham and Alex Ferguson famously often did not see eye to eye; Cantona's frustrations erupted in angry outbursts, culminating in his infamous kung-fu kick on a taunting fan; and Ronaldo sent England crazy with his petulance, wicked winks and diving.

Could we have chosen other Sevens? Well, trawling the record books, there were only three other decent candidates – Johnny Berry from the Busby Babes era, Willie Morgan from the Seventies and Stevie Coppell, also from the Seventies and early Eighties. But none of them had the edge to become one of the Sevens – they were, for the most part, 'what-you-see-is-what-you-get' characters. They did not have the devil in them that went hand in hand with genius.

Berry was not a true Babe, in that he was not United bred. He was bought in from Birmingham for £15,000 aged 25 in 1951 and retired from the game after Munich seven years later. In his time at Old Trafford, he made 276 appearances and scored 45 goals and was renowned as being a tricky little winger with a lot of guts. As team-mate Dennis Viollet would say of Johnny, who played four times for England, 'No one had more heart than Berry.'

Willie Morgan was another who gave fine service, but who was hardly of the calibre of George Best, the man he was brought in to replace from Burnley for a fee of £100,000 in 1968. Willie made 304 appearances for United, grabbing 34 goals, and represented his country, Scotland, at the 1974 World Cup Finals.

Stevie Coppell – who took over from Morgan at Old Trafford – was another right-winger renowned for his speedy, direct play. Of the three outsiders for a place in the Magnificent Sevens hall of fame, he remains my personal favourite – an intelligent, constructive player who lit up the Tommy Docherty era of bright, attacking football. Coppell made 496 appearances for United, scoring 70 goals after joining the club from Tranmere for £60,000 aged 20 in 1975. Coppell, who earned 42 England caps, is also famed for appearing in a Manchester United club record 206 consecutive league games between 15 January 1977 and 7 November 1981.

Yet Berry, Morgan and Coppell – the cream of the outsiders for a place in the Magnificent Sevens – remain decent bread-and-butter men in comparison to the five greats – Best, Robson, Cantona, Beckham and Ronaldo – five names you would surely gladly move heaven and earth to see even in this era of high prices and high-tech alternatives. With the help of new interviews and material, my aim is to cast a fresh eye over the famous five who make up United's Magnificent Sevens – and to shed new light on their achievements, their failings and their ultimate legacies.

Frank Worrall, 2008

1

George Does It Best
(1946-68)

*'I was born with a great gift, and sometimes with that comes a
destructive streak. Just as I wanted to outdo everyone when I played,
I had to outdo everyone when we were out on the town.'*
GEORGE BEST

'Unquestionably the greatest.'
SIR ALEX FERGUSON

The more I examine the evidence, the more I arrive at a
rather unexpected conclusion: the closest model we have
in modern-day football to George Best is Roy Keane. Not in
terms of their skills or defined role on the pitch itself, of course,
but certainly if you're talking about their psyche. Best and
Keane had problems at both club and international level when
their respective Manchester United and Irish teams went into
decline. Their innate professionalism – or maybe you would call
it their search for perfectionism – meant they could not tolerate
playing with men they saw as losers.

Up until 1968 – and for this book's purpose, George's life
story splits obligingly into the glory years until that wonderful
Wembley night and his subsequent downfall until he died in
2005 – Best did exactly as it said on the tin. He was simply the
best – possibly in the world – and was certainly a marvellously
innovative pioneer of the glorious magic surrounding United's

number 7 shirt. Yet after the European Cup win against Benfica in 1968, having been named European Player of the Year and Football Writers' Player of the Year, he self-combusted. As United struggled with an ageing, no-longer hungry team, he lost his motivation. That nagging inner dynamo that perpetually spurred him on to be the best meant he could not bear to be in a team that would never again reach the same dizzying heights.

Now, let's consider Keane the footballer, who won a European champion's medal in 1999 and was never to reach the same heights as a player again. Even that dreamy night in Barcelona left Keane with a nagging feel of failure; he would always maintain he did not deserve a winner's gong as he had been ruled out of the final due to suspension. After 26 May 1999, Roy Keane would continually strive to earn that medal and United's failure to take him there would lead to his open criticism at what he saw as the underperformance of his colleagues up to 2005, and his ultimate sacking by Sir Alex Ferguson for speaking out once again in November of that year.

The similarity of the two United icons is also mirrored in their international careers. George Best got sick of turning out for Northern Ireland because he knew they would never achieve anything of note. He would miss games for his country under the pretence of injury rather than play in a poor side. Likewise, Keane blew up over the inadequacies he found in the Republic of Ireland's approach to matches and tournaments. He publicly perceived it to be an amateurish 'we're only here for the craic' approach that turned his stomach and made him ashamed to be an Irishman. It would lead to the furore in the 2002 World Cup Finals and the bust-up with Mick McCarthy that saw him sent home.

Yet, while Best would self-destruct in an unrelenting downwards spiral right up to his death from liver failure in

2005, from the late 1990s Keane found a contentment through his family life – a sanctuary outside of the game. He would play out his career until the end and he, too, would still end up being kicked out of United, but he would not be finished in football or life outside it like poor George, who had become a social misfit until his sad demise.

Poor George? On the surface you could argue that that is nonsense – how can someone have so much going for them and yet be so fragile mentally? It is the question many sports leaders have asked of their charges over the years – they are trained to turn their rough diamonds into sparkling winners, not to become virtual nursemaids.

Former Aston Villa manager John Gregory publicly lambasted his wayward centre-forward Stan Collymore for complaining about his bouts of depression. Now, I am no admirer of Big Stan, but I did feel for him. Gregory held the much-maligned Collymore up for ridicule, saying, 'I find it difficult to understand how anyone in Stan's position, with the talent and the money he has, is stressed. I wonder how a 29-year-old at Rochdale, in the last three months of his contract, with a marriage and three kids, copes with stress. I wonder what he'd be thinking, looking at this.'

Similarly, on paper at least, George had every opportunity to enjoy life to the full. What did he have to gripe about, given his bewildering array of hedonistic riches – the Miss Worlds, the sex, the drink, the cars, the houses? Or as the two quintessential 'laddish' quotes of George's life – both from his own lips – would have it, 'I spent 90 per cent of my money on women, drink and fast cars. The rest I wasted…' and 'A waiter delivering champagne to my hotel room saw thousands of pounds of casino winnings and the current Miss World both arranged tastefully on the bed. The waiter looked at the scene, shook his head and asked the legendary question, "Where did it all go wrong, Mr Best?" '

Years later, when the money had dried up and the birds had flown, a wiser George, armed with much more knowledge of his condition, would nod rather more sagely and say, 'Yes, perhaps that waiter saw something in me that I didn't.'

He suffered badly because of his demons and was also prone to periods of depression. Just as frequently, George was often told to 'pull himself together and just to drink orange juice', but as any intelligent mental health professional will tell you, that does not necessarily help addicts. A psychoanalyst friend of mine told me that they are not in a position to choose to abstain; the craving for the required substance is too powerful to withstand.

Towards the end of his life, George would admit he regretted much – all the high-octane antics could not compensate for what he had missed out on; that he would have liked to have spent more time watching his son Calum grow up; that he loved the moments when he could do a crossword or take a walk with his dogs and spend quality time with his family. In essence, he regretted missing out on what would be termed 'a normal life'.

My psychoanalyst friend puts it like this, 'When not drinking, it is the dream of every alcoholic to find peace in everyday activities and to be seen as a decent human being. But the only peace many do find is by taking another drink – it is a never-ending vicious circle that can lead to them eventually not knowing what is real and what is drink-induced fantasy. Alcoholics are seriously ill people – life is not fun for them, it is more often tortured and black. Many are on a slow, painful, suicidal journey.'

It hadn't started out like that when George moved to

4

Manchester from Belfast aged 15 in 1961, when he literally had the world at his feet. True, there were hints of another side to his character behind that cheeky-boy grin. His first trip to United would last all of 24 hours, ending with him and fellow homesick Irish urchin Eric McMordie heading swiftly back to Belfast. Painfully shy, George was frightened by what he had found at Old Trafford: much bigger boys on the training field and an alien city that did not understand his broad Ulster brogue. Scared maybe and, even at his young age, he would reveal another common trait of the alcoholic-to-be – a feeling of betrayal wrapped up in a series of resentments. As my psychoanalyst adds, 'Injustices, or perceived injustices, are just about the biggest bugbear of any alcoholic. They will drink on them and part of the recovery programme for alcoholics is how to lose the power a grudge has upon them and their lives. You can always tell an alcoholic by the number of grudges he will harbour ... unfortunately, some die because of them.'

As he climbed back on the ferry to Northern Ireland, the young George complained to McMordie that United had not treated them well. It would be a criticism levelled at the club by many – including some aggrieved surviving Busby Babes – over the years and, in George's case, it was undoubtedly a fair one. United had expected a couple of naïve 15-year-olds to make their own way over to Manchester with no travel arrangements and no one to meet them when they disembarked the ferry at Liverpool. He and McMordie had initially ended up at the Old Trafford cricket ground by mistake when they finally arrived at Manchester and, by the end of what George described as an 'intimidating' first day, which finished with them holed up in a lonely guest house, the duo decided to head home.

That United behaved so badly is puzzling given George's obvious potential. Only weeks earlier, Bob Bishop, who had discovered the 15-year-old George playing for Cregagh Boys' Club, had sent the now legendary telegram to Matt Busby, saying, 'I think I've found you a genius.' You might think Busby would have been spurred into action by those unambiguous words and looked out for young Georgie. The boy did return to Old Trafford later the same year, but United could easily have missed out on their greatest talent since Duncan Edwards.

George's homesickness is easy to explain. Born on 22 May 1946, he came from a close-knit family – he was the eldest of six children – and enjoyed a relatively peaceful childhood growing up in a council house on the Cregagh. His father Dickie was a proud man who worked in the Harland and Wolff shipyard; his mother Ann worked in a tobacco factory. Dickie enjoyed football – he played as a full-back at amateur level – while Ann was a fine hockey player.

George would take the usual route to the football field, kicking tennis balls about in the street from the moment he could walk but, surprisingly, he preferred to watch his mother playing hockey than his father on the football pitch. The young George was not affected by the sectarian troubles that would blight the province; they did not take a hold until some time after he had left for England. That is not to say George was unaware of the hornet's nest of emotions religion could stir up in Belfast. Much to the delight of his parents, he made it to the local grammar school, Grosvenor High, but soon became disillusioned with life there.

Part of the problem was that he missed his former primary school friends and the school played rugby, not football – but he also had to face up to religious bigotry. Each day, he had to walk to the school through a Catholic area wearing his Protestant school uniform. 'They would throw stones at me and call me a Proddy bastard,' he said. 'I played truant more and more often and, eventually, mum and dad let me go to the local secondary modern school.'

That meant football when lessons finished and watching Glentoran with his grandfather whenever possible. His English club was Wolverhampton Wanderers and his goalscoring exploits at youth level mirrored those of his Molineux hero, Stan Cullis. At 14, George once scored 12 goals for Cregagh Boys when they won 21-0. Inevitably, the Northern Ireland-based scouts for the big English clubs sat up and took notice and it wasn't long before he was on the boat to Liverpool, then on to Manchester and Old Trafford.

When he finally joined United aged 15 as an amateur on 16 August 1961, George still was only 5ft 1in and weighed just 8st 7lb; Busby ordered his staff to fatten him up – quickly. Landlady Mary Fullaway, who would look after him on and off for his first five years in Manchester, summed it up, saying, 'I wanted to sit him down and fill him full of meat and potatoes.'

George himself had worries of a different nature regarding his size and, yet again, even at this early age, they highlighted his complex character make-up. He said, 'I knew I was good enough and that I could be a great player. But I did feel conspicuous about being so thin and small because I thought the girls wouldn't like me! I know it is hard to believe but, at first, I was shy and scared to chat them up because of it.' It was a 'failing' that would not last long as he filled out thanks to landlady Mrs Fullaway's hearty suppers.

George signed pro forms with United on his 17th birthday in 1963, three days before that year's FA Cup Final, in which United would beat Leicester City 3-1. His first wage was £17 a week – the shy, insecure lad from Belfast was finally on his way to a life he could never have imagined as the first pop star of football. With his delicious skills – he would jink one way, then another, that wonderful low centre of gravity taking him past man after man in the junior and reserve teams – it was only a matter of time before Busby gave him his big break.

Bobby Charlton became aware of just how good the Belfast boy with the dribbling skills would become when he asked the United coach Wilf McGuinness what he thought of the '63 crop of youth team kids. McGuinness said, 'Well, bloody hell, if you think you're a good player you should see this lad who has come in from Belfast.' He then proceeded to tell a stunned Charlton that the boy called George Best would be even better than him.

Four months after the Cup Final at Wembley – which Georgie had watched as an awestruck youngster – the boy Best was making his first team début. The date was 14 September 1963, the opponents were West Bromwich Albion and the match was at Old Trafford, Manchester. Busby had played it cool on the day of the match – in the hope of not making the youngster too nervous – giving no indication that he planned to play George. But a couple of hours before kick-off at the pre-match lunch, he finally whispered the immortal words into George's ear, 'You're in today, son.'

The local paper, the *Manchester Evening News*, best summed the day up, commenting on his 'natural talent' and saying he 'played the game pluckily and finished it in style'. It was certainly a day Albion's experienced full-back Graham Williams would never forget. George nutmegged him and tormented him as United won 1-0 to stay ahead of Albion at the top of the table. Williams would say, 'I wanted to kick him but I couldn't get close enough to him.' Years later, so the famed story goes, Williams met Best at a charity event and pleaded with him, 'Will you stand still for a minute so I can look at your face?'

'Why?' asked George.

'Because all I've ever seen of you,' explained Williams, 'is your arse disappearing down the touchline.'

Busby then employed something of the Alex Ferguson logic by dropping his protégé for a few matches – or, more accurately, protecting him against himself and an ever curious press. George was put in cotton wool until three days after Boxing Day, when he scored United's first goal as they steamrollered Burnley 5-1 at Old Trafford. In 1990, when talking to respected journalist Ross Benson, George gave us an inkling of the 'fix' he would get from walking out for United. His words offer a useful insight as we try to understand what made this complex, emotional man tick. Much in the same way as Jimmy Greaves would a few years earlier admit that he turned to drink after losing the high of playing football in front of thousands, so George spoke of how he felt delirious that winter's day in Manchester. 'I felt marvelous ... I remember walking out of the tunnel and hearing the roar of 54,000 people ... It is like turning on a radio and turning the volume up ... I can still recall the way the hairs on the back of my neck stood up. I was numbed. At the same time, I felt exhilarated.'

Yet, without that adrenalin rush when he left the game, George would be lost. He would lose the fix, and search for it in the bottle, in the bedroom, shops ... in fact, anywhere he thought he might experience that same temporary, exhilarating high. It would be a journey with only one outcome – the inevitable, tragic finale in London's Cromwell Hospital in 2005. Greavsie himself would later confirm the 'black hole' existence footballers felt after retiring, saying, 'I look back at George ... I look back at myself ... same problem as George, same as Gazza ... we all had the same problem ... but I think it might have been lack of pressure, for want of a better word, why we succumbed. I think we missed it. I missed it. It wasn't the pressure of playing that made me start drinking heavily, it was probably the emptiness of not playing.'

One other comment from his chats with Benson is worth noting – how George saw himself as much more than just a winger. He knew the importance of working for the team, tackling back and getting stuck in. He said, 'I learned from experience ... I learned to release the ball to a player in a better position and then run through, making space for the return.'

Over the years, many people have dismissed George as a genius, but a greedy one and, even worse, a lazy one. Immediately prior to starting this book, I looked over a video collection of some of George's performances, and noted rather quickly that that simply was not true. OK, he might not have passed to Law or Charlton if the chance was on for himself, but he did his fair amount of graft for the team.

Graft ... who would have thought we would be using that word to describe Georgie-boy? But he was renowned at United for his work-rate – as a youngster at United he would spend hours working on improving his left foot and, by the late Sixties, that peg was almost as effective as the right one. He was also not afraid to tackle back and give as good as he got from the so-called 'hard men' of the day – indeed, within the club, he was known as one of the best tacklers.

As George would say later, 'Sir Matt always said that I was probably the best tackler at the club, and that was a hell of a compliment. I enjoyed the physical side of it. I had people trying to kick me and, if they took the ball away from me, it was an insult. I wanted it back.' And George made it quite clear what he thought of the thuggish defenders who would try to kick him up in the air. 'I had nothing but contempt for the so-called hard men. For "hard men" read "men who couldn't play".'

Busby had this to say about Best's footballing gifts and strength of character on the pitch. 'George was gifted with more individual ability than I have seen in any other player ... he was certainly unique in the number of his gifts. He was skinny-looking but strong and courageous to a degree that compensated amply. Every aspect of ball control was perfectly natural to him from the start, and he had more confidence in his ability than I have seen in any other sportsman.'

His old pal, chat-show host Michael Parkinson, assessed his determination and talent in this way: 'He was quick, two-footed, beautifully balanced. He could hit long and short passes with equal precision, was swift and fearless in the tackle and he reintroduced the verb "to dribble". He was as imaginative and whimsical in midfield as he was economical and deadly given a chance at goal.'

I asked Bobby Robson where George stood in the all-time rankings. He said, 'Certainly in the top three or four. He was the greatest player from the British Isles and would push Pelé, Puskas, Di Stefano and Maradona for the best ever. I will never forget the first time I saw him and was left almost gasping at his skills. He was that good – his talent would take your breath away. What I particularly loved about him was the way he would take a game by the scruff of the neck and change its outcome. He was always at the centre of things – never merely on the edge of things.'

I put the same question to Sir Alex Ferguson, who said, 'No question about it, he was a genius, someone you would gladly pay to watch. He would have you on the edge of your seat. George will always be a legend here at Old Trafford.'

Despite their differences, when I asked Tommy Docherty about George, he was similarly effusive. 'There is no argument – he was one of the greatest players ever at Man United. In his prime, no one could match him. If I had had him at the top end of his career, I would have built the team around him – and probably have made him my captain.' An interesting one that – about the captaincy – given that Busby's refusal to even consider Georgie as his skipper led to festering resentment and a feeling that he was not appreciated enough.

Arsène Wenger was also a fan. He told me, 'George Best was an artist at the top of his trade. I used to watch him and be beguiled by the effect he could have on a match … how he could turn things around when it seemed all was lost. I think the closest we have to him in the modern game is Thierry Henry and Ronaldinho, but George was different class.'

That doyen of football writers, Brian Glanville, mused about George like this: 'On a football field, he could do anything and everything, the very personification of "Total Football" before it was invented. For, no more than 5ft-8in tall, he could out-jump far bigger opponents to head spectacular goals. His ball control was consummate, his acceleration devastating, he could flip a coin over his shoulder and catch it in the top pocket of his jacket. Kicked, tripped and constantly fouled by tormented defenders, he rarely retaliated and was never intimidated.'

The Times also deftly summed up his footballing genius, all-round talent and mastery in a measured obituary on 25 November 2005, saying, 'George Best was the most talented British football player of his and arguably of any generation. He appeared to play and read the game at a different pace from those around him. He possessed dribbling skills which, in the words of his team-mate Pat Crerand, could leave opposing defenders with "twisted blood", and a balance which enabled him to ride or avert the most ruthless tackles, which his reputation and ability to humiliate the hard men of the game inevitably attracted.

'His goal-scoring record was phenomenal for a winger. Best was quick, brave and a sublime passer of the ball when he could curb his natural inclination to hold on to it for as long as possible. At his best, he gave the impression that thought and execution were a seamless whole and, at all times, he approached the game with the passion and excitement of a young boy. Even the incomparable Pelé once called him "the greatest footballer in the world".'

Ah, yes, those goalscoring feats – George made 466 appearances for Manchester United in all competitions, scoring 178 goals, from 1963–74. By the end of 1964, he was a permanent fixture in the first team and a key component of the so-called Holy Trinity of himself, Denis Law and Bobby Charlton. He was United's top scorer for six consecutive seasons, and also topped the First Division scoring charts in 1967–68 with 28 goals. Not bad for a bloke not considered to be an out-and-out winger. Along the way, he helped United to win the Football League Championship in 1965 and 1967, and the European Cup in 1968. In 1964, he had also pocketed an FA Youth Cup winners' medal, inevitably scoring one of United's goals in their 5-2 aggregate victory over Swindon Town.

Which leads us nicely to his greatest goals and matches. The ones that stand out for me are the 1966 European Cup quarter-final away leg to Benfica, the 1968 European Cup Final, the 8-2 FA Cup win at Northampton in 1970 and the miracle show and strike for San Jose Earthquakes in 1981 – the latter two we will discuss in the next chapter.

His brace of goals in Lisbon in 1966 was perhaps a watershed for George. From being a boy of magical potential, George Best was, literally overnight, transformed into a world-famous footballer and celebrity. Christened 'El Beatle' by a Portuguese newspaper, life would never be the same again for the boy who had to deal with a level of fame and fortune that no previous footballer had experienced.

Looking back at his performance in Lisbon sent shivers down my spine; it was remarkable, even more so when you think George was just 20 at the time and that this was the Benfica of Eusebio, who was presented with the European Footballer of the Year award before kick-off. United had won the first leg 3-2 at Old Trafford, but would it be enough to take to Portugal? Busby's instructions had been to keep it tight for the first 15 minutes and see how things went. With just 12 minutes gone, George had scored twice – once with a header, and the second a moment of magic as he beat three men before shooting past the goalkeeper. Afterwards, Busby turned to George and said wryly, 'You obviously weren't listening.' George's brace in the 5-1 triumph brought about Benfica's first ever home defeat in the competition – they had been unbeaten in 19 matches – and propelled him to stardom.

Football writer David Miller would brilliantly go on to describe George's display as 'fantasy brought to life'. It was not difficult to see how apt that analysis was; George's second goal of the night was undoubtedly one of his best ever, and even he himself accepts that as he explained in his final autobiography, the excellent *Blessed*: 'I dipped a shoulder and swerved inside a defender and I just knew from that point that I was going to score … As I left the second defender trailing behind me, I looked up to see the keeper coming towards me … I knocked it past him … given the situation and the circumstances and the enormity of the game, it has to be one of my favourite goals ever.'

Even in 1966 there were portents that told us George's story would not be a straightforward *Roy of the Rovers* tale like, say, Bobby Charlton's. By now, he was on £160 a week, had a white 3.4-litre Jag, 70 shirts, a 1,000-strong fan club, a full-time secretary and half shares in a booming fashion boutique. Ian Wooldridge, that perceptive and incisive sportswriter of the *Daily Mail*, outlined the dangers facing Georgie-boy. 'He could be destroyed by a broken leg while playing on the wing for Manchester United today,' Wooldridge wrote, 'or he could destroy himself while still searching for something to replace the stern Presbyterian discipline which once packed him off to church thrice every Sunday. It is the second thought that disturbs him daily.'

George backed up Wooldridge's fears by admitting, 'Wednesday 'til Saturday is murder. I know I've got to stay off the town and get to bed by eleven. But it drives me nuts. I don't read. Well, only the sports pages. The only thing that keeps me sane is remembering that there'll be a party on Sunday and Monday and Tuesday.'

Conquering Europe would have to wait for George. United fell to Partizan Belgrade in the semi-finals after their glory win over Benfica, losing 2-0 in the away leg – a match in which George injured a knee and missed the rest of the season. It was an injury that would trouble him throughout his career. United won the home leg 1-0 but went out 2-1 on aggregate, a result that left Busby devastated. He would describe it as his 'lowest ebb' since Munich. More despair would follow that season – with George sidelined, United could only finish fourth in Division One and missed out on Europe.

But after the darkness came the light – and it would now shine brighter than ever before for George and United. The following season, he collected the second of two League Championship medals and then the 1967–68 campaign would prove to be the zenith of George's career. After narrowly overcoming Real Madrid 4-3 on aggregate in the European Cup semi-finals, George and United once again faced Benfica, this time in the final, taking on the two-times winners at Wembley. It was all-square at 1-1 after 90 minutes, with the match heading into extra time after Graca cancelled out a Bobby Charlton header.

Later, George would claim he knew United would win as Busby and his assistant Jimmy Murphy came on the pitch to boost morale at the end of full-time. George said, 'I still felt fresh and full of running. Looking at our players and glancing across at theirs, I knew we had it.' His instinct was correct – now George Best would come into his own, leaving an indelible footprint on world football. Two minutes into extra-time, he used his tremendous pace to leave Benfica captain Mario Coluna in his wake to put United ahead again, majestically slipping the ball around the keeper and gently tapping it over the line. He danced away in triumph, his blue shirt – a special one-off kit for the final – hanging loose over his blue shorts. Two more United goals, the first from 19-year-old Brian Kidd and the other from skipper Charlton, taking the final score to 4-1, followed his moment of personal joy.

Ten years after the Munich air crash, which killed eight of Busby's young team, United and George Best had reached the pinnacle of European football that had been the object of the manager's dreams and ambitions. The Red Devils had become the first English team to win the European Cup and Busby revelled in the moment, triumphant that his own holy grail had now been put to bed. With tears in his eyes, Busby said, 'The players have done us all proud. After Munich, they came back with all their hearts to show everyone what Manchester United are made of. This is the most wonderful thing in my life and I am the proudest man in England. The European Cup has been the ambition of everyone at the club … now we have it, at last.'

George had been United's star player on the night and, just a fortnight after being chosen as the football writers' Footballer of the Year, he was also named European Footballer of the Year. Later, he would almost purr with pride as he spoke of the magical evening in north London. 'That night at Wembley we knocked it about as well as any of the great sides I've ever seen. That night, at least, we were as good as the Real Madrid of the Fifties, the Spurs double team ... anyone you care to mention.'

Truly, in May 1968, Best and Busby had the world at their feet ... but, amazingly, this would be the last footballing honour either man would ever win. At 22, it should have been just the start for an avalanche of further honours for George, not the end of it all. Many years later, Busby would admit how special George was to him, but also how much more he thought he should have achieved. 'Every manager goes through life looking for one great player, praying he'll find one. Just one. I was more lucky than most. I found two – Big Duncan and George. I suppose in their own ways, they both died, didn't they?'

Fair enough, but after 1968, Busby himself should surely have gone on to claim another European triumph? But, just as their glory years were intertwined, so was their decline. Busby seemed exhausted by it all – the despair of Munich, the rebuilding, the false European dawn of 1966, the final crowning glory of 1968. He had nothing more left to give; he was finished and so – although you would never have guessed on that wonderful, captivating Wembley night – was Georgie Best.

By 1972, George had announced his retirement from the game – although he returned to United a year later – and by early 1974 he had left Old Trafford for good. Twenty-nine years later he would even sell off those precious European Footballer of the Year and Footballer of the Year trophies at auction.

So, with the world at your feet, exactly where, why and how did it all go wrong after 1968, Mr Best?

2

Past His Best –
George's Lost Years
(1969-83)

'Getting knocked out of the European Cup feels like the end of the world.
You just want to crawl into a corner and die.'
GEORGE BEST, 1969

'The first 27 years were sheer bliss and the last 27 have been a disaster.'
GEORGE BEST, 2000

The decline kicked in quickly after the European Cup Final victory of 1968. There had been signs that Best was living a hectic life during the previous months but it was as if the club's – and his own – success kept him in check. As soon as their joint fortunes began to ebb quickly away, so did George's willpower and desire to maintain his particular level of genius. As we have already noted, the relative decline of United, the Busby empire and George Best shows the strength of the link between all three, a link that was beyond the power or skill of any one man to break.

In later life, George would admit that he had no fond memories of the celebratory events that followed the final, because he drank himself into oblivion. He said, 'I went out and got drunk ... to be quite honest I don't remember very much about the victory night. I was celebrating and I had every reason to. The skinny, shy little boy who came off the ferry from Belfast

19

seven years before had done his job ... and more. If you look at the results leading up to the game at Wembley, at the goals that were scored, and who scored them, at the final itself, you will see the contribution I made.'

Now no one is arguing against the idea that George deserved to celebrate – even if he ended up completely wasted – after such a night. Most footballers would. But there is a certain hard-to-like arrogance and overblown ego that accompanies his comments that, once again, highlight his problem. As my psychoanalyst friend says, 'An addict – whether it be drugs, alcohol or whatever – has two sides to them. The lovable, almost humble side – the one that is never bloated with ego; and the other rather more unpleasant edge, the one that is ego-ridden, the one that sees the addict blowing his or her own trumpet with rather an unpleasant, "look-at-me" approach. It is a mix of on one side the low self-esteem of the addict, on the other the massive ego, that makes him or her want to prove they are the best.'

I can understand what she is saying in terms of George's state of mind the night of the European Cup Final. He would go on to say, 'It adds up to one thing – if I hadn't been playing for them, I don't think Manchester United would have won the European Cup.' There is a stark difference between George Best and Roy Keane – Roy survived the anguish of *not* playing in United's European Cup-winning side of 1999. He reconstructed himself and, essentially, he became the very essence of a team player.

George Best, on the other hand, imploded after the 1968 triumph, and it was his immature personality and distorted view of himself and his team-mates that sped him down that road to destruction. Is he right that United would not have won the European Cup in 1968 without him? He scored one goal; Charlton grabbed two. OK, George was the star, but United won it without Denis Law that night – just as they won it without Keano in 1999, playing with a midfield that lacked balance and penetration. No, I think there is every chance United would still have won that night at Wembley.

Georgie-boy was rapidly becoming too big for his boots. And the tragedy for him and United was that Busby was too tired and burnt out to keep him on the straight and narrow any more. After 1968, Busby seemed to see him like a prodigal son, as someone whom he knew was riddled with faults, but someone he loved like no other. He turned a blind eye when Best went AWOL or when he didn't cut it in training. Why?

Despite his undoubted craft and inner resilience – what you might term his toughness – at heart, Sir Matt Busby was a cerebral man. When he was made a Freeman of the City of Manchester in 1967, he said this in his thank-you speech: 'Football's great occasions for me are unequalled in the world of sport. I feel a sense of romance, wonder and mystery, a sense of beauty and poetry. The game becomes larger than life. It has something of the timeless magical quality of legend.' It is not difficult to extend that love of 'the timeless magical quality of legend' also to include his favourite footballing son, Georgie Best.

Busby's own son Sandy explained it this way. 'I think Dad found something of the Duncan Edwards in George ... the same brilliance, the same mastery of all the football arts and, in those days at least, the same professionalism. That sounds daft now, but in those days George lived for football, nothing else ... just like Duncan. Dad nearly did give up after Munich; Duncan's death was a terrible shock, and it was only Mum who talked him round. But it was Bestie who restored his faith in football in many ways.'

One particular way in which Best restored Busby's faith was

by helping ease the screaming demons of Munich in his own head by playing a key part in bringing home the European Cup. The pursuit of the trophy had become Busby's great obsession – he led English teams into Europe against the great reservations of the domestic football authorities. He would later admit to feeling guilty about surviving the crash that had killed so many of his Babes – Geoff Bent, Roger Byrne, Eddie Colman, Mark Jones, David Pegg, Liam Whelan, Tommy Taylor and superstar-in-the-making Edwards – especially as he had been the man who had dragged English football into the maelstrom of European competition.

After the crash, doctors in Munich had insisted the news of the deaths be kept from Busby as he recovered from what had been life-threatening injuries. Later, he would recall the anguish he felt as he learned the full tragic truth from his wife Jean. 'I said, "What happened?" She said, "Nothing." So I began to go through the names. She didn't speak at all ... she didn't even look at me. When they were gone, she just shook her head. Dead ... dead ... dead ... dead ... dead ... dead ... dead ... dead.'

Devastated by the loss of his babes, he vowed never to return to football. 'Well, Matt, just please yourself...' said his wife. 'But the boys who have died would have wanted you to carry on.'

It was only after winning the European Cup that he finally felt some sort of peace, admitting, 'That moment when Bobby Charlton took the Cup, it, well ... it cleansed me. It eased the pain of the guilt of going into Europe. It was my justification.'

Busby also believed strongly that George Best would not have strayed so dangerously had Duncan Edwards survived Munich. Edwards would undoubtedly have been the skipper of the side that George excelled in, and Busby was confident he would have kept the wayward Irishman in line, 'He was like George in a lot of ways. The bigger the occasions, the better they both liked it. While other players would be pacing up and down the dressing room rubbing their legs, doing exercises and looking for ways to pass the time, Duncan and George would always remain calm. They would glance through a programme or get changed casually and wait without a trace of tension.

'Duncan was a good type of lad. When I brought [centre-half] Ronnie Cope into the team for that last match at Highbury, I asked Duncan to keep an eye on him and he revelled in that responsibility. Off the field, Duncan did not want to know about the high life. He just wanted to train, play or go back to his digs or home to Dudley. He lived for his football. Maybe some of that would have rubbed off on George if Duncan had survived Munich.'

Given the nature of his own personal exorcism, it is easier to understand why Busby took his hand slightly off the tiller at United after 1968. But for United and Best, the consequences would be little short of disastrous. Without a clearly defined path, United would struggle to regain the glory days; in fact, they were on an inexorable journey of decline that would lead to relegation from the top flight, while George – now working without Busby's discipline – would accelerate towards his own personal oblivion, missing training, getting drunk, fighting, running away and getting involved in some outrageous love affairs, including a just-married bride whom he took upstairs from a hotel bar while his team-mates plied her husband with drink.

In much the same way as you could argue Ferguson should have retired from Old Trafford in 1999, so Busby should have walked away in 1968. The reason why neither left is also much the same – who could possibly have taken over? The club had been built up by Busby, then was rebuilt by Ferguson three decades later. Who had the qualities and talent to walk in their shoes? Nowadays, you could make a case for Martin O'Neill; back then, the only man suitable was the late, great Jock Stein. But, after giving the nod to United in the early Seventies at a secret motorway rendezvous, he then changed his mind at the last minute when his wife Jean demanded he stay at Celtic Park because she simply could not bear the idea of moving away from Glasgow.

At the start of the 1968–69 season, the problems at United were crystal clear – the club needed direction from the manager and some inspired buys in the transfer market. In the previous four years, Busby had splashed out just once – for goalkeeper Alex Stepney. It meant there was nothing to keep the players on their toes – the established stars knew they would play week in, week out, as there were no serious rivals breathing down their necks.

The season would be a wash-out for George. He was sent off for fighting in the World Clubs Cup against the South American champions Estudiantes of Argentina. United's league form was poor and they finished the campaign in eleventh place. They got as far as the semi-finals in the European Cup and, by the end of the season, the glory days were clearly at an end.

George wanted Busby to buy class acts – he knew that Mike England and Alan Ball wanted to come to Old Trafford. Instead, they would end up at Spurs and Everton respectively – and Busby would plump only for winger Willie Morgan. The boss also laughed off George's suggestion that he should be made captain of the team. George could see the downward trend, and his views are eerily similar to those voiced by Keane at Old Trafford. George said, 'I think quite a few players thought we had done what we set out to do, and relaxed a bit. I certainly didn't see it that way. I was only 22 … I wanted to keep winning things, and felt we had every chance of retaining the European Cup.

'My goals became all important, because others weren't scoring them so frequently. Instead of revolving around me, the team now depended on me and I lacked the maturity to handle it. I began to drink more heavily and, on the field, my list of bookings grew longer as my temper grew shorter.

'When the bad times started, I couldn't bear the thought of going out on the pitch. I used to drink so I didn't have to think about it. Which came first? The bad times then the drinking, or the drinking then the bad times? I'm still sure it was the thought of playing in a bad team, of not winning anything, of not having a chance to play in Europe that drove me to it. All right, you could say that if I'd trained and lived properly, United might have stood a better chance of doing well. That's true, but I just couldn't see myself doing it single-handed.'

It would be 31 years before the club were once again crowned champions of Europe and, just eight months after the 1968 triumph, United would announce that an exhausted Busby would move upstairs at the club. Chairman Louis Edwards said, 'Of course, we knew that it had to come but this does not mean that Sir Matt will be any less involved with Manchester United. In fact, the post of General Manager carries even wider responsibilities....'

Indeed, it did – for Busby's hapless successor, Wilf McGuinness, it would take on the form of a poisoned chalice. Every time he made a decision – including dropping George for poor commitment at training or going AWOL – Busby would overrule him. It would be the same problem for McGuinness's successor Frank O'Farrell, and the situation was only truly resolved when Tommy Docherty – hardly a shrinking violet and certainly not in thrall to Busby – took command.

I asked a couple of United experts – Andy Bucklow and Martin Creasy – what they made of the messy end of the Busby reign and how the restructuring at Old Trafford upset George. Bucklow is a senior journalist on the *Mail on Sunday*, and has followed United's fortunes for 40 years. He had some sympathy for Busby's situation in dealing with Britain's first pop star footballer, but felt he should have built his team around George. Bucklow told me, 'It has become common legend down the years that an increasingly benign Busby was too tolerant of his errant, adopted son Best, a tolerance seen by many as an indicator of the decline of the great man's managerial powers. There is, no doubt, a generous dollop of truth in that. George – and his increasingly challenging boozing and birding activities – certainly broke the mould when it came to the disciplining of star players.

'Sir Matt's mettle had been tested before, certainly, most notably by the transfer demand from another member of the Holy Trinity, Denis Law, and, even earlier, by his no-nonsense dealings with Johnny Giles, who was summarily dispatched to Leeds following a row over being played out of position.

'Indeed, during the transitional days of the early Sixties, some of the other more experienced players bought in were openly disrespectful of Matt on coaches going to away games. But these were all football-related activities. Best's off-field behaviour, just as much as his sublime skill, transcended all that had gone before from any previous member of the awkward squad, but Busby should have clamped down on him much harder, and much earlier.

'For all Sir Matt's experience, he never did quite get a handle on Best as the first of the pop star footballers. Sir Matt's later dealings with Best would have been an irrelevant footnote in history had United enjoyed any sort of continuing success after the 1968 European Cup Final win. The old man's failings were more down to failing to build for the future with the Irishman at the fulcrum of a new team, not being too accommodating of his greatest player. Had that happened, Best, as he later admitted himself several times, would have had the incentive to carry on, providing countless more treasured memories for the archives.'

Martin Creasy is a United nut – what you would call a 'superfan'. He has followed the club since the 1960s and has been a season ticket holder since he was a youngster. The first time he witnessed the sublime skills of Georgie-boy was at Stamford Bridge in the 1967–68 season 'when he was kicked all over the park by Chopper Harris and it finished 1-1. George played a part in United's goal, which was scored by an 18-year-old Brian Kidd.' Creasy makes the important point that 'the fact that the number 7 shirt at United is iconic at all is down to George Best. Every subsequent superstar number 7 was proud to wear the shirt in his honour,' and goes on to defend the Irishman's reputation. He told me, 'George was clearly irked during his retirement years when people would say to him that he blew his United career because of the playboy partying and boozing. He would reply that he spent his 11 best years at Old Trafford, a lot more than most players, and he went on to play for years after that.

'As fans, we were regularly put through the wringer as George's personal life unravelled. But, on reflection, I don't think there would have been a happier ending for United, or Georgie's Old Trafford career, if nothing stronger than orange juice had passed the Belfast boy's lips. United were in terminal decline after 1968 and even Besty at his mesmerising best could have done nothing about that. If he was going off the rails, the team was already heading for the buffers. There's no way he could have carried that team. It was a combination of things – lack of motivation, ageing players, injuries – they all played their part.

'It became obvious that achieving Sir Matt's dream of winning the European Cup was enough for those players. The blood, sweat and toil and emotional rollercoaster that ended on that glorious May evening at Wembley in 1968 just couldn't be followed.

'When a player of George's calibre implodes the way he did, the first person under the microscope is the manager. Sir Matt felt the same as a lot of his players. He had completed the dream and he was starting to feel old in an age when the coach was coming to the fore. He believed United needed a younger man at the helm with the energy to get out on the training ground with the players.'

But wasn't Busby too lenient with him when he skipped training after heavy drinking sessions? Creasy said, 'People always said Sir Matt had an iron fist in the velvet glove, but it was never apparent in George's case. He must have been tearing his hair out. He certainly tried everything – sending Georgie back into digs with a landlady as he did when he was a teenager. George even stayed with Paddy Crerand and his family for a while, but that didn't work either. Frank O'Farrell and Wilf McGuinness had no chance of getting through to George, who had been treated more like a son than a player by Sir Matt. Maybe that was the problem, although the only two people who can answer that one for certain are sadly now no longer with us.'

Of course, George knew that the years after 1968 were wasted in terms of career progress. He would say, 'In the end, I became a monster to myself [but] I gave millions of people hours of pleasure for years.' Indeed he did, and the fact that he could still turn it on and enchant the fans after 1968 seemed to bring him some solace, although he would always feel he – and United – could and should have achieved much more.

One of those magical days when he proved he could still turn it on like no one else came in the FA Cup fifth round tie at Northampton in 1970. Inevitably, all eyes were on Georgie-boy after he returned from yet another suspension – this time George had been banned for knocking the ball out of referee Jack Taylor's hand after a League Cup semi-final defeat to Manchester City. Some players return from suspension a little rusty, and it takes them a little while to adjust back into the hurly-burly of top-rank competition. Not George. With a point to prove, he scored six goals that day, the pick of them being the final one when he left a defender for dead and then dribbled round the keeper. Stopping the ball on the goal line, he saluted the United fans like an all-conquering matador before rolling it into the net.

But the days of joy would be fewer and fewer and it would eventually all end in tears at Old Trafford one bleak midwinter's day in 1974. McGuinness and O'Farrell had come and gone, Busby had returned for a temporary stint at the helm, and then, finally, the United board made an appointment that made sense. Enter the Doc, a brash, abrasive Scot, the man who would take United down, but bring them back stronger, the man who would bring the smiles back to Old Trafford with his brilliant, adventurous team of 1976. Gordon Hill and Stevie Coppell would spend their time marauding down the wings and Stuart 'Pancho' Pearson grabbed the goals up front with Sammy McIlroy.

The Docherty era meant a new start at United, a sweeping away of the cobwebs that had gathered as the Busby years had ended in rusty lethargy. For George, though, the new regime would spell the end. Eleven years at the club and not so much as a word of thanks from the new boss, let alone the offer of a testimonial. Yet, looking look back on the bust-up between

George and Docherty, many feel – including me – that the Doc got it right. Not easy to say, or to admit, as we are not talking about any journeyman player here. George had given his heart – and talent – to Manchester United, and may have been able to offer even more in the ensuing years.

The time had come for someone to finally stand up to George and say, 'Look, you can still be the greatest player in the world or you can piss it all up against the wall by continuing as a spoilt playboy. Which is it to be?' Docherty was the man who finally had the guts to tell Georgie the truth rather than wrap him up in cotton wool, protecting him from the realities. The facts were undeniable – George was out of control; his excesses had to be curbed once and for all. Credit to Docherty for his bravery, and for seeing the bigger picture, that of United's long-term goals.

Inevitably, the pair would disagree about the catalyst that led to the final parting on 5 January 1974. Docherty claimed George had missed training due to a New Year's Eve party that had extended into 2 January, and claimed that when the Irishman eventually did materialise, he had a girl on his arm and stank of booze. George denied all the allegations, saying the Doc had given him an extra day off and that he did not arrive with either a girl nor boozed up.

What's absolutely clear is that after United had beaten Plymouth Argyle in the FA Cup on that 5 January, Best sat alone in the empty stands at Old Trafford, tears streaming down his face. He knew the game was up; he had threatened to quit in the past, and had even announced his retirement at a press conference in Marbella in May 1972, just days short of his 26th birthday. But this time it was for real and his tears were a mix of regret, at what had been and what should have been, and rage. He would later lay the blame for his ignominious departure firmly on Docherty's doorstep, saying, 'Tommy Docherty is the reason I finally, unequivocally, quit Manchester United ... I walked out on the club I loved, that had been my family, my life for 11 years, because of Tommy Docherty.'

OK, Bestie was one of the kindest, most generous people you could have hoped to have met when not sozzled, but when under the influence he was, without doubt, stubborn, proud and unwilling to budge an inch ... no wonder it all ended up pear-shaped.

But Docherty certainly was not the cause of George's downfall; George himself was the only man responsible for that. At the time, he could not – would not – see it. In later life, he would admit he had often looked at life through the wrong pair of glasses, but he would never forgive the Doc. My psychoanalyst friend tells me that 'at times of complete breakdown – rock bottom – addicts will sometimes find a way to free themselves of their demons. Alcoholics will go to AA, drug users to NA; it is a window for release, brought about by the complete hopelessness of one's situation.'

Fair enough, so if George hit rock bottom during his life, surely the first occasion would have been around the time of January 1974? But his despair was not enough to 'save him'. 'Some people have such a strong ego, such a strong, overblown sense of self-pride, that they will not try to find a way out,' says my friend. 'They do not think there is anything that wrong with their life – their illness, whether it be alcoholism, drug abuse or co-dependence, is so powerful that it keeps them in a state of denial.'

And so it proved with George. He left United to spend more time trying to fill the aching hole inside him with purely hedonistic solutions – more women, more drink, more highs. His career as a serious work of art was over; post-'74, he became a rolling, drunken mercenary of a footballer, parading his fading talents to the highest bidder, whether that be in Scotland, America or the lower leagues. It was a criminal waste of his talent.

There followed spells with Stockport County, Fulham, Hibernian, Los Angeles Aztecs and San Jose Earthquakes, before George finally retired from the game in 1983 after a brief stint with Bournemouth. Brian Glanville summed it all up like this: 'He had prematurely retired, and when he returned to play for Fulham and in Los Angeles, his girth had increased, the dynamic acceleration had gone and the game was deprived of his marvellous virtuosity.'

Of course, there were also still moments of joy – as we have already mentioned, George would claim his goal for San Jose against Fort Lauderdale in 1981 was his finest ever. George was 35 by now, a little more rotund, a little slower, but the natural skill was still there. He took the ball from a team-mate in the centre circle and then took on a handful of Fort Lauderdale opponents. As he edged towards the box, another three defenders approached – he swerved around them as if they simply weren't there and then lifted the ball over the hapless goalkeeper. Every time I see it, it reminds me of John Barnes's goal for England in the Maracana in Brazil – only it is a better goal than even that piece of genius.

The pick of George's lost years would probably be 1976 and 1977, when he joined Fulham. Brian Glanville says, 'In late 1976, he went back to England [from America] and, along with Bobby Moore, turned out for Fulham, playing 42 games in two seasons and scoring eight goals. He was inevitably slower, but still skilful and adroit.'

Five years after he had left United, George Best would ask the club for a testimonial. They refused. The decision would create a chasm that would see George stay away from Old Trafford for the best part of two decades and increase his resentment at what he saw as the cold-shoulder treatment from the club. While I think Docherty was right to kick him out in 1974, I believe George had a strong case to be granted a testimonial in 1979 – and one can understand his bitterness.

He played for the club from September 1963, when he made his début, until 1 January 1974, when he turned out in his last match, the disappointing 3-0 Division One defeat by Queen's Park Rangers at Loftus Road. It was a total of 11 years' service, but the United board refused him a testimonial on the grounds that he had not played enough games in that timespan.

It was a ridiculously unfair decision; players are usually granted a testimonial after ten years of service, and George had given one more. Moreover, the club's reasoning was hardly logical when you consider that Paddy Crerand had been given a testimonial – and yet had played 160 games fewer, and for only eight years, from 1962–70. George would eventually find allies back in Belfast who were willing to help him out – the Football Association of Northern Ireland.

In 1988, a testimonial match was held for him at Windsor Park, Belfast. Among the crowd were Sir Matt Busby and Bob Bishop, the scout who had discovered George, while those playing included Ossie Ardiles, Pat Jennings and Liam Brady. George scored twice, one goal from outside the box, the other from the penalty spot. With the help of the £72,000 raised by the testimonial match and dinner in Belfast, George was finally able to sort out a life that had been shattered by financial and emotional problems in the 14 years since he had quit United.

It was good of the Irish FA and the locals to treat him so warmly. He had not always had the interests of Northern Ireland at heart during his career – in fact, it would be the truth but a massive understatement to say that his career for his country never managed to achieve anything like the supreme class of the one he had for Manchester United. Without doubt, he was the greatest player to ever pull on the green shirt of Northern Ireland, but he would appear for them just 37 times, scoring 9 goals. The first of those caps arrived on 15 April 1964 when, aged 17, he played, along with Pat Jennings who was also making his début, in Northern Ireland's 3-2 victory over Wales at Swansea. The last game was against the Dutch on 12 October 1977, when, aged 31, he played in the 1-0 defeat at Windsor Park.

Two highlights stand out for me in what was a generally undistinguished international career – the games against Scotland at Windsor Park in 1967 and against England in 1970. George tormented the Scottish defence in that British Home International Championship encounter in 1967, single-handedly destroying them with a dazzling display of skill and mischief and laying on the winning goal for Dave Clements. The brilliant Scottish defender Tommy Gemmell suffered a personal nightmare against George that day. He said, 'George Best was the greatest player I ever faced and, drunk or sober, he could take you to the cleaners. Do I remember it [the match]? I'll never forget it. If ever a defender was destroyed by an attacker it was [then] ... The unfortunate defender was me, the attacker was George Best and the details are still seared on my mind after all those years. It was a muddy pitch but it would not have mattered what the state of the surface had been, the outcome would still have been the same, because the Belfast-born George Best – starring for one afternoon only in his native city – was simply tremendous.

'I started the game at right-back and Bestie began on the left wing. He tore me apart. Inside, outside, I couldn't even catch him to kick him.'

Then Georgie-boy had the audacity to take the mickey out of the great Gordon Banks in another Home International in May 1971, which England won 1-0. Banksie, the goalkeeper who had thwarted the great Pelé with that miraculous, low, right-handed save in the World Cup a year earlier, almost conceded a bizarre goal against George. The mischievous Georgie was lurking as Banks prepared to punt the ball upfield. The England keeper tossed the ball into the air and, as he draw his leg back, Best nipped in and lifted it into the air. As Banks looked around helplessly, Georgie nodded the ball into the goal. The referee disallowed it for foul play, but Banks would later admit he was lucky to get away with it.

That was the beauty of George Best. Reputations on the pitch meant nothing to him; he simply weaved his own magic, oblivious to rivals with world-class pedigrees who would try to stop him. More was the pity – given the isolated incidents of extraordinary skill and perception – that he never put his heart into playing for his country. It was as if he could not always raise his game because the standard of his team-mates did not match up to his own stratospheric levels, just as he had complained about turning out with a fading team at United in the early Seventies. On another level, his lack of commitment would cost him in terms of posterity, with some critics arguing that he could never be compared to, say, Pelé and Maradona because he had never cut it at international level.

At the time, with mounting problems in his life both in and outside football, his role in footballing history was one of the last things on George's mind. He became one of the first people to have 'Antabuse' pellets sewn into the lining of his stomach – the drug that they contained – Disulfiram – was supposed to make him violently sick if he drank alcohol. But two separate attempts at the implant treatment, in Scandinavia and the USA, failed to stop him drinking and, by the mid-1980s, a bookmaker George knew offered him odds of 6-4 on making it to his 40th birthday.

The game for George had now become more about survival than establishing a permanent legacy. George's sad decline was lived out in the full glare of publicity and, despite the best intentions of many who sought to save him from himself, George careered inexorably off the rails. He was once the world's most gifted and lauded footballer, and could now do little to avoid becoming the most pitiful.

3

The Good, the Bad and the Bubbly

'Not only have I lost my dad ... we've all lost a wonderful man.'
CALUM BEST, GEORGE'S ONLY SON, 25 NOVEMBER 2005

'Anyone who has seen him as a football fan will never forget it.'
PRIME MINISTER TONY BLAIR, 25 NOVEMBER 2005

For me, it will go down as one of those 'Where were you when JFK died?' moments. Friday, 25 November 2005, the day the genius with the twinkling feet died; the day George Best could fight on no more. I was in the offices of the *Mail on Sunday*, writing something up, when the news flashed up on the television screen around lunchtime. In thick red capital letters: 'GEORGE BEST DIES! GEORGE BEST DIES! ' Sky TV's coverage made me feel like throwing up at that moment. Capital letters and an exclamation mark, as if it were relaying the numbers from the lottery or some bingo show. Hardly subtle, even less compassionate. All morning there had been updates, with earlier messages across the screen stating, 'GEORGE BEST CLOSE TO DEATH! GEORGE BEST CLOSE TO DEATH!' The exclamations somehow reduced the tragedy of the event to the level of a freak show.

Arguably the greatest footballer these shores have ever

produced gave up the fight for life at the tender age of 59 after multiple organ failure. The private Cromwell Hospital near Earl's Court put out a statement saying George's death ended 'a long and very valiant fight'. George had been treated in the hospital since entering with flu-like symptoms almost eight weeks earlier. He then suffered a kidney infection and, towards the end, his condition deteriorated sharply with the development of a lung infection that led to internal bleeding. He had been particularly susceptible to infection because of the drugs he had had to take after his 2002 liver transplant.

It had ended in tears – ours – as we had always known it would. Given George's emotional make-up and his self-destruct mechanism, the final script could not have been any different. Of course, the tributes were predictably fond and caring. Republic of Ireland Prime Minister Bertie Ahern said, 'George should be remembered as the very best at what he did. He was quite simply a football genius.' Sir Bobby Charlton said his former Manchester United team-mate had 'made an immense contribution to the game, and enriched the lives of everyone that saw him play,' adding, 'Football has lost one of its greats, and I have lost a dear friend. He was a marvellous person.' A statement from Manchester United said, 'For the goals, the audacious dribbles and all the wonderful memories, Manchester United and its legions of fans worldwide will always be grateful.' And it was announced that a minute's silence would be observed at every Premiership football match the following weekend in George's memory.

Yet you could argue that the tributes – worthy and warranted in a football sense – were rather over the top if you looked back at his life and cast a more critical eye over the trail of misery he brought to himself and others; the fights, the boozing, the affairs, the drink-driving, the prison spell, the abuse of a second chance with the new liver. But George Best would not be tainted by all that; he would ultimately be remembered as a hero – he would even have Best Belfast City Airport named after him and be given a virtual state funeral in Northern Ireland!

Why? Because of his God-given talent, but also because we accepted him for what he was. A genius, but a mischievous, wayward, immature man, a Peter Pan of football. We excused him many of his misdemeanours precisely because he was George Best, and because he lived a life that few of us would have been able to survive without some deviations from the straight and narrow. He was football's first pop star and even Busby would admit it was something he as a manager had never been faced with before, saying, 'What were we to do, shoot him? I always looked for a cure with George. It would have been easy to have transferred him, but that wasn't the answer. Special rules for George? I suppose so, but only in the sense that he was a special player. I mean, you make it different once you say someone is a good player, and the man next to him is a genius … George is a genius.'

I first saw George Best when I was a young boy, sat on my dad's shoulders in the Scoreboard Paddock at Old Trafford. It was the late Sixties and I felt a shiver go down my spine as he swirled past defender after defender in a league match against Chelsea. My memories of the night are always in black and white, but George would bring colour to my life for many years.

His downfall was his character – his unwillingness to face reality. It was always preferable to take a drink and return to his own fantasy world, a world of safety and warmth that takes many alcoholics to their death. In November 2001, George emerged with what would be his final autobiography, *Blessed*. It was his first attempt on paper to deal with the demons inside his head, demons that, he would finally admit, only went away when he'd taken enough alcohol on board. I was lucky enough to be asked to review the book for the *Sunday Times* and wrote these words: 'Where did it all go wrong, Mr Best? This brilliantly raw book on the life of arguably Britain's greatest footballer gives us some of the clearest clues yet. The Belfast genius lays bare his tortured soul, his battle with the demons and his fears. Above all, it is an immensely sad book, belying its uplifting title.

'Blessed? It reads more like a tragic obituary penned by George himself, though, God willing, it won't come to that for some time. But make no mistake, it could. And Georgie, in his heart, knows that. The 15-year-old boy who arrived at Manchester United and promptly rushed back to Northern Ireland, homesick and full of trepidation, is still running. From himself. Let's get one thing straight, right now. George Best's problem was never alcohol, it still isn't. As Jimmy Greaves, another alcoholic (thankfully, still recovering) would tell you, George's problem is alcoholism – that aching inner loneliness and spiritual turmoil that takes him to that life-threatening first drink. Only by confronting the alcoholism will he ever kick the bottle and find that elusive peace.

'This book is 366 pages long but only in the last 30 does he deal with the alcoholism, the onset of liver sclerosis, the admission that he is in the last-chance saloon, the revelatory discovery that he may be the problem, that the bottle is but a symptom of his inner illness. Sure, the first 336 pages are entertaining, with anecdotes focusing on his magical European Cup Final goal in 1968 … But they are countered by the pathos of the wrecked relationships, the squandered thousands, the jail term and his deep unhappiness.

'Alcoholism is essentially an illness of ego, and George still has plenty of that. He mocks AA, claiming it could not work for him because he is too famous. How could he, the great

George Best, be anonymous? Well, it worked for Greavsie, Tony Adams, Anthony Hopkins and Eric Clapton, and they are hardly nobodies. Maybe the answer is staring Bestie in the face, and maybe it's not having anti-alcohol tablets stitched into his stomach.

'Yes, this book is a good read, but it's also a tortured one. Blessed? Only if you're still around in a few years, Georgie.'

I still consider it my best review, although I take no great pleasure in being proved right with my analysis and ultimate prediction. I knew what George was going through and had an understanding of why he could not find a way because I shared his journey for many years. I, too, was diagnosed as an alcoholic and, indeed, remember many drinks with George and his cronies in the Phene Arms, just around the corner from his flat in Chelsea. I recall he was a good pool player but that he would also become deeply morose after the drinks set in, and would end up arguing over nonsense. Inevitably, the landlord would help him home at closing time, or whenever he could take no more, whatever the time of day.

Then I remember going to Alcoholics Anonymous and seeing George there. He had been in first in the early Eighties, but this was a decade later. It was his second attempt at AA, something he kept secret – something that has not been revealed until now. If he were not dead, I would not have mentioned it; AA is an anonymous programme after all.

He often told the story that he went to AA but did not continue going because people would come up to him and ask for his autograph. I can tell you that is simply untrue. No one asked for anyone's autograph at the meetings. There were bigger 'stars' than George Best who used AA – Clapton and Hopkins for two.

No, it was just Georgie playing silly buggers, making up a

story for his ever-growing anecdotal library, and, if truth be told, also making up an excuse. George Best did not leave AA because he was being pestered; he left AA because he did not want to stop drinking – because he could only tackle his demons so far before it became too painful.

Looking at it another way, George Best left AA because he was *not* pestered enough. I remember one night at London's biggest meeting near Knightsbridge when George was sat a couple of seats away from me. Film stars and pop stars were sat in front of the two of us. The format is that a selected person 'shares' for 30 minutes on their life – basically telling how they got to AA, how they are 'recovering' and their hopes for the future – and then the meeting is thrown open to the 'audience'. This particular night, George's hand kept shooting up, but he could not get in to share. After about another 20 minutes, he stood up and said, 'Look, if you've not got time for me to fuckin' have my say, I'm fuckin' off.' And with that, he turned and walked out of the hall in a rage. I and another couple of people went after him, trying to persuade him to come back, saying that he would get his turn. He told us to 'fuck off away', and made his way back to the Phene Arms.

No one had bothered him and that – rather than what he would claim was a constant pestering – would be the reason why George Best decided AA was not for him. His ego could not take it if he was not the centre of attention; his illness had him hung, drawn and quartered. He was self-obsessed to the extreme. But if we accept that, we must also have compassion for this clearly tortured man. Ultimately, he was a sick man, not a bad man.

My psychoanalyst friend puts it this way, 'If someone said to you, "Don't drink out of that bottle, it contains bleach, and will poison you and eventually kill you," you would leave it alone, wouldn't you? Yet George was constantly being told that he was drinking stuff that would kill him, but could not leave it alone. He was a prisoner of the bottle, a prisoner of alcohol, and he died an alcoholic, from alcoholism. It's all very sad.

'So, while in one sense George could not live with the limelight, in another he could not live without it. He needed the allure of celebrity to satisfy his illness; the illness that told him he had to be the centre of attention to quell that feeling inside him that continually told him he was not good enough.'

George knew he was trapped with the bottle, and that AA could have provided the answer if he had stayed; he was just too far gone to make a commitment. Then he would show his knowledge of the illness he was a victim of by once saying, 'If a thousand drinks are not enough, then one is too many for an alcoholic like me.'

The alcohol had really taken a hold of George by the end of the Sixties. Many pundits believe that he lost his way when his best pals – team-mate David Sadler and Manchester City star Mike Summerbee – both announced engagements in 1969, leaving him deprived of his two 'best social companions'. But it is likely he would still have hit the bottle big-time even if they had stayed by his side. They held him back a little from the excesses that would follow but, even by 1969, he had his own key to the Brown Bull pub in Salford.

Before George made it his local, the boozer had been struggling – a real spit-and-sawdust pit that was never full. George's presence turned it into one of Manchester's places to be – the landlord would look after him, and he had the pick of the bedrooms where he could take any pretty young things who took his fancy from the nearby Granada studios. George was heading nowhere quickly – by 1970, his interest in training was fading and the drink was becoming the most important thing in his life. He was banned from driving for six months after crashing his car on a boozy night out, and the fact that he was recognised wherever he went only added to his need to find solace in drink and women.

Busby was at his wit's end with his star man – he even suggested that George should go to see a psychiatrist for help. George treated that with the contempt he felt it deserved, laughing out loud at his manager's suggestion. In truth, Busby had come up with a sound idea – George clearly suffered from clinical depression and may have found some answers on the couch.

Unfortunately, the only couch he deemed worthwhile was one that also included a pretty young woman, and they were freely available. The women in his life were invariably beautiful and feisty but would eventually tire of his antics. He could not commit to one woman for life; his illness would not allow that. He needed fresh reassurances that he was still desirable, that he was still worth loving. He had many brief flings – what he would term 'nameless faces on the pillow', and he once boasted of having sex with 7 women in 24 hours in Manchester, George's own self-confessed Magnificent Seven – but George would eventually admit that the Romeo years only left him 'with a deep feeling of emptiness'.

The mainstays of his life were his first wife Angie, his second Alex, the model Angie Lynn and the 'mother-figure' Mary Shatila. Yes, there were countless others who stayed a little longer than a night – including Miss Worlds Mary Stavin and Marjorie Wallace and actresses Juliet Mills and Sinead Cusack – but those four were his strongest relationships. He had a habit of ending his numerous autobiographies during the years with a word of thanks to the woman he was involved with at the time – in 1990 he paid tribute to Shatila as '... my lover, my friend and my strength...' while 11 years later he would admit that 'I owe Alex some good years for all she's been through....'

These women who stood by him got a raw deal. He could not stay faithful – booze, he admitted, was his constant 'other woman' and, under its influence, he would embark on wild affairs – yet they all retained a certain love and affection for him. The relationships would follow a similar path: he would be the naughty little boy, she would be the scolding parent; he would be the patient, she would be the doctor; he would be the one who could not be saved, she would be the one who would try desperately to bring him salvation. Then, when the woman would realise he was beyond change, they would split up. It was an unenviable, vicious circle.

The four women also had their own lives before they met George – and three of them would give it all up to try to tame him. His first wife Angie – whom George described as independent and determined before they married in 1977 – was the personal fitness trainer of pop legend Cher; Alex was an air hostess with Virgin Atlantic; and Shatila was brilliant with money – she rescued George from bankruptcy. Only Angie Lynn would continue her career as a model – much to George's disgust – and they would constantly engage in rows over his jealousy. His wife Angie bore him his only legitimate child, Calum, but she could not live with his excesses in America – which, for a bohemian like George, was a true hedonist's paradise and possibly the worst choice of destination – and similarly struggled with him in Fulham in the late Seventies and early Eighties. She left him with the words, 'You're wasting your life, George. You're not going to waste mine as well...' and the marriage was annulled in 1984. She would later add, 'My priorities changed. I had a baby. I couldn't look after another baby.' In turn, George would also one day admit, 'I don't know how she put up with me so long.'

Yet, many years later, Angela would show how George retained the love of his women even after they had split by saying of his relationship with Alex, 'Alex is a sweetheart but, of course, she is a nutcase to take George on. She is a very nice girl. She deserves a medal for marrying him. I just thank her every day for looking after him because he would have been dead years ago if Alex hadn't been around.' Angie thanked her for looking after her ex-husband – the patient/doctor love continued even years after they had parted.

Both Angie and Alex suffered physical and mental abuse from George, and it is telling that his son Calum, having witnessed his father's excesses, had little time for him during his growing years and chose to live with his mother in California until completing his education.

Of the four women, Angie Lynn was the girl George could never tame, the one most similar to him in attitude and outlook. She refused to give up her independence for him and would even visit a late-night club frequented by prostitutes and addicts, much to George's displeasure. He would ask her why she visited such a dump. 'To get away from you,' she would reply and, like him, she would disappear for days on end without explanation. The very fact that she was not an easy touch made him all the keener – he would admit to being 'infatuated' and 'besotted' by her. Their time together would also be remembered for George's infamous Christmas of 1984 spent at Her Majesty's Pleasure at Pentonville – the jail spell following a threefold sequence of events that started with drink-driving, continued with failing to appear in court and concluded with him assaulting a police officer.

After they split in 1987, Angie would eventually make a new life for herself in Ibiza, but George would retain an admiration for her, praising her for never going to the papers to cash in on their time together, saying, 'That's why I admire Angie Lynn so much. She's never spoken about our relationship and she certainly went through real hell with me.'

After the tempestuous days with Angie Lynn, Mary Shatila brought a welcome period of stability to George's life. Boasting 'a business background', she helped George sort out his financial nightmare – he had clocked up enormous debts through gambling and failed business ventures, including his nightclubs and clothes boutiques – and she advised him over his bankruptcy and encouraged him to begin a new career as a public speaker. Yet the leopard could not change his spots – he repaid her efforts in his usual way, this time by seducing her sister.

He was still living with Mary when he started seeing Alex, and his first words should have sent alarm bells ringing. He introduced himself to her in Tramp nightclub with the words, 'I love you.' Her first sight of the fallen idol had been his infamous appearance on the *Wogan* show, where he told the benign Irishman that his favourite pastime was 'screwing'. The next day, he was on the front pages of the tabloids for being drunk and disorderly on TV.

George then sold the story of how he had bedded Alex on his first date to the *News of the World* for £15,000. The move – apart from being hardly chivalrous – was also dishonest as they had not slept together at the time. Then there was the case of their initial wedding day – it was cancelled when they stood each other up. 'He has been on a two-week bender and has turned into a monster,' Alex told the *Sun*. 'He is being horrible to me.' Finally, on 24 July 1995, they would marry in a low-key civil ceremony at Chelsea Town Hall. George was 49, Alex just 23. By April 2004, they had divorced, on the grounds of his adultery with an unnamed woman, although that was merely the tip of the iceberg as far as Alex was concerned. During those nine years, she had nursed him and loved him as best she could – especially when he needed her most, after his liver transplant in July 2002. A generous, loving man when sober, he could not resist the call of the bottle, and started drinking again with his new liver. It brought out the lurking, dangerous Mr Hyde from within and, as Euan Ferguson would report in the *Observer*, the outcome was frightening, 'He beat Alex and broke her arm, and cut much of her hair off while he was drunk; and towards the end, after she had nursed him through and past the operation, draining the bile from his tube with plastic gloves and a measuring jug, and tried to sort out his shambolic finances, he went on a few benders and disappeared off with other women and ended up, of course, in the papers again.'

Alex would be slammed in some quarters of the press after George died when she changed the name of her autobiography from *Always Alex* to *Loving George*. Some argued she was cashing in on his memory, but she is actually OK, a good sort. She did not even ask for the title to be changed – it was down to her publishers. She did her best for Georgie-boy and showed an understanding of alcoholism and the alcoholic that could only really come from someone who had loved one in vain. She said, 'It is, of course, a disease. It's partly genetic, I've been told, and read. George's mother was an alcoholic. And it doesn't go away. I've spoken to other alcoholics, who may have had years off the sauce, but they all say that they think of it every day. Many of them, though, have had counselling, or done the steps [of recovery in AA]. George wouldn't hear of it. He's actually an extremely shy man, and never wanted to deal with it in that kind of confrontational way, and that's why it was never dealt with; it just seemed to go away some times, possibly because those times he was almost dead. And to anyone trying to deal with it, I would argue very fiercely that "cutting down" is never the answer, no matter what they tell you; the only answer is a complete halt, for ever.'

More the pity that George could not even hear the truth when it came from the person closest to him in the whole wide world. Such was the power of the illness over him. It is also interesting that Alex should mention the idea of alcoholism being a hereditary illness. His mother Ann would die at the age of 54 from alcoholism – five years fewer than George – on 12 October 1978. 'Dickie, I don't want to live any more,' she told her husband as she went to bed on the night of 11 October. The following morning, when George's dad brought her up a cup of tea, she was dead in the bed.

George admitted to being racked with guilt. He had spent many of his summers in Mallorca, soaking up the sun and the women, rather than returning to see his family in Northern Ireland during the late Sixties and early Seventies; after Ann's death, he mentally castigated himself for staying away.

George had learned from his sister Carol that Ann had started drinking and it appears that, given his own struggle with the bottle, he simply could not cope with seeing his beloved mother deteriorate, too, so he did not visit her. In *Blessed*, he would say, 'I felt guilty because I knew Mum worried about me and I'd given her plenty of cause over quite a few years … I felt guilty because of all the bad publicity I had been getting, which I knew upset Mum more than anyone else in the family. I felt that her death was all my fault … that if I hadn't gone to England, hadn't done the things I'd done, and if I'd only gone home more often, it wouldn't have happened. It's a terrible thing, guilt, and it would be a long while before I could see things as they really were and accept that there was nothing I could have done.'

It is hard not to feel compassion for a man who can come out with words like that; I know he was a bounder in many ways, but even towards the end of his own life he was tormented by demons. He was still the lost little boy missing his beloved mum. It would also make him question whether he had been born an alcoholic – whether the symptoms of the mental illness that dragged him towards drink had been genetic. When talking to journalist Ross Benson in 1990, he said, '… my mother's death does pose the worrying question – Is my drink problem genetic? Was I programmed from birth to be an alcoholic?'

But my psychoanalyst friend observed, 'Really, it doesn't matter whether he was genetically an alcoholic or not. You can argue all day long whether it is a hereditary illness or not, but the bottom line is the here and now – and finding a way out of the alcoholism. There were programmes of recovery back then, but George clearly did not want to find a way out. He did not want to quit drinking – and there is nothing more you can do if an alcoholic will not abstain.'

And the fact of the matter remains that Ann was a different sort of alcoholic to George in one sense; she was a late arrival to the bottle, never having touched a drop of alcohol until she was past 40, while George had been a sufferer from his early 20s. George would be buried next to her in Belfast's Roseland Cemetery.

George's other sister, Barbara McNarry, who launched the George Best Foundation in 2006, confirms Ann did not start boozing until she was 43. Barbara said, 'She started drinking partly due to the pressures of being a hard-working mum and dealing with a famous son. She turned to alcohol for support. It started as one or two and escalated from there. Ten years later, she was dead.'

Barbara knows the power of alcohol addiction – she certainly noticed how it took a stranglehold on her famous brother. She added, 'His addiction ended his life prematurely. He allowed alcohol to get a grip of him and it never let him go. He was only 59 and if it wasn't for alcohol he would still be enjoying the fruits of his genius.'

The end game for George would really begin in 2002 when he had his liver transplant. In the preceding years, he had reinvented himself as a TV pundit – commenting on matches on SkySport – and a newspaper columnist (he had a weekly column in the *Mail on Sunday's Night & Day* magazine). Even as the good times rolled, there had been signs that the drinking would still cost him dearly – SkySport, for instance, always had former footballer Clive Allen standing by in case George was under the influence.

By 2002, his liver had all but packed up, wrecked by years of alcohol abuse. After examination and analysis by specialist Professor Roger Williams at the Cromwell Hospital, George was accepted for a new liver. The operation – performed at the end of July 2002 – almost cost him his life as he underwent 10 hours of major surgery and needed 40 pints of blood during the transplant operation. When he recovered enough to be allowed home, George would vow never to drink again – and he also hit back at those who had criticised him being given a second chance, saying, 'I would never say to anybody you don't deserve to live, no matter who they are. As for calling this self-inflicted, I didn't decide one day that I would drink myself to death. It is as a result of alcoholism. I know myself I will never drink again. The only reason I would is because I want to kill myself or I want to go through this again – and I don't want either, so there's no reason to drink.'

He added that he was grateful to the anonymous donor of the organ, and that he did feel guilty that someone else had to die for him to survive. He also expressed hopes for a bright future and said he was planning to have children with wife Alex as soon as he was feeling better.

They proved to be fine words, but no more; in his war against alcoholism, the final battle was looming and he was facing defeat. It was not long before he was back on the booze – and then the chaos would once again set in. Affairs resulting in a split from Alex, talk of punch-ups and debts – it was as if he were reliving the Sixties. Only now he was burnt-out, haggard, physically destroyed – the game was almost up for George Best, one of the most seminal figures in international football, now widely described in newspaper reports around the planet as 'Britain's most famous alcoholic'. It was the ultimate, sad footnote to the demise of a genius.

Irony of ironies – and one George, a keen observer of topical events and a talented exponent of crosswords and puzzles, would have enjoyed – a day after he died, the Government passed a law allowing bars to stay open 24 hours. He would also have appreciated the level of devotion and love apparent at his funeral when he made the final journey back home, although, no doubt, George being George, he would also have been a little embarrassed by all the fuss.

That just about sums him up – a man who could not live with the fame his genius brought, but also could not live without it. A complex, beguiling character … at the same time, gentle and bullying, generous and spiteful and loving, but feeling unloved. In his last interview before he died, he would ask to be remembered only for the joy he brought to those on the terraces at Manchester United, saying, 'When I'm gone, people will forget all the rubbish and remember only the football.' He was asking a lot of us all – but then he also gave us a lot on the pitch, didn't he? Thanks always for those treasured footballing memories, Georgie-boy….

4

A Man Out of Time

'Only Captain Marvel can save us now. Give it to f***ing Robbo...'
UNITED FAN AT THE FA CUP FINAL 1990, AFTER IAN WRIGHT
HAD PUT CRYSTAL PALACE 3-2 AHEAD

'My better performances came when I wore the number 7 shirt
and I came to regard it as my lucky number.'
BRYAN ROBSON

After the breathless years of George Best, the spotlight shifts on to Robbo – the man who launched a thousand clichés, chief of them being that he was 'Captain Marvel'. I'll admit right now that, after Georgie-boy, the prospect of trudging through Robson's life did not have nearly as much appeal. On the surface, he was a man out of time – a throwback to the days when footballers were simple guys who lived their lives to the Mars bar motto – 'work, rest and play'. They give their all on the pitch, and then have a few beers. Not much to say about life, good at their jobs, but hardly complicated, let alone enlightened or enlightening beings.

After trawling through Robson's career, I am left with these conclusions about Robbo the footballer: he was too courageous for his own good; foolhardy, even, in the way he would launch himself into tackles he could not win, but that he also earned the right to be a member of United's Magnificent Sevens club.

And I was left in no doubt that he will always be a Red legend because of the fact – and excuse the cliché, they do seem to occur rather too easily when talking about Robbo – that he would die for the club. Also there is the small matter of the fine achievements he recorded in what was an undoubtedly lean era at Old Trafford.

Put it this way – if Robbo had been starting out for United when Ferguson arrived, rather than approaching the end of his career, he would have won many more medals, and the legend of Roy Keane would possibly never have been written. As it was, he suffered a less garlanded existence under the perennially underachieving Ron Atkinson.

Robbo the human being? As we have said, an essentially straightforward man, not simple, but certainly no illuminating conversationalist like, say, Cantona, nor a man with a mischievous nature like Best. Speak to Bryan Robson and you are struck by the honest constraints of his being; phrases such as 'the lads', 'the gaffer' and 'a pint' are prominent when he discusses his career. Here is a man with no fancy edges to him, a man who could have easily been describing a life down the pit as the vagaries of a professional footballer.

He has always been a mighty decent human being but still fits into our unpredictable but magnificent Number Sevens by virtue of his gung-ho approach to the game and his love of 'a pint' – but more of that later.

The Bryan Robson story begins on 11 January 1957 when he was born in the footballing stronghold of Chester-le-Street – the same area that provided the game with Jackie Milburn; his nephews, the Charlton brothers; and Paul Gascoigne. Robbo would be brought up in a council house in the village of Witton Gilbert; he would later admit his childhood was a happy time and he remained devoted to his father, Brian, and mother,

Maureen. Brian was a long-distance lorry driver, Maureen a school dinner lady and a proud mother who would almost single-handedly bring up Bryan, sister Susan and brothers Gary and Justin – also good footballers. Bryan was not an academic achiever, but he had a passion to win from an early age. His fall-back would have been to have become a P.E. teacher but he knew he wanted to be a pro footballer and his determination propelled him towards his chosen career – although some thought he, like Georgie Best, was too small to make the grade. Robbo would prove the doubters wrong, not for the last time in his life, as he progressed through the school teams – infant, junior, Birtley Lord Lawson Comprehensive, then the Washington and District team, which he eventually captained.

He was an outstanding talent despite his size and soon the scouts were queuing to barter for his services. There was a chance to join the Toon army, Burnley, Coventry and Sheffield Wednesday, but Robbo took the path that would epitomise his career and, indeed, his life choices – the sensible ones. He talked his options over with his parents and opted to join West Bromwich Albion. They were the most personable of the clubs that approached him – they looked after triallists best, putting them in guest houses rather than hostels and taking more of an interest in them.

Why not Newcastle, the team he supported, his local team? Robbo did not feel right there; he went by gut instinct and that was to prove a solid yardstick throughout his time as a pro footballer.

They built him up at the Hawthorns – they needed to, he was only 5ft and 7st as a 15-year-old – and he did his bit by working hard to become a two-footed player. He had the opposite problem to that of George Best – Robbo was naturally left-footed and had to put in the practice hours to bring his right foot up to standard. That old fox, Don Howe, was manager at the time and he took the decision to give Robson his big chance in the summer of 1972. He would not become an immediate millionaire, not on a fiver a week, although the club did pay his board and lodgings. Two years later, he would turn pro and his wage 'rocketed' by £23 a week.

Robbo made his first-team début aged 18 on 12 April 1975 in the Second Division clash at York, and kept his place in the following match, making his home début against Cardiff, and scoring in the 2-0 win. Now 5ft 10in he was growing in stature as well as height and, by the end of that season, had played his part as new boss Johnny Giles took Albion back into the First Division.

But anguish would follow the joy at winning promotion – he broke his leg for the first time against Spurs in 1976 and, with rotten luck, broke it for a second time on his comeback for the reserves just five weeks later. It would be the start of a series of injuries that would blight his career and lay him open to the accusation that he was injury prone. He was certainly too brave for his own good, maybe even too rash – he would throw himself into tackles from which most pros would shrink. Paradoxically, it was this element of the beast in Robbo that made him a beauty in the eyes of the supporters, but it was also his own undoing. Having said that – and Robson himself has argued this point long and hard – he did compete in over 700 club games in a career spanning a remarkable 23 years from 1974 to 1997 and also played for England on 90 occasions.

I think we could probably agree that Robson was, in his own way, the bravest player ever to grace English football – although you could argue that, from a different perspective, he was also perhaps one of the most foolish to himself. His body didn't half take some batterings over the years, but he was moulded from tough stock. Never afraid of a battle, he led Albion – and then United – from the front line. To use another footballing cliché, he was a man you would have been glad to have in the trenches with you.

In April 1977, he added a broken ankle to his growing list of injuries, sustained in a tackle with Dennis Tueart of Manchester City. At least, he thought it was a broken ankle – in actual fact, it turned out to be his third broken leg in seven months.

Three broken legs by 1977 – and yet his top-class career, with Albion, Manchester United and finally Middlesbrough, would continue for another 20 years. Clearly, this was not just another run-of-the-mill footballer we are talking about here – no, Robson was more of a superman as he defied the physical setbacks that would surely have spelt the end for most characters.

The six-million-dollar man of football? Well, it was more like a £1.5 million superman. That is what Manchester United gladly paid for this all-action hero on 1 October 1981. In the four intervening years, after he had recovered from those broken legs in 1977, West Brom would reach dizzy heights under a new manager, the flamboyant Ron Atkinson. Just as George Best's fortunes had been tied up with those of Busby, so Robson would find his life inexorably intertwined with that of the man who took over at the Hawthorns in early 1978. An average footballer himself during an average career, Atkinson had proved himself more than capable at the managerial game by transforming the fortunes of little Cambridge United. As Robbo was variously known as a 'marvel', so Atkinson was dubbed 'Big Ron'. He liked his jewellery, his tan and his smart clothes; he also earned the moniker 'Mr Bojangles'. He had style and no little substance – he would take the Albion to a high of third place in Division One and offer the fans an attacking, entertaining style of flair football that they simply lapped up.

Atkinson's team contained the all-out pace and aggression of Robson, the style of Len Cantello, the wing wizardry of the late Laurie Cunningham and the rampant bull-in-a-china-shop raiding of centre-forward Cyrille Regis. He also added the reinforced steel of Remi Moses to complement Robson and Cantello in midfield.

In 1981, Atkinson was lured to Old Trafford as the successor to the dour, dull Dave Sexton. Atkinson would persuade Moses to join him at United in September of that year and, a month later, Robson would follow him to the Theatre of Dreams. The exodus was complete – and West Brom supporters were far from happy, especially at the loss of Robson.

Mike Tuck is a Baggies fanatic – he has followed the team since he was a lad in the late Seventies – and he admits that it was a sickener when Robbo left. When I tracked him down, Robson had just been sacked as manager of West Brom, in September 2006. He told me, 'It's a bit sad to see Robbo get the boot now, but it was nothing to what us fans felt back in '81. He was our main man – the player we had put our hopes on, the one who was our future, who would lead us to glory. We had an inkling he would follow Atkinson but we prayed he might stay loyal. In the end, money and Man United came calling and it takes a lot to say "No" I suppose.

'1981 was like the beginning of the end for us; it took the club a long time to recover. It was bad enough when Cantello went but then, when Cunningham, Moses and Robson also quit, I felt sick to the stomach. I remember talking to Cyrille Regis at his house. It was like that back then – you could actually see the players and have a word with them. It wasn't so much "them and us" as it is now. I lived near Cyrille and he was happy enough to let me and other Baggies' fans chat with him and sign autographs for us. I can't imagine that happening with today's so-called superstars!

'We always knew Robson would be a great talent, that he would play for England. He was such a brave, dynamic player. In the final analysis, I am just grateful that we once had him as a player at the Albion. He was one of our greatest ever players.'

Having notched up nearly 200 league games for the Baggies, scoring 39 goals, Robson's arrival at Old Trafford was greeted in typical champagne style by Atkinson. The night before it was announced that Bryan would be signing for United in a deal that would smash the British transfer record, Atkinson invited his two favourite sports journalists to a hotel in Haydock Park for a drink and a natter. It was part of his weekly régime; he liked to keep the wheels well oiled with the press, and he was well aware that having the press on his side made his life easier and provided an excellent method of communicating his ideas, plans and dreams through his favoured journalists to the fans.

Paul Hazeldine was one of the two journalists who accepted Atkinson's request for a chat at Haydock Park that night. He subsequently became Editor-in-Chief of a series of newspapers in the Midlands. Back then, he was a football writer for the *Sunday Journal*, which had its main base in Manchester. Paul admitted he enjoyed being one of the few taken into Atkinson's confidence. He told me, 'Every week, Ron would invite me and another football writer along to talk about how things were going at United. Invariably, it ended up with us being smashed and having to get a cab home – which Ron paid for, along with the rather large bar bill!

'This particular night was a Wednesday as I recall, the last one in September, so we knew we would have a good few drinks with the boss as there was still time to recover for the weekend. But it was a bit different from the start that night. Usually, it was just me, the other football writer and Ron in the bar, but that night we were welcomed at the hotel with the news that Ron had booked a table.

'Clearly, it was going to be something special on the agenda, but I would never have guessed exactly what Ron had up his sleeve! The three of us sat down at the table, ordered a meal apiece – all on Ron's expenses account – and got stuck into the wine. All of a sudden, Larry Lloyd and Duncan McKenzie, the former Forest and Everton footballers, arrived and joined us. They were good mates of Ron's, but it was the first time I had seen them on a night out with us.

'As the night wore on, we were all feeling the effects of the booze when Ron turned towards me with that big smile of his, the golden rings and bracelets flashing on his arms and hands and said, "Paul, if you had the chance of signing any player in the world for United, who would you go for?" I couldn't think of anyone off-hand; I think the booze had dulled my mind a bit! "Maradona," I suggested.

'"No, someone who is more reliable than him, and who is a more rounded, all-round performer. OH, FOR FUCK'S SAKE, COME ON, MAN!" Ron bellowed at me, his face still like the proverbial cat that had got the cream. "I've just signed Bryan Robson to be my lynchpin at Old Trafford – for a record fee of one-and-a-half million fuckin' quid!"

'We two reporters felt our faces dropping in shock, although Lloyd and McKenzie were clearly in on the secret; they were grinning like mad. Then Ron got up and told the whole restaurant what he had done and poured champagne into my glass until it was overflowing, all the while laughing like a crazy hyena. It was typical of the man – he was a big, brash man – wonderful company, great to be with but also just what United needed at the time. A fun antidote after the dreadful, dull days of Dave Sexton. And what a signing Robson proved to be for

United, hey? He was cheap at the price when you think of the service and efforts he put in for the club. A brilliant buy, no doubt about it – and that night with Big Ron is one I will treasure until my dying days.'

Typical of Atkinson the showman – the flash production would continue after Robbo agreed to join United the next day, 1 October 1981. He would officially sign for the club on the pitch before the match against Wolves the following Saturday – in front of a crowd of 47,000. The record fee of £1.5million would not be broken for six years, when Liverpool paid £1.9 million for Newcastle striker Peter Beardsley in the summer of 1987. Robson would also take the number 7 shirt – which he regarded as his lucky number – from the unfortunate, injury-jinxed Steve Coppell.

Robbo looks back on that pitchside signing with a certain fondness, as well as embarrassment, after the historic moment was splashed over the world's press the following day. He says now, 'I'll never be allowed to forget that picture. I've had so much ribbing over the years because, at the time, I was one of the many footballers who had the permed look. Keegan, Souness and McDermott were among those who famously became curly mops. But the reason I had my hair permed was for the convenience, not for the fashion.'

The combination of Robson and Atkinson would be the key to United's success – or lack of it, when considering the highest level of achievement, such as League Championships and European trophies – during the next five years. Robson would admit to 'being on the same wavelength' as his manager; they both liked to work hard and play hard. He denies the accusation often levelled at Atkinson that he did not rule United with enough discipline – that there was perhaps too much 'fun' and leniency. Robson is also unhappy with the allegation that

United, during his and Atkinson's reign, was 'a boozer's paradise from the top down', although, at other times, he moderates his dissatisfaction with his regular admissions throughout his career that he was more than partial to 'a pint'.

He would make his first team début for Manchester United on 7 October 1981 in the League Cup clash at White Hart Lane. It would be the first of 465 appearances for the Red Devils in which he would score 98 goals until he quit the club on 31 May 1994. That first season itself would end with Robbo playing in 32 games and scoring 5 goals. He quickly grew in stature, replacing Ray Wilkins as club captain (and England skipper, too) in 1982 and led United to three FA Cup wins in 1983, 1985 and 1990.

The 1983 final against Brighton and Hove Albion remains my personal favourite of the three – he scored twice in the 4-0 replay victory after it had ended 2-2 first time around at Wembley. Frank Stapleton and Ray Wilkins had scored for United in the first match with Brighton's goals coming from Gordon Smith and Gary Stevens. Smith will also be remembered as the man who 'lost' the Cup for the Seagulls after his astonishing last-minute miss in that initial encounter, when he found himself clean through with only United keeper Gary Bailey to beat. Instead of winning the Cup, he hit his shot straight at the relieved Bailey.

I was at both matches and remembered a certain apprehension over the replay the following Thursday night. The Seagulls – amusingly referred to as 'Seaweed' by the United faithful – would be reinforced by the return of influential centre-back and skipper Steve Foster. In the end, Robson led the charge and United eased to their first trophy under Atkinson and their first in what had otherwise been a decade of underachievement. The replay was on Sir Matt Busby's 74th birthday – the grand old man of Old Trafford could not have asked for a better present, and a charged-up Robson was happy to oblige. The result was also the biggest winning margin in a Wembley FA Cup Final until United themselves equalled it with a 4-0 win over Chelsea in 1994. Dutch midfielder Arnold Mühren scored the fourth goal from the penalty spot. Mühren admitted it was the high point of his career at Old Trafford. He said, 'To be honest, for me every game was a big party but my absolute best moment was winning the FA Cup in 1983 against Brighton ... and scoring!' And he told me he was in no doubt about the influence of Robson on that achievement. He said, 'Yes, he was one of the greatest all-round players of all time. It was a pleasure and a privilege to play with him – we had a strong midfield with me, Robbo, Remi Moses and Ray Wilkins. We should have gone on to even greater things – but I do not think our squad was strong enough to cope. But I will never forget the thrill of winning the FA Cup that year with Robson.'

Was it Robson's finest hour for United? Not according to Robbo himself. He said, 'One of the classics for myself was for United against Liverpool at Anfield in 1988. We had a man sent off and were 3-1 down but we got back to level terms. Gordon Strachan actually missed a great chance later on to win it for us. It was definitely one of the all-time great games as far as I'm concerned. In those years, we always did well against them in one-on-one games. We also did really well in the Cups around then because in one-off games we could beat anybody. But Liverpool had a great consistency and probably a slightly stronger squad.'

Others are convinced that Robbo's greatest moment arrived against Barcelona (and Maradona) in 1984, when United beat the Spanish outfit 3-0 in a European Cup Winners' Cup quarter-final second leg clash at Old Trafford, with a brace from Robson after they had lost the first leg 2-0. That year was also memorable for Robson in that he signed a new deal at United that would secure his future financially and at the club – it was for seven years and would net him a cool £1 million, big money back then.

Others, though, argue that Robbo's high came in 1991 with Alex Ferguson's United running out 2-1 European Cup Winners' Cup Final winners over Barcelona in Rotterdam.

Sun journalist Dave Morgan, a United follower since the Seventies, believes that the Brighton replay was the first major inkling of just what Robbo could do – how he could almost change the course of a game single-handedly, taking it by the scruff of its neck and imposing his presence upon it. Morgan told me, 'I was at Wembley for the FA Cup Final replay in 1983. Apart from the joy of spending the evening taunting the Seagulls' ineffective returning skipper – "Stevie Foster, Stevie Foster … What a difference you have made … what a difference you have made!" – there was also the pleasure of watching two-goal Robbo fire United to the glory we'd expected to savour five days earlier.'

Yet he argues that the win over Barcelona in 1984 was even more memorable, and uses it as an example of the chasm in class between Robson and the United midfielders of the current era. He said, 'More unexpected and more memorable would have to be the victory over Barcelona at Old Trafford the following March. There was Robson, flying in with a diving header to set us on the road to a stunning comeback against the Hand of God merchant and his mates.

'Who can forget him being carried off shoulder-high by the fans he served so well? Can we expect to see the likes of Darren Fletcher and John O'Shea leaving the pitch perched in a similar position? I think we know the answer to that one, don't we? Oh, to have a Robbo in the ranks these days instead of some of the shallow, no-marks who have plied their distinctly average trade at the Theatre of Dreams.

'He wasn't blessed with the most talented company during the Atkinson era. Just imagine how things could have panned out if he'd been surrounded by more talented peers – say, the true class of the late Nineties.'

Mail on Sunday writer Andy Bucklow is in no doubt that the 1991 win was vital to Robson's legend. He told me, 'Yes, his finest hour as United's tour de force arrived in Rotterdam in the 1991 triumph over Barcelona. It was United's first European triumph in 23 years and, when Bryan lifted that trophy, the huge weight of unfulfilment dropped off his shoulders. The one-man band had finally recruited enough support to become a headline attraction.

'The Rotterdam game has long gone into United folklore as "Sparky's Revenge" on Barcelona – the club which had deemed Mark Hughes surplus to requirements. But looking at the bigger picture, it was entirely fitting that Robson, now in the twilight of a glorious but injury-ravaged career, should be the first English captain to lift a European trophy after the five-year exile following the Heysel disaster.

'Most pundits and some staunch fans, including me, it has to be said, didn't give United too much of a chance and with good reason. The Reds had endured yet another very average league season under Alex Ferguson, reaching the dizzy heights of sixth and 24 points behind champions Arsenal, following his first trophy as United manager – the 1990 FA Cup a year before. To put it into perspective, the teams finishing immediately above the Reds were Crystal Palace, Leeds United and ... er, Manchester City. In contrast, despite a few high-profile absentees, Johan Cruyff's Barcelona were a class act and stood nine points clear at the top of the Spanish La Liga.

'Everyone will remember it was Mark Hughes who was to prove their downfall with his two very different goals. Hughes, a man on a mission, quite rightly took the plaudits. But just pause to remember who took the free kick which led, via Steve Bruce's sizeable head, to the vital opening goal. It was Robbo. And who was it, seven minutes later, who provided the clever pass to enable the Welshman to break free from the Barça defence and round the 'keeper to make the score 2-0? Robbo again. Barça pulled one back but United hung on to lift the trophy.'

Yet Bucklow believes Robson's powerhouse show against Barça seven years earlier remains his proudest moment. He said, 'I can understand why Robson himself rates his performance against Barcelona in the 1991 Cup Winners' Cup Final higher than his career-defining display against the same team seven years earlier. It meant United were once again a force to be reckoned with in European football.

'But anyone privileged to witness both might beg to differ. The Barcelona of 1984 included one Diego Maradona, coming into his prime two years before the appearance of the Hand of God. And that Barcelona side were defending a 2-0 lead, helped along by a farcical early own-goal in the Nou Camp from accident-prone central defender Graeme Hogg.

'But this unforgettable occasion saw Robbo at his imperious, inspirational best and, backed by a then capacity crowd of more than 58,000, any thoughts Barcelona might have had that this was a foregone conclusion were soon dispelled. For the opening 20 minutes, the Spanish succeeded in stemming the Robson-inspired onslaught. Then a Ray Wilkins corner was helped across the goalmouth to the far post. And there, inevitably, was Robson, his body horizontal as he dived, to head in the ball in from close range.

'But the skipper knew the job was not even half done and, only five minutes into the second half, a dangerous low cross from Wilkins was fumbled by Barça keeper Urruti and, first on the scene, was Captain Courageous Bryan Robson to pounce on the chance and slam the ball home to make it 2-2 on aggregate. It was one of those nights when Robson was everywhere at once as he drove the midfield inexorably onwards.

'Frank Stapleton rifled the ball into the Stretford End net from an acute angle for 3-0 and you'd have thought United had regained the European Cup such was the tumult of noise from the terraces. Robson was carried off the pitch shoulder high by a sea of fans who invaded the pitch.

'This was the pick of numerous high-profile games when Robson dragged his talented, but often mentally lightweight and under-achieving team-mates to another level. He was that good on this particular night that he even dragged himself up to another level, if indeed that was possible. For me, it was that game, and that season more than any other, that epitomised his time at Old Trafford.

'As happened so often, glory soon turned inevitably to gory and the man seemingly destined to drag Big Ron's charmers to Cup Winners' Cup glory was all too familiarly *hors de combat* for the semi-final against Juventus and, despite a brave fight, an injury-ravaged United went down 3-2 over two legs.'

Two FA Cup wins would not be enough to save Atkinson. As Robson would later admit, the weight of expectation demanded more – much more at Manchester United. He would say, 'Their success in the Fifties and Sixties cast a shadow over the teams of the Seventies and Eighties.' Indeed it would. Big Ron had brought a touch of the cavalier to Old Trafford; the football was often exciting, but there were doubts over the quality of his squad – the first 11 were good enough but injuries contrived against him – and, by 1985, the writing was on the wall.

United had been overwhelming favourites to win the league in the 1985–86 season after winning their first ten league games, opening a ten-point gap over their rivals as early as October. But the team's form collapsed and they finished the season in fourth place. The poor form continued into the following season and, with United on the edge of the First Division's relegation zone, Atkinson was shown the door.

Just how would Robson cope without the man who had been his mentor for the previous eight years? He had conceded he was on the same wavelength as Atkinson – they both liked a laugh and 'a pint' – but the man chosen to sort out what some considered to be a 'rabble' at Old Trafford was on a very different frequency. Alex 'I come from Govan' Ferguson was hardly easy-going like Big Ron; no ... Big Alex would demand 100 per cent and more from his players, both at work and out of it. It was difficult to see how Robson and he would build a successful working relationship.

Ferguson quickly stamped his own style and personlity on the team: he would soon lambast Robson for allegedly coming into training with the smell of alcohol on his breath, although Robbo would hit back, telling him he was wrong. The Scot would then weed out Norman Whiteside and Paul McGrath and kick them out of Manchester United without any ceremony.

Things settled down between Ferguson and Robson; the Scot trusted him enough to keep him on as captain as he set about revolutionising the fallen giant that Manchester United had become since the glory days of Busby. Robson felt more at home in the Atkinson era, but he would become a better player and earn more valuable silverware under the command of the fiery Scot who had previously turned unfashionable Aberdeen into an outfit that would not only rival Rangers and Celtic, but also win European glory. You could definitely claim that, on paper at least, Robson and Ferguson would not be a happy marriage but, in retrospect, it was. Just as Paul Gascoigne would surely have benefited under the patronage of Ferguson, so did Robson.

But how did the driven, demanding Scot get the best out of the tough-as-old-boots Englishman, and how did he enable the young Bryan Robson to rise to the very top of the national and international game?

5

Ferguson and England

*'I'd never been afraid of anyone but Ferguson was a frightening
bastard from the start.'*
BOBBY MCCULLEY, EAST STIRLINGSHIRE FORWARD, JUNE 1974

*'When I first went to United, Bryan Robson was somebody I looked
up to, still do. But I was young, and when you're young you smell blood.
It was like, "Robbo, I'm after you, I'm taking you."'*
ROY KEANE, 2006

Alexander Chapman Ferguson walked into Old Trafford on 6 November 1986, surveyed the wreckage that was the legacy of the Atkinson era, smiled and shrugged his shoulders. Then he shared a joke with one of the club's groundsmen – he would make a point of treating all the staff the same, whether the chairman or a cleaner. Ferguson, then 44, knew he had his work cut out – but so what? What was new? It had always been that way, from his first match in professional football as a striker for Queen's Park at 16, through to his début as a manager at East Stirlingshire in June 1974 at the tender age of 32.

He had proved himself as a striker of quality, rising through the ranks of Scottish football and earning himself a move from Dunfermline to Glasgow Rangers in 1967. The fee of £65,000 was a then record transfer between two Scottish clubs. But controversy was fast becoming his middle name; after he was blamed for a goal Rangers conceded in the 1969 Scottish Cup

Final, he was forced to play for the club's junior side instead of the first team. His reaction to the slight? According to his brother, Ferguson was so upset that he threw away his loser's medal.

He would gain revenge on Rangers when he took the reins at Aberdeen in 1978. In eight years at this bleak, northernmost outpost of British football, Ferguson broke the Old Firm monopoly of Rangers and Celtic with seven domestic titles and one in Europe. Pre-Ferguson, the club had not won the title since 1955 – but he changed all that when they lifted the league trophy in 1980. It was the first time in 15 years that the title had not been won by either Rangers or Celtic and Ferguson now felt he had the respect of his players, later saying, 'That was the achievement which united us. I finally had the players believing in me.'

Aberdeen then followed that up with back-to-back titles in 1984 and 1985. They also lifted the Scottish Cup three seasons in a row from 1982–84, and their greatest success came when they beat Real Madrid to lift the European Cup Winners' Cup in 1983. Such was the pedigree of the beaming Scot who arrived at Old Trafford on 6 November 1986.

Eighteen years later, Robson himself would lead the tributes to the man who breathed life back into United, saying on the occasion of his 1,000th game as United manager in 2004, 'He's had an incredible impact. It's not just having 1,000 games, it's the standards that he's set, and not just with United but with Aberdeen. It doesn't surprise me because he lives and breathes football. With the amount of hours he spends in the office in the training ground, his life revolves around football.'

Back in 1986, Robson would swiftly learn how Ferguson did indeed 'live and breathe' football. When he took over from Atkinson, United were second from bottom in the old First Division and relegation was a frightening possibility. Ferguson quickly instilled a discipline in the squad that had been lacking, and warned them that their drinking would have to stop and their levels of fitness increase, or they would be on their bikes. The iron fist worked; United climbed up the table to finish the season in 11th place.

And Ferguson's chief ambition at United? Robson quickly learned he wanted one thing more than any other at the start of his reign. He said, 'His aim was to knock Liverpool and Everton off their perch and make United number one again.'

In 1987, Ferguson really started to make his mark by signing Steve Bruce, Viv Anderson, Brian McClair and Jim Leighton. United and Robson were flying and they would finish runners-up to Liverpool by nine points.

Yet it would not be until 1990 that Robson would lift the first trophy during Ferguson's reign – once again it would be the FA Cup, the competition he had last won five years earlier under Atkinson. Typically, Robbo scored United's first goal in the FA Cup Final against Crystal Palace in the first match, which ended in a 3-3 draw. United won the replay 1-0 with a goal from Lee Martin, and Robson became the first player to lift the FA Cup three times at Wembley as captain.

The FA Cup triumph had proved a job saver for Ferguson and provided him with a much-needed lifeline. By now, Robson was 'working on the same wavelength as Ferguson'; he had become a close confidant of the United manager after that initial spell of unease between the two almost four years earlier. Indeed, Robson looks back on that 1990 win over Palace with pride, but also relief, as it meant Ferguson would survive at the club. He had grown to believe in the man who put such emphasis on personal discipline both on and off the field. Robson said, 'I have great memories of FA Cup Finals, especially as I never lost one as a player – but that 1990 Final is the one I treasure most of all. Not many people gave Palace a chance, but it showed how good players in smaller clubs can be. Ian Wright and Mark Bright were in their team, so it was no wonder they gave us such a tough one with those two against us.

'We had to go to a replay, but I was just so pleased for all the youngsters in the team who had been given a tough time in the media. There was a lot of stick going around and people were saying the team was underachieving and so on. People like Paul Ince and Gary Pallister were having to put up with all sorts of criticism.

'There was also talk along the way that Sir Alex Ferguson would have been sacked if we hadn't won the competition, although I found out later that it wasn't the case. The victory was the launching pad for the club to go on to become the powerhouse it is now. It gave us a lot of confidence to go on and the following year we won the European Cup Winners' Cup and it snowballed from there.'

Ferguson had certainly been under immense pressure from the fans and the press as he entered the Christmas of 1989 with a 5-1 Division One defeat at Manchester City hardly helping his cause. In January 1990, many pundits were predicting Ferguson would be sacked, with the late Liverpool skipper Emlyn Hughes leading the chorus of disapproval. In the *Daily Mirror* that winter, Hughes wrote a piece attacking Ferguson's management under the headline 'FERGIE – OBE (OUT BEFORE EASTER)'. It did prove one thing – while the much-missed Hughes was a giant out on the pitch, he lacked similar skills in sports journalism.

Ferguson approached what will go down as one of the defining games of his reign confidently in January 1990. Other writers were arguing that defeat to Nottingham Forest in the third round of the FA Cup that month would spell the end of the Scot. Ferguson survived thanks to a goal from reserve striker Mark

Robins in the 1-0 win at the City Ground on 7 January 1990 and the die was cast for what would become an unprecedented haul of domestic trophies in the following decade.

During the next season, injury would limit Robson to 17 league appearances, but he was fit for that legendary Cup Winners' Cup Final in which United beat Barcelona 2-1, thanks to his driving force and Mark Hughes's brilliant brace. It had been a wonderful achievement in Rotterdam and yet the nagging doubts remained on the Ferguson–Robson partnership – chiefly, of course, because the club still had not won the league for a demoralising 23 years. In 1992, it looked as though the nightmare might finally come to an end, but Leeds pipped United at the post for the title. Robson's disappointment was compounded by injury forcing him to miss out on the League Cup Final victory over Nottingham Forest.

Time was becoming an adversary to one of United's finest servants as 1992 came to an end. Bryan Robson's starting role was under threat from the combative Paul Ince, who had designs on his central midfield role, and he was being given less and less opportunity to prove he still deserved that key berth in the team because of injuries. Even his role as captain was increasingly in doubt; Robbo was still club captain and skippered the side in most of his first-team appearances, but Steve Bruce was making a confident claim for the role because of his effectiveness when Robson was sidelined with injury.

Yet when all seemed lost, providence smiled on Robson and Ferguson, in the shape of the remarkable Eric Cantona. The Frenchman arrived at Old Trafford with a swagger, as if he owned the place, at the back end of 1992 and his influence would blow away the cobwebs that had surrounded the club for those agonising 26 years. He was the catalyst who would bring the title back to United – but just as importantly in the story of

Bryan Robson, ensure that Robbo would always be a legend at the Theatre of Dreams by paving the way for him to lead the club to their first league title since 1967.

In May 1993, United won the inaugural Premiership by ten points from Aston Villa. Then, a year later, Robson at 36 would win a second title medal although his prominence was now inevitably fading as age and injuries finally took their toll. Captain Marvel knew the game was up that summer – he had made enough appearances for that second Premiership champions' medal, but newcomer Roy Keane was now impatient to take his place in central midfield. At £3.75 million the previous summer, he had also become a British record signing when he left relegated Nottingham Forest for United. The 22-year-old Irishman had been told by Ferguson that he was being signed as a long-term replacement for Robson, but had been used out of position – including several spells at right-back – to accommodate the ageing Robson in the team.

By the end of the 1993–94 season, Keane had had enough. He was a tough talker and an even tougher performer and he told Ferguson he wanted to play in central midfield the next season – in Robson's role. He was like a proud young boxer whose time had finally come to give the defending champion a good hiding.

The bell finally tolled on the Robson era when Ferguson left him out of the FA Cup Final against Chelsea in May 1994. He had scored one of their four goals in the FA Cup semi-final replay victory over Oldham but Ferguson told him he wanted to give his youngsters a boost by naming them instead of Robson in the final squad. Robbo revealed that the boss had told him he was not going to be involved by saying, '"You can have a drink tonight if you want … I've got to look after the young lads who are coming through and make them feel part of it. Here's a few quid. Get yourself a drink."

'"I don't want your money, I don't want a drink," I replied. I felt more angry than insulted.'

It was a sickener for Bryan who – along with Steve Bruce – had led United to the Premiership title for the second consecutive year as they beat Blackburn to the crown by eight points. Robson had set his heart on leading United to FA Cup glory – and the added distinction of being the man who had led them to the first league and cup double in their history.

United duly became only the fourth team of the 20th century to win 'the Double' – but Robson would not be an active part of it as they thrashed Chelsea 4-0 at Wembley, with the incomparable Cantona bagging a brilliant brace.

Ferguson would later admit it was one of the hardest calls of his career, while Robson would leave United with a bitter taste in his mouth. He was 'very angry' and 'upset' that Ferguson had treated him 'so badly', although he would, in later years, refine his indignation, conceding that while Ferguson may not have been right, he certainly *had* the right to make whatever decision he thought best for Manchester United. Robson's 13-year spell at United was over and he left the club to become the player-manager at Middlesbrough. It was a sad ending to the reign of one of United's greatest servants – and number sevens – but the Bryan Robson story was not over ... not by a long chalk.

Having examined Robbo's service to his club, what about his country? Robbo's international career was certainly as eventful, if not nearly as rewarding in terms of silverware, as that he enjoyed at United. He made his début for the national side in the 2-0 European Championship qualifier win over the Republic of Ireland on 6 February 1980 and bowed out 11 years later, again at Wembley, in the 1-0 triumph over Turkey on 16 October 1991. Robson won 90 caps and played in 46 wins, 27 draws and 17 defeats, scoring 26 goals. He was booked just once and was never sent off, a fine record considering the all-action, take-no-prisoners style of his game.

The FA's official site sums up his international career rather splendidly in three paragraphs after conceding that his efforts were 'lung-busting': 'More's the pity then, that in 90 games for England, the memories come tinged with a wistful sense of what might have been had injury – so often caused in the line of fire – not cost him so dearly.

'Two of his three World Cup campaigns were cruelly cut short this way. The one he did manage to see through, his first, in Spain in 1982, began with him smashing home a fairytale goal after just 27 seconds against France – the first of two strikes in a 3-1 success in Bilbao.

'But England would exit in the second round despite not losing a game. In 1986, a dislocated shoulder suffered in the stalemate against Morocco ended Robson's hopes in Mexico. Achilles problems caused his early exit against the Dutch in Italia '90.'

Again, injury would blight the cause for this extraordinary performer. The FA conclude their accolade to him with these words, 'At his brilliant, driving best, Robson was probably the most complete midfielder of his day, with the vision to dominate in midfield and the tackling skills honed by playing as a left-back in his early days.'

He scored the first of his 26 goals in the 1981 defeat by Norway. His best ever was arguably the spectacular right-foot volley against East Germany in a friendly in 1984.

The team's composition in the first and last matches of Robbo's reign shows how England's formation and style changed over the years. Against Ireland, under the stewardship of the shrewd Ron Greenwood, the line-up was: Ray Clemence; Trevor Cherry, Dave Watson, Phil Thompson, Kenny Sansom; Bryan Robson, Terry McDermott, Laurie Cunningham; Kevin

Keegan, David Johnson, Tony Woodcock. Steve Coppell was substitute and Keegan scored both goals – ironically, Robson had replaced Coppell as number 7 at United and would take the captaincy off Keegan for England.

By the time of his swansong in 1991, England looked quite different under the depressing, long-ball direction of Graham 'Turnip' Taylor: Chris Woods; Lee Dixon, Des Walker, Gary Mabbutt, Stuart Pearce; David Platt, Bryan Robson, David Batty, Chris Waddle; Gary Lineker, Alan Smith – the latter of whom scored the winner.

I would argue that by the time it was all over for Robbo, he was playing in a superior England team to the one he'd started in. Certainly the midfield appeared stronger with Batty, Platty and Waddle in there. Yet Taylor was a much less talented manager at this level than Greenwood; he did not know how to handle major stars and his tactical nous was certainly debatable. In that last match, Robson claims Taylor asked him to play as a virtual left-winger and certainly gives the impression he felt that he had played under better managers. Robson would leave disheartened and would later say, 'The position didn't suit me and the manager didn't suit me.'

Back in 1981, Greenwood knew straight away he had a winner in the young Robson. He included him in all eight of the qualifying games for the 1982 World Cup in Spain, the results of which earned England a place in the finals. During one of the qualifiers – the shock 2-1 defeat in Norway – Robson scored his first England goal. Robbo's goal did not make headline news that night; his effort was shaded by the torturous, now legendary screams of commentator Bjorn Minge on Norwegian TV. At the final whistle, he shouted himself hoarse with the immortal words, 'Lord Nelson! Lord Beaverbrook! Sir Winston Churchill! Sir Anthony Eden! Clement Attlee! Henry Cooper!

Lady Diana! Maggie Thatcher – can you hear me, Maggie Thatcher! Your boys took one hell of a beating! Your boys took one hell of a beating!' If Robbo's début goal will forever be intertwined with Norway's major claim to fame, it did not bother the United man one bit. He said, 'All that mattered to me was that I scored but that we lost. It was a bad one to lose but at least we were able to make up for it and reach the Finals in Spain.'

Robbo played a major role in helping England reach the second round in Spain, the quarter-finals in Mexico four years later, the European Championship group stages in 1988 and the World Cup semi-final at Italia '90. That goal against France after just 27 seconds in 1982 remained the fastest in World Cup Finals history until 2002, when Hakan Sükür scored after ten seconds for Turkey in the third-place match against South Korea. For Robson's achievement, he received an inscribed gold watch, which he still occasionally wears.

But does that list of creditable achievements make him a legend at international level? Some would argue yes, particularly those wearing red-and-white United shirts. But others beg to disagree. They contend that Robson should have done better, but that injury cost him dear. They point to him missing the 'Hand of God' match against Argentina – arguably England's seminal match of his era. Diego Maradona had scored both goals to knock England out in the 2-1 quarter-final, but Robson would surely have made a difference had he played. He had initially been hurt in a warm-up game, and was never fully fit. Robson then suffered another injury in the 0-0 draw in England's second game against Morocco and played no further part in the World Cup that year.

Chief among his critics is journalist Nick Chapman, who works for *Sun Sport* and is a regular follower of the national team both at home and abroad. He has supported them around the globe since 1980, taking in World Cups in Spain, Mexico, France, Japan and Germany and European Championships in Germany, England, Belgium and Portugal, plus a host of qualifying matches and friendlies from Liechtenstein to Macedonia, and so is ideally placed to comment on the Robson era from 1980–91.

Chapman believes that Robson should have achieved much, much more. He concedes there were moments of brilliance – when Robbo was rightly acclaimed a hero – but that, ultimately, the fans and the country felt let down. This is what he had to say when I asked him to give me a guided tour of the ups and downs of Bryan Robson's England days. Chapman told me, 'The 1970s were a tough time for English football, a period in which international failure had become the norm and sporting figureheads were hard to find. It was also a time in which the world was being introduced to British hooliganism and responding with violence of its own. But tough times often unearth tough people – and so it was with Bryan Robson.

'A transfer to Manchester United had raised his profile by the time Ron Greenwood's side headed for the 1982 World Cup Finals in Spain. But his standing among England fans was secured less than a minute into England's opening game of the tournament. I was still trying to persuade a Frenchman out of my seat behind the goal when Terry Butcher headed on a Steve Coppell throw-in from the right and Robson hooked home England's first goal of the tournament after 27 seconds. He scored again during that astonishing 3-1 victory over the hugely-fancied French in Bilbao and his inspiring, all-action performance in midfield dominated discussions as we drank the hotel bar dry that night. Bryan Robson was our new national hero – official!

'But England's next match, a 2-0 win over Czechoslovakia, gave us a hint of what was to come from Robson throughout his international career – an energetic, committed performance brought to a sudden halt by injury just before half-time. As much as we grew to admire Robson the midfielder, Robson the captain and Robson the inspirational battler, we England fans also grew to understand the man we called Captain Marvel would also always be Robson the unreliable. He was Robson the perpetually injured.

'I followed England to Mexico in 1986, with Robson firmly established as England captain and the driving force behind Bobby Robson's highly-favoured side. To fully appreciate Robson's impact on us that summer, you have to understand what England fans were forced to tolerate during the early days of our month in Mexico.

'I was based in Mexico City and flew north for each of England's three group matches in Monterey. On the day of our opener against Portugal, my plane was met at Monterey Airport by heavily-armed members of the Mexican army. They escorted myself and half-a-dozen other England fans off the plane and into a military truck. We were then shadowed by more trucks laden with Mexican troops as we were driven past a column of tanks to the stadium, which was ringed by barbed-wire fencing and patrolled by hundreds more soldiers in full combat gear. Welcome to Mexico.

'What we needed from England was victory and an inspiring performance to lift the feelings of fear and trepidation that were gripping the travelling support. What we got was wholly different and desperately disappointing.

'Robson went into the tournament recovering from a shoulder injury. He lasted only 79 minutes of that miserable 1-0 defeat to Portugal. The second match – a desperately poor 0-0

The young George Best in March 1963.   © *Action Images/MSI*

Above: George Best holds aloft the European Cup after Manchester United beat Benfica 4-1 in 1968; Best scored one of the goals in extra time.
© *Action Images/MSI*

Below: Matt Busby's Manchester United with the Cup.

© *Action Images/MSI*

Above left: George Best in 1972.   © *Action Images/MSI*

Above right: George and Angie Best in 1982   © *Action Images/MSI*

Below left: Out on the town. With Noel Gallagher of Oasis at an awards ceremony, 1999.   © *Action Images/MSI*

Below right: Remembering a legend. Thousands throng the streets of Belfast as George Best's funeral cortege leaves Stormont, 3 December, 2005.   © *REUTERS/Andrew Parsons/Pool Picture Supplied by Action Images*

Above: Bryan Robson celebrates after scoring in the 1983 FA Cup final replay, Manchester United v. Brighton & Hove Albion. Manchester United won 4-0.   © *Action Images/Sporting Pictures/Dave Hodges*

Below: Robson, captaining Manchester United, shakes hands with Barcelona captain Diego Maradona before their European Cup Winner's Cup second leg quarter-final match in March 1984. Manchester United won 3-0 and went through 3-2 on aggregate.   © *Getty Images*

Above: Robson triumphant after Manchester United win the 1991 European Cup Winner's Cup Final.

© Action Images

Below: As Middlesbrough manager, Bryan Robson shakes hands with Terry Venables after inviting the latter to become first team coach at the struggling club, December 2000.

© Getty Images

Above: The young Eric Cantona turns out for Auxerre during the
1988/89 French championship.   © *Action Images*

Below: The 1994 PFA awards, at which Andy Cole wins Young Player o.
the Year while Cantona wins Player of the Year.

© *Action Images/Tony Henshaw*

Eric Cantona clings to the goalpost to celebrate scoring against
Liverpool upon his return to Manchester United from suspension
in 1995.

© Cleva/Fotosports International

Above: Eric Cantona, king of beach football, playing in Rio de Janeiro, Brazil in 2005. © *Reuters/Sergio Moraes/Action Images*

Below: Beckham, still in a number 7 shirt, this time in action for England in a World Cup qualifier against Georgia. © *Mark Leech/Offside*

Above: Beckham and Dwight Yorke celebrate their win over Bayern Munich in the Champions League final, May 1999.

© *Manchester United via Getty Images*

Below: Beckham joins the elite club of England centurions in March 2008.

© *Cleva*

Above left: Cristiano Ronaldo in action as Manchester United beat
Panathinaikos 1-0 during a 2003 Champions League encounter.

Above right: Ronaldo seen in June 2005 with the Indonesian boy
Martunis, who was found after the Boxing Day tsunami wearing a
Portugal football shirt with Ronaldo's name on the back.

Below: Ole Gunnar Solskjaer, Ronaldo, Sir Alex Ferguson, Roy Carroll
Darren Fletcher and Eric Djemba-Djemba in the dressing room after
Manchester United's 2004 FA Cup Final success against Millwall.

Above: Wayne Rooney is sent off by the referee in the England-Portugal World Cup clash, 2006, after shoving Ronaldo during an altercation over Rooney's foul on Carvalho.   © *Mark Leech/Offside*

Below: Ronaldo and Rooney are soon reconciled; here Ronaldo applauds at the end of the 2007 FA Cup semifinal tie with Watford, during which Rooney scored twice.   © *Cleva/Backpage Images*

Ronaldo with the Football Writers' Association Footballer of the Year
award for 2007. © *Action Images/Alex Morton Livepic*

draw with Morocco – saw the injury hit him again, this time four minutes before half-time. Captain Marvel's tournament was over. Of course, the injury was not Robson's fault, but it's hard acknowledging that when you are thousands of miles from home, thousands of pounds out of pocket, being treated like a terrorist and watching your team spectacularly underperform in a tournament you expected them to win.

'Mexico was the first time Robson's importance had been called into question by angry, frustrated England supporters. And it was also the first time I experienced genuine doubt being cast on Robson's credentials. It seems unbelievable in these days of security guards, exclusion zones and terror alerts, but in Mexico City I spent many a night drinking in hotel bars with players from other participating nations.

'One such night saw myself, my friend Paul Fry and a group of Scots from our hotel rubbing shoulders in the Sheraton Hotel bar with pretty much the entire Danish squad. I was chatting happily to a small group of players that included Michael Laudrup and Jan Molby, when they offered up the opinion Robson was the most over-rated player in Europe. He couldn't pass, they said, lacked real quality and was a one-trick pony – his "trick" being a combative, gung-ho nature. In one conversation, the Danes had highlighted everything that was bad about English football ... and good about Robson. It was impossible to argue against.

'Robson played no further part in Mexico, but at least his luck – if not his success – changed two years later when, having obviously failed to learn my lesson, I headed with my father Barry for Euro '88 in Germany. The tournament was different, the continent was different – but the unfriendly, threatening, official welcome was the same.

'Just as in Mexico two years earlier, the thousands of travelling

England fans needed their team to lift the gloom. Sadly, just as in Mexico, they failed the task. Ironically, I consider this tournament the pinnacle of Robson's international career. I suppose that isn't quite so surprising when you appreciate it was the only tournament in which injury didn't severely limit his appearance and effectiveness.

'He was one of the few to come out with any credit from our opening 1-0 defeat to the Republic of Ireland – how *did* Ray Houghton's wickedly deflected shot go in?

'But it was his performance in the 3-1 defeat to eventual winners Holland in our second match in Düsseldorf that lives with me to this day. Make no mistake, England were thoroughly outplayed by a classy, exciting and exuberant Dutch side boasting Gullit, Van Basten, Rijkaard, the Koemans, Mühren … But when Robson equalised early in the second half and turned in the kind of perpetual motion, battering-ram performance that had become his trademark, we England fans actually began to believe it could be our day.

'Marco Van Basten thought otherwise and completed his hat-trick in a 3-1 victory, but at least we had witnessed Robson at his peak, at his badge-thumping, never-say-die, fight-to-the-last best.

'Two years later, it was all over … 155 minutes into Italia '90, the injury jinx struck again. This time it was an Achilles problem that forced him off during the 0-0 draw with the Dutch. He flew home shortly afterwards and you knew the end of his international career was approaching.

'When Robson had led England to Mexico '86, he was exactly what English football needed – an inspirational leader, a driving force in midfield, a wholehearted, honest player of whom we could all be proud. How sad, then, that we were left five years later wondering what might have been.'

Interesting, provocative words from a man in the know. But

others remain convinced Robson did the best he could and was worthy of the Captain Marvel tag even for England. Another England fan, Tom Bray, says, 'Untimely injuries robbed him of the chance to really make his mark on the world stage, ruling him out of the 1986 and 1990 World Cups, but Robson remains one of England's most inspirational captains. A dynamic midfielder who was equally adept in a defensive role as he was in marauding forward to score – as he demonstrated 26 times for England – he was a captain who led by example.

'Widely regarded as the best midfielder of his generation, Robson would frequently inspire through the intensity of his performance and his leadership the moniker "Captain Marvel". He was held in such high esteem that Bobby Robson, manager of England for the 1990 World Cup, still believes they would have won the tournament had his namesake not suffered an Achilles strain in the second group match.'

Robson – who led England 65 times – David Beckham (58), Billy Wright (90) and Bobby Moore (90) are the only players to captain England more than 40 times. Robson would have challenged the Wright/Moore record of 90 captaincies but for the injuries that marred his international appearances. Robson's first match as skipper was on 17 November 1982 when he took the armband for the European Championship qualifying game against Greece in Salonica. England won 3-0, then went on to beat Luxemburg 9-0 in their next match.

Another writer, James Lawton, believes Robson deserves more credit for battling on with England despite the crippling array of injuries with which he had to contend. Lawton said, 'Three times he went on to the great stage as the embodiment of English hopes. On the first occasion, in Spain in 1982, he had the impact of a wrecking ball. In Bilbao, a place which reserves its warmest welcome for warrior footballers, he destroyed the

France of Michel Platini with two goals of ransacking authority.

'England, however, trailed out of the competition without losing a game and, in 1986 and 1990, Robson, the fabled Captain Marvel, was cut down by injury, the first time in Mexico when a protective harness on a dislocated shoulder failed to carry him through the lightest of challenges against Morocco.

'Even then he was so loath to leave the theatre of football war he refused the orders of Manchester United to return to England to start immediate treatment, preferring to encourage his team-mates on the road to their dismaying confrontation with the hand of Maradona and the feet of his genius.'

It is perhaps telling that in all-time England great teams and squads, Robson is well favoured. Bobby Robson loved him and had no hesitation in naming him in 'the perfect 23-man party from the 160 players who have been included in England World Cup squads.' Robson's squad read: Goalkeepers – Gordon Banks, Peter Shilton and Ray Clemence; full-backs – Jimmy Armfield, Don Howe, Ray Wilson and Roger Byrne; centre-halves – Jack Charlton, Billy Wright, Bobby Moore and Terry Butcher; wingers – Tom Finney, Stanley Matthews and John Barnes; midfielders – Bobby Charlton, Wilf Mannion, Martin Peters, Johnny Haynes and Bryan Robson; centre-forwards – Geoff Hurst, Jackie Milburn, Jimmy Greaves and Gary Lineker.

Not a bad selection, Bobby. But Robbo ... hero or flop overall for England? Whatever you say about Bryan, he certainly provokes extreme reactions, whether supportive or critical. He was a man born to lead, but with several facets to that style of leadership – the good, the bad and the ugly – and he provoked widely dissenting views both as a player and a manager. Is it possible to find a general consensus, a little agreement, on his rightful place in the pantheon of the Magnificent Sevens?

6

Too Much Bottle?

'I used to drive home from Manchester United training along the M56 and there was a left turn for Wilmslow, where I lived, and a right turn for Hale, where Norman Whiteside, Paul McGrath and Bryan Robson lived. I used to say that it was left for under three pints a night and right for more than ten.'
FORMER MANCHESTER UNITED STAR GORDON STRACHAN SUMS
UP THE OLD TRAFFORD CULTURE IN HIS PLAYING DAYS

'I dismiss as total rubbish that the ethics of the club under me were the wrong ones.'
BRYAN ROBSON AFTER LEAVING MIDDLESBROUGH, 2001

Apart from Captain Marvel, Robbo, during his years at Old Trafford, was referred to in some quarters as one of United's so-called Three Musketeers of the 1980s, along with Norman Whiteside and Paul McGrath, both of whom were booted out of Old Trafford after Alex Ferguson took charge. Robson adamantly maintains that he was not a boozer. He points to the fact that, if he was such a boozer, how come his game was all action and speedy aggression? How could he have reached such heights if he was anything less than a total professional.

In 2006, while still boss at West Brom, he had this to say In answer to his critics: 'Throughout the whole of my playing career, I never missed a day's training with a hangover. Even so, the reputation follows me around. Perhaps if I'm seen out, it's assumed I'm on a bender, but most managers, like most normal people, go out for a meal and a few drinks now and then. It's called living.'

As I have mentioned earlier, I myself was addicted to alcohol at one stage in my life and I attended AA meetings with George Best. Bryan Robson, however, was someone who liked a drink now and again and he does not strike me as a man who would drink alone in his lounge at home with the curtains drawn to keep out the light.

Robson's friend and sometime teammate Whiteside wrote in the dedication to autobiography *My Memories of Man Utd*: 'My drinking buddies Robbo, Big Paul and those I can't remember!' Clearly, he remembered Bryan Robson at the bar with him. Big Norm also regales us with his take on the Atkinson era. Whiteside said, 'Big Ron was so laid back, it was unbelievable at times how things were. There were never any cross words exchanged and he practically let you do what you liked between Sunday and Friday, as long as you contributed to the game on a Saturday afternoon … Ron didn't just want to be the manager, he wanted to be a friend of the players as well and again this was perhaps a bad thing.' Bad? Maybe. It certainly puts a different gloss on the situation than the one earlier presented by Robson.

Whiteside's memories of the new days under Ferguson also make stark reading. After 'the rather easy life we had under Atkinson', Big Norm admits Ferguson's arrival blew away the cobwebs of lethargy as the new boss made 'quick, early decisions … training had been stepped up, discipline and personal appearance were paid more attention to.' It is hardly the fairly seamless transition Robbo has described.

Whiteside also says, 'The friendship between Paul [McGrath] and myself was cemented way back in the days when we both lived with Mr and Mrs Fannon and, along with Bryan Robson, we could have been Manchester's Three Musketeers … Robbo could go out drinking at night, wake up in the morning, go training and never be up nor down.' That last phrase strikes me as important – 'and never be up nor down'. I put it to my psychoanalyst friend and she observed, 'Yes, he was just a man who liked a drink and the social side of it ... the companionship.'

Whiteside informs us that when he and Robson were injured they would go 'out for a few pints to forget the misfortunes we suffered with injuries', but that is no surprise. Out injured is a painful place to be for footballers – Roy Keane would admit to me that he used to mope about the house and feel down, that the last place he wanted to be was at the ground in the company of footballers going about their day-to-day business. While Keane chose the house to mope about in, Robson and Whiteside would go to their local.

Robson's closeness to Whiteside and McGrath is illustrated by the fact that he wrote a foreword for both men in their respective books. In *Ooh! Aah! Paul McGrath*, Robson recalls their friendship, saying, 'After training, we'd go for the occasional drink, once a month or so, myself and Norman and Kevin Moran. Paul would come with us.' Clearly, Robson was no McGrath in drinking terms.

The big Irishman admitted he valued Robbo's advice during his time at United, and his company out on the town, 'At United, it was Kevin Moran, Norman Whiteside and Bryan Robson who kept me sane, who kept me on the straight and narrow ... We were a regular foursome in the drinking holes of Hale and Altrincham....'

When Ferguson took over at Old Trafford, he clearly had an image of Robson as a man who liked his pint. Robson admits as much, describing how the boss took him in his office to explain his position on the demon booze. '"Look, Bryan," Ferguson said, "I've heard you like a drink and I've no problem with that as long as it's not in the week. I don't want players coming in with alcohol on their breath."

'"Fair enough, Gaffer," I said. "If that's what you want, that's the way it will be."'

Robson admits that the manager wanted them to abstain almost totally – although he would allow them a glass of wine with a meal on a Saturday night. It was certainly a different scenario to the good old, bad old days of Big Ron.

When you talk to Robson about booze, he says, 'I could drink loads of pints without falling over and making myself look stupid. It didn't take the edge off my game because, if I'd had a session on the Monday, I wouldn't have another drop for the rest of the week. The morning after, I'd train hard and sweat it out. When you are comparatively young and fit, you can cope with it. I always made sure the drink didn't affect my job.'

When I asked Arsène Wenger about the way a footballer should treat his body he said, 'It is very important for footballers to live the right way. Everything in moderation and the right food and the right nourishment. I do not want my players drinking too much as it affects their minds and their bodies.'

I asked an AA spokesman for his views on the effect of alcohol on sporting prowess. He said, 'Of course, alcohol can affect a sportsman's performance. OK, they may sweat it out, or think they do, but let's remember it takes 48 hours for it to leave the system. Alcohol can also increase aggression, adversely affect your judgement, co-ordination and reaction times to a great degree. Plus there is the dehydration and the tiredness – the body is suffering whatever you may think.'

And a spokesman from former England and Arsenal star Tony Adams' Sporting Chance clinic said, 'For the sportsman or woman, the effects can also be only too obvious – and often very publicly obvious – in an arena where the focus is on physical activity. Loss of form or performance is easily spotted by team-mates or managers. But most of all, though, they are reluctant to admit it even if they know it, deep down ...'

Robson suffered more injuries than any other footballer I have ever known. He was, without a doubt, the bravest performer I have ever seen on a football pitch – but was he also perhaps one of the most foolhardy?

United fan Dave Morgan argues the case that Robson could have achieved much more if he had come under Ferguson's more disciplined tutelage and driving ambition earlier. He says, 'You can't help feeling that had he been in more illustrious company while wearing the red shirt, then he wouldn't have been under such pressure to win games single-handedly. That, in turn, would have reduced his time on the treatment table during his 12 years at Old Trafford.

'He can only have been even better. What if more of Robbo's years at Old Trafford had coincided with the Fergie era? His would have been one of the most richly rewarded careers ever.'

But Morgan does not believe that Robson's gung-ho bravery deserves a barracking. He contends, 'It's easy to accuse Robbo of being too gung-ho, but I don't think we'd have had him any other way. A real blood-and-thunder hero for whom the name of Manchester United meant everything.'

The *Mail on Sunday*'s Andy Bucklow also makes a case for remembering with fondness Robson's walks on the wild side. Bucklow says, 'If anything, Robson was probably too brave for his own good, and there was always a suspicion that he pushed himself a tad too hard to make up for the deficiencies of others. It is total conjecture but one can't help wondering that, if had he been at his peak as part of the all-conquering United sides of the mid- to late Nineties, the injuries wouldn't have been quite as frequent. For the best part of a decade, the man was Manchester United in a way that even Roy Keane wasn't. Both, at times, carried the team, but Robson shouldered the heavier load.'

Robson eventually left Old Trafford to manage Middlesbrough in 1994. What I admire about Robbo is that he is a battler to the end, a man of true grit. Yes, someone you would want in the trenches with you.

He did well at 'Boro in the early years. Along with chairman Steve Gibson, he transformed a rundown, ramshackle club that earned promotion to the Premiership and ended up being able to attract gems such as the Brazilian Juninho, the Italian Ravanelli and the unpredictable genius of Paul Gascoigne and Paul Merson. 'Boro would move from the derelict Ayresome Park into the brand-new Riverside Stadium a year after Robbo's arrival. He took them into the stadium and the Premiership as Division One champions – no mean feat in his first season as a manager. A year later, the crowd had soared to an average of 29,000 from well below the 20,000s in the bad old days, and Juninho had signed for £4 million along with £6 million Nick Barmby.

By the summer of 1997, Robson had taken 'Boro to two Cup finals – they lost to Leicester in the League Cup and Chelsea in the FA Cup – and back to Division One. They were relegated after losing three points as a punishment for failing to fulfil a fixture against Blackburn, claiming that most of their squad was suffering from 'flu – an excuse rejected by a sceptical FA. The board kept faith in Robson and were rewarded with promotion back to the Premiership as Division One runners-up the following season. They also made it to another Wembley final – again losing 2-0 to Chelsea, this time in the League Cup.

1999 saw 'Boro's best finish under Robbo – they ended up ninth in the Premiership and things looked rosy with Gazza and

Merson now on board. But, by 2001, Robson's tenure was over – during the preceding season he had been forced to call in Terry Venables for help as 'Boro struggled in the relegation zone. Eventually, they avoided the drop but the damage had been done. In the 2001 close season, Robson handed in his notice after seven years as manager and was replaced by Steve McClaren, who would go on to become England manager five years later.

Robson was perceived as damaged goods over his decision to bring in Venables. It was seen as a sign of weakness, although you could also argue that it was a sign of strength and integrity. Robson cared enough for the club to put to one side what would inevitably be seen as surrender; he cared enough to ask for help.

He explained his thinking by saying, 'A lot of people, some of them close to me as well, have said that I sacrificed myself by doing what I did in bringing Terry on board. I didn't see it that way. When things weren't working out, I thought we needed a different voice around the place. I didn't want to let it stagnate, to stand back and do nothing, then still go down. I was looking at the likes of Brian Kidd, Archie Knox and Don Howe, coaches I've worked with. I know how good they are. I had to make a change.

'It was no slight on my staff either. We'd all been at 'Boro for seven years. But certain players had got too familiar with the set-up. I had to turn it round. Terry was the one man I could think of to do it. So I went for him. Could I have walked out then? If I had, Terry wouldn't have accepted the job. I was determined to get it right on the pitch. Then, if I had to leave at the end of the season, so be it. I never felt threatened or isolated by the arrangement. We worked together and it worked out.'

'Boro fans on the whole appreciated – and understood – what Robson had done in the cause of their beloved club. An editorial on the fans' website *boroforecast.com* summed it all up as Robbo walked away in 2001: 'Last season was Robson's last throw of the dice … and he knew it. His uncanny ability to entice some of the football world's biggest names to Teesside, his greatest strength, continued to the end. And that includes Terry Venables. In desperate trouble in mid-December, Robson turned to his mentor to steer this great club of ours out of trouble. His willingness to play second fiddle to Venables, a great coach, for the 'Boro cause speaks volumes. There was no going back once Terry arrived and everyone knew it. Not least Robson, who never once rocked the boat.

'Whether Robson deserves to stand alongside the very best the club has offered – George Camsell, George Hardwick, Wilf Mannion, Brian Clough, Graeme Souness, Juninho – is open to debate and discussion for a long time, but Robson, in his way, has been the equal of them all. His presence alone early on, his ability to locate and lure the likes of Juninho, Fabrizio Ravanelli, Paul Merson and Alen Boksic should never be underestimated.

'Perhaps had Venables been there then, there would be a different story now. In all probability, Robson was let down by his motivational skills at the highest level and also, at times, by his players of the highest level. His demise and withdrawal to the background under Venables was, for the true fan, painful indeed. Think what it must have done to the man himself.

'Yes, it probably was time for a change; it was the manner that was unfortunate. Unlike several leading Premiership managers, Robson never once whinged and neither should the fans have done. 'Boro supporters should have looked back not to where they once were, but to where they where when Robson came. And to where we are now, and for that we should be grateful. The Robson era will in time, I've no doubt, be looked upon as a golden era of memories for 'Boro's fans. And the squad he will now pass into the hands of another untested manager, who, like Robson himself, has the same Man Utd connections, is as good a start as any for a fledgling manager, despite worries over the average squad age.

'Bryan, thanks for the memories, lad.'

It is a touching tribute to Robson's efforts up on Teesside and you would have thought the man's honesty and willingness to graft would have brought him a sooner-rather-than-later return to management. In the event, it was not to be – it would be over three years before the Manchester United legend would once again manage in the Premiership. During that period, Robbo suffered continual jibes about his drinking and there were rumours that he was going off the rails. One newspaper suggested he had even had an affair with a television presenter in 2000 and that his wife had attacked the girl – alleged to be Clare Tomlinson of Sky Sports – with a crutch when she learned of the indiscretion (Clare was using crutches as she had a broken ankle at the time of the alleged liaison).

Others whispered that he was just not up to it when it came to management. Paul Merson, one of the men on whom he had staked his reputation when he had signed him for £4.5 million from Arsenal in 1997, had fired the starter's gun in the 'Robbo's a boozer' stakes when he made damaging comments before his move to Aston Villa for £6.75 million in 1998. The recovering alcoholic said he was relieved to have escaped a club for boozers – a glorified pub team – stewarded by Robson. It was a claim Robson would vigorously deny, but it was also one that would be associated with him as he tried desperately to find a way back into the game that had seemingly turned its back on him.

Merson had said, 'A lot of the players like to have a drink and a bet. The situation is too much for me – the danger signs are there. I know if I keep on being exposed to drinking and gambling, I am in danger of going back to my old ways. I made Bryan aware of my feelings in a conversation ... but this isn't an overnight decision on my part ... I had three meetings with the club last year about getting away and no one ever knew about it. Things were sorted out behind the scenes and everything was kept hush-hush.'

Robson would admit his hurt at the criticism, and received backing from his former skipper at 'Boro for two seasons, Andy Townsend. Robson said, 'It was a total nonsense. There was a code of conduct at the club and, if the players stepped out of line, they were punished. And there weren't too many players who stepped out of line.'

Former Republic of Ireland international Andy Townsend added, 'Too much has been said and written about the man by people who have not worked under him. The problem is that Bryan picked up this tag because of the backbiting that goes on in football. Whenever things don't go to plan, the negatives are always the first thing flagged up – and that's all the ammunition people had to hit him with. Let's face it, you couldn't criticise Bryan Robson the player.

'But there was never a problem. If there was, do you think players like Fabrizio Ravanelli and Juninho would have played for him? Do you think he would have achieved what he did with the club? He achieved an awful lot with Middlesbrough. That place was on its knees until Steve Gibson came along and asked the most respected footballer of his generation to take over as a manager. Yes, money was available, but he needed to get the football side up and running. I played under a lot of managers. Bryan knew what he wanted from his team and he knew its limitations.'

Genuine support for Robbo, indeed, and much welcomed by

him as well. Robson, aged 47, emerged a wiser, more hardened man and manager when he walked back into The Hawthorns as manager of West Brom in November 2004. He had taken the hard knocks – including a short spell at Bradford City, too short to really judge him on it – but his enthusiasm was uncurbed as he returned to the club he had first joined 32 years earlier as a 15-year-old apprentice. He said, 'I was disappointed not to have been offered a job like this before. I had seven good years at Middlesbrough. They were 14th in the old First Division when I took over, didn't have a training ground and we enjoyed two promotions and three Cup finals. Since then, I think I've improved as a manager. I'm determined to do this job and I'm coming back into it with an appetite for it.'

The wheel had come full circle and chairman Jeremy Peace had no doubts about Robson. Peace admitted, 'I had a lengthy chat with Middlesbrough chairman Steve Gibson. We have researched Bryan extensively and we are satisfied with his credentials for the job. Bryan played Premiership football until he was 39 and didn't miss a day of training through illness.'

Robson had not been top choice for the rebuilding work at The Hawthorns – the board had wanted Glenn Hoddle to take on the role – and it would end in tears when he was sacked in September 2006. In the intervening years, he had proved he *could* do a Houdini act when required, by saving West Brom from what looked certain relegation in the 2004/05 season. The following year, the club was relegated and, when they made an indifferent start to the 2006/07 season, the writing was on the wall for the great battler. Peace said, 'After much deliberation, it has been decided that a change is necessary if the club is to achieve its aims for this season and beyond. With promotion a priority, the board felt that, given the club's league position, the best way forward was to agree to make a change now.'

Robson, typical of the man, did not hold a grudge. He said, 'I've really enjoyed the short time I've been at the Albion. The fans have been different class and I just hope, with the squad of players in place, that they get back up to the Premier League, which I really believe they will do this season.'

Baggies fanatic Mike Tuck summed up the feelings of many Albion fans when he said, 'It was the right move. He's a good bloke ... we all knew he had given his best, but I just don't know if he is cut out to be a manager. You know, at the end of the day, we stayed up that season by the skin of our teeth. We may have been the only team to be bottom of the Premiership at Christmas and still survive, but we also did it on the lowest number of points and because Charlton beat Crystal Palace in the last five minutes.

'The season we were relegated we didn't win any of the last 13 games so, to be fair, he needed to get off to a flyer to the new season in the Championship. Maybe it would be best if he called it a day now and let the memory of his playing days be the ultimate legacy of his footballing career, the yardstick by which he should be judged.'

That was an unlikely scenario given the nature of the man, the inbuilt fighting machine that epitomised Robson the player, Robson the man and, ultimately, Robson the manager of men. He would not want to skulk away without proving himself; it was simply not in his nature.

I can certainly sympathise with the idea put forward by Tuck – maybe the ultimate role for Robbo would be as a number two to a top-class number one. Look how successful he was as Venables' assistant for England in Euro 96. Don't forget that, before it went pear-shaped at Boro, William Hill were giving odds of 6-4 for him to succeed Venables as England coach. Having said all that, Sheffield United became probably the last club to take a punt on

Robson as their No 1 in 2007. They appointed him with Brian Kidd as his No 2 just days after the resignation of the mischievous Neil Warnock. Blades chairman Terry Robinson said he was convinced Robson had the motivational skills to make them thrive again – but once again it would end in tears. Robson would leave the club after turning down a 'head of football' role in February 2008, just eight months after he had joined. The Blades lay 16th in the Championship, seven points off the relegation zone and fans protested against Robson after he had won only 14 times in 39 games.

It is also interesting to note that Sir Alex Ferguson rated him as a motivator, offering him the opportunity to take part in coaching sessions when he left the Riverside. Maybe Robbo's Achilles heel is that he loved too much being in the thick of it when he was captain of United and England, and never really wanted to stop being one of the lads? That would also point to him becoming a number two – a middleman between the lads and the boss. I'll never forget the time he helped out Gazza when the Geordie man-boy – who was then playing for 'Boro – was suicidal on a railway station late at night. He said he was going to throw himself in front of the next train, only to discover the last one had long gone. Robbo takes up the story: 'I was at home in Manchester, he was in Hertfordshire. The first thing I did was see if someone could get to him quickly. I phoned his dad but he couldn't help. Then I spoke to Jimmy 'Five Bellies' and he was busy doing some promotional stuff. Finally, I spoke to Sheryl [his former wife] and she agreed to pick him up and take him to a hotel.

'I panicked at first, but I knew I had to do something and, as I drove down, I spoke to the medical staff at 'Boro. The feeling was that I should take him to the Priory, so I phoned ahead and told them we were coming. Paul was in a real state when I got to him, but we arrived at the Priory at about 3.00am and the doctor was waiting for us. He was brilliant. He had a chat with both of us and then I left it to them. As a club, we're going to get on with that and, as a manager and a friend, I'm going to try to help Gazza as much as I can.'

It was 1998 and the beginning of what has been a rocky road to recovery for Gazza – and it was all down to Robbo. The Priory taught him that he was an alcoholic and the basic principles of the AA programme – then let him out with the warning that his survival depended upon him continuing to attend AA meetings.

Robson, the true friend ... yet when Gazza hijacked the team bus and crashed it into a concrete sleeper, causing thousands of pounds of damage, Robson would show the other side of his nature. He says, 'That was just irresponsible, and I had a real go at him in front of the other players and then fined him a fortnight's wages.'

Bryan Robson, the true friend, but also Bryan Robson the man who could deal out the tough love. Bryan Robson, a former United great; Bryan Robson, always a United legend. On 20 March, 2008, it was revealed that Robbo was coming home for good to his spiritual home of Old Trafford – that he would be rejoining the club he served with such distinction as their global ambassador. It was a fitting reward for a man who had never seemed truly at ease after leaving United in 1994. A true, well deserved, fairytale ending to the Bryan Robson story.

7

From Caveman to Cavemen

*'I remembered how the old Marseille manager had warned me ...
"Remember, when the sun is shining he plays, but it rains a lot in England."'*
HOWARD WILKINSON, FORMER LEEDS MANAGER

*'I even offered him the chance to pick the team himself ...He said, "Oh no.
That is your job. Leave anybody out but not me. I have to play."'*
HOWARD WILKINSON

On the wall of his bedroom, one poster stood out when Eric was a youngster in the south of France, the one of his ultimate hero, the one you would have expected to be of a French footballer; but, no, the man he most wanted to be, the one he most admired, was the one and only Bruce Lee. Many years later, fans of Manchester United would guffaw when the news of the Frenchman's idol was relayed to them; guffaw and nod sagely. Yes, it all made sense now, exactly why their ultimate hero, because of his rebellious and winning ways, had kicked out that dark midwinter night in 1995.

But that was Eric 'the King' all over, wasn't it? A walking, talking mass of contradictions, a man who was great yet fallible, a man who talked of philosophy and beauty, yet a man who would sometimes spark into life with anger and brutality; a man who, to many United fans, remains the greatest ever, but too often – to other football fans – also the most repulsive. One thing is for sure – this was no normal man and no normal footballer. United had been crying out for a superman to lift them from the depths of normality for 26 years. 26 long, miserable years since they had last won the league title.

Cantona arrived at Old Trafford in 1992 and, within a year, the wait that had lasted from 1967 was finally over. The nightmare had passed. Cantona was the final piece of the jigsaw, the catalyst for what would become known as The Ferguson Years; two decades of non-stop glory. And for five of them, with Eric in the team, half a decade of non-stop cabaret.

At £1.2 million, he would prove arguably Ferguson's best buy. OK, you could make a case for Peter Schmeichel at £650,000 and Roy Keane at £3.75 million, but without Eric, their impact may not have been as wondrous. He laid the foundations upon which they would build. He walked into Old Trafford like he owned the place in November 1992; 26 years old, but with more baggage than anyone else might pick up in two lifetimes. He had picked up the tag 'Le Brat' for his adventures in his native France and had managed to fall out with Howard Wilkinson at Leeds within nine months of arriving in the UK.

His temperament would be what endeared him to Manchester United's vast army of fans – indeed, most of us can relate to the rebel, we just usually do not have the guts, or if you look at it another way, the foolhardiness, to act like one. Eric did what he wanted, how he wanted, when he wanted; he remains the ultimate rebel with a cause and has earned a permanent place in the hearts of United fans.

At Old Trafford, he would win four Premiership titles in five years, including two league and FA Cup 'doubles' and, in 2001, he was voted Manchester United's player of the century. To this day, United fans still refer to him as Eric the King, the Frenchman taking up the mantle that once belonged to the also legendary Denis Law. The equally loved Bobby Charlton described Eric's qualities in the mid-Nineties, saying, 'We're just very grateful he's here. He's such a great player. I'm still pinching myself. A player like that only comes along once or twice in a lifetime, and you don't leave him out or put him in the reserves. You respect his skill. Eric is the brainiest player I've ever seen; he sees such a lot when he has the ball. The big thing he has given United is the ability to make attacks count, not waste good positions until the right option appears, and we now finish almost every move with an effort on goal. The other thing is his ability to release players, even when the pass doesn't look on. If you make the run, Eric will probably get you the ball.'

Cantona was born on 24 May 1966 in Paris – his parents named him Eric Daniel Pierre – just two months before England's greatest footballing triumph, when Bobby Moore would lift the World Cup at Wembley. But he grew up in the Mediterranean city of Marseille in the Caillols suburb. His father's family originated from Sardinia, his mother's from Spain – that production line perhaps helping to explain the volatility of his mixed Latin temperament. Yet from an early age, Eric was no 'brat'; indeed, he much preferred painting and reading in the cave high above the city of Marseille that the family called home.

His father Albert loved painting and hunting. By trade, he was a psychiatric nurse, but he also loved to play football, earning a reputation as a fine amateur goalkeeper. Albert would tell Eric, 'There is nothing more simple than football. Look before you receive the ball and then give it and always remember that the ball goes quicker than you can carry it.'

Eric's mother Eleonore would spend her time bringing up him and his brothers Jean-Marie and Joel. They were poor, but Eric loved his young life, later claiming he was the 'son of rich people' because of the variety of cultural and artistic activities open to him with his family.

By the age of five, he was playing football in the streets and fell in love with the game, saying, 'You start wanting to play [it] when you are three, four or five ... you know you have a passion when you can't stop playing the game, when you play it in the streets, in the playground, after school, and when you spend your time at school swapping photographs of footballers ... playing football in the streets gave us a tremendous need for freedom.'

He would first make his mark with the locally renowned Caillols junior club, which had helped another French legend, Jean Tigana, emerge. 'It was obvious that Eric was something special,' Yves Cicculo, the club's president, would say. 'He had all the qualities of a player. At the age of nine, he was playing like a fifteen-year-old. When he was with us, we won lots of tournaments – and I can honestly say that he alone made the difference. He was hot-headed but a genius. He's always been his own man. I have to admit he was a little difficult occasionally. He knew he was better than anyone else.'

The makings of the legend were being wrought. They would be further shaped and moulded by Guy Roux, the man who has helped so many French youngsters make the top grade. Roux would take Cantona under his wing at Auxerre Football Club, more than 400 miles away from the boy's hometown of Marseille. Similar to Sir Alex Ferguson at Manchester United, Roux would preside over an academy of young talents and nurture them. At the tender age of 15, Cantona would continue his footballing education under the watchful, precise eyes of the grand master of French football.

He was often homesick but also determined. His grandmother's father had been a freedom fighter in Franco's Spain before fleeing to France and Cantona would show some of the same stubborn fighting qualities through his tears of missing his family in Auxerre. Roux had no doubts about the boy's ability, admitting Cantona was 'the most brilliant of our youth trainees' and saying, 'He will play for France ... he had class and saw the game very clearly. He was always trying things. When they came off, it was magnificent – but often they didn't and he gave the ball away ... we had to teach him discipline.'

By 17, he was playing for the French national youth side and within a year had made his début for the First XI at Auxerre. In 1984, he put his career on hold as he carried out his national service. After discharge, he was loaned out to FC Martigues in the French Second Division. Rejoining Auxerre and signing a professional contract in 1986, his performances in the First Division were good enough to earn him his first full international cap. He was called up for a friendly against West Germany in Berlin and scored France's goal in a 2-1 loss.

He was also part of the French U21 side that won the 1988 U21 European Championship and, shortly afterwards, decided he wanted a change of scenery at club level, securing a deal to Olympique de Marseille for a French record fee of 22 million francs (£2.4 million). Cantona had certainly rewarded Roux's belief in him, making 81 appearances for Auxerre and scoring 23 goals. He helped them to finish fourth in the league in 1987, but was also fined for giving his own goalkeeper a black eye and suspended for three months after a dangerous tackle.

Cantona admitted that he enjoyed life at Auxerre and that he enjoyed just as much the challenge his temperament presented to boss Roux. Even then, the big man had a mischievous nature. He said, 'I remember that my joy during the whole of my career at Auxerre had no connection with the money that I was able to earn. How proud I was to take part in matches counting for the Championship of France's First Division. What joy to know that the managers of such an up-and-coming club didn't hesitate to place their confidence in a young player they had previously loaned to Martigues in the Second Division.

'Guy Roux is a man who likes challenges. He knows that one or two confrontations annually between the young players of the club and the team in the First Division can show up one or two of the established stars. That is why, without doubt, I began to exist in the eyes of Guy Roux one fine day in the spring of 1982.

'The club was finishing its second season in the First Division. Roux organised a match involving players from the lower teams against the likes of Bats, Szarmach, Garande – the club's stars. When I went on in the second half, it wasn't my intention to show anybody up. I only wanted to play well – nothing more. The defender, Lucien Dennis, 15 years older than I am, will remember the miseries which I caused him that day. Off balance, the defender tried to foul me at every opportunity. His team-mates let him know about it quite gently because you don't try to rough up somebody who's making his début and is just trying to show his ability.'

Cantona would then go on to prove Marseille were also right to gamble on him by helping them win the league and Cup double in 1989. Again, there were the inevitable downs as well as the ups both at club and international level. Eric's short temper quickly surfaced when he insulted the coach of the national team, Henri Michel, on TV and, despite apologising, was banned from internationals for a year. Peeved by Michel's decision not to pick him for a clash against Czechoslovakia, he said, 'I will never play for France again as long as Henri Michel is manager. I would like it to be known that I think he is one of the most incompetent managers in world football. I was reading an article by Mickey Rourke ... that the people who award the Oscars are a bunch of shitbags. I think Michel is not far from being included in that.'

Then, during a friendly game for Marseille against Torpedo Moscow, Cantona ripped off and threw away his jersey after being substituted. He was suspended indefinitely by Olympique Marseille chairman Bernard Tapie, who said, 'A player who throws his shirt on the ground, even if he has scored three goals in the match, must be sanctioned because that's not what we expect from sport. This doesn't correspond to the idea which I have of football in general and of football at Olympique Marseille in particular.' Tapie's true morals would, ironically, be highlighted when he himself was caught up in the bribes scandal that would engulf Marseille in 1993.

Tapie responded to Cantona throwing his shirt to the ground by banning him for a month. He moved to Bordeaux on loan and then to Montpellier with a similar agreement. At Montpellier, a fight with one of his team-mates led to six players demanding Cantona be sacked. However, with the support of team-mates – including Laurent Blanc and Carlos Valderrama – the club kept him on and Cantona repaid them by helping them win the French Cup in 1990. His excellent form persuaded Marseille to take him back, or, as Cantona saw it with customary modesty, 'They had been forced to appreciate me.' It couldn't last – he was sold for £1 million to Nîmes where he became captain.

Life at his fifth club followed a similar pattern. In 1991, he disputed a decision with a referee and threw the ball at him. The French FA suspended him for four matches, taking into account his previous poor disciplinary record and reputation. He told the disciplinary panel they were treating him unfairly, to which the panel chairman replied, 'You can't be judged like any other player. Behind you there is a trail of the smell of sulphur. You can expect anything from an individualist like you.'

Eric responded by insulting each member once again – hissing 'idiot' in each ear – and his ban was increased to two months. He was at his lowest ebb and quickly announced he would retire from football in 1991. Salvation would come thanks to Michel Platini, who had by now taken on the job of France national boss after the hapless Michel was sacked. Platini knew France's success – or lack of it – would hinge on the form of the brilliant Cantona; he needed him playing regularly at club level if he were to pick him. He needed him to reverse that self-imposed, self-pitiful retirement decision.

Platini visited Cantona at home and urged him to return to football for the sake of the French nation. He suggested to Eric that he might be more suited to the more physical English game. Cantona agreed to give it a go and Platini used Gérard Houllier – who would eventually go on to manage Liverpool but was then French national technical director – to help find the enigmatic Cantona a club in England. Cantona, meanwhile, agreed to the cancellation of his contract with Nîmes on 16 December 1991.

The die was being cast for the English air to be braced with that unique 'smell of sulphur' – Cantona was on his way to his destiny at Old Trafford. But first there were stop-offs in Sheffield and Leeds. He arrived grumpy at the prospect of a week's trial with Sheffield Wednesday – why did the great Cantona need a trial? – and when the myopic Trevor Francis, boss of the Owls at the time, asked him to try out for a further week, Eric was off ... initially back to France, but ultimately to Leeds after the intervention of Howard Wilkinson.

Aged 25, Cantona joined Leeds in February 1992 initially on a loan deal that would see the Yorkshire club pay Nîmes £100,000 and pay Cantona's wages until the end of the season. Ironically, Cantona would help them win the old First Division

Championship that season (1991/92) at the expense of Manchester United and his move to Leeds was made permanent, with an extra £1 million exiting the Elland Road coffers.

Howard Wilkinson and Eric Cantona? Even in the same sentence, the names hardly gel; they grate. One was an English footballing pragmatist and a seemingly dull, dour Yorkshireman; the other a French romantic, a dreamer, a painter, a poet, a motorcyclist philosopher – an enigmatic footballer who believed the beautiful game was just that, an opportunity for expression and joyful highs. From the very start, it was, on paper at least, a marriage of convenience – yet you would have to concede it was a major success for the short term it lasted. With Cantona in tow, Sergeant Wilko remains, to this day, the only Englishman to lead a team to the Premiership title – and it was Leeds' first top-flight title in 18 long years. For Cantona, the shop window of Elland Road would ultimately lead to his dream move to the club he was always destined to grace and to lead – Manchester United.

Wilko is an educated man, one who left Sheffield Hallam University with a BEd (Hons) Education degree in 1975, and his work as technical director of the FA would suggest he was no fool. Indeed, when I once asked Cantona about Wilko, he smiled that enigmatic smile and admitted, 'He was OK. Yes, I knew he had a degree and that he had brains. We used to have some good talks and he was good to my family and me. It just didn't work out at Leeds; he had his ideas on how the game should be played, I had mine. He wanted to win at any cost; I wanted to win with style. Parting was inevitable.'

So there you go: ideologically poles apart, undoubtedly. Wilko was a fan of a more direct, one-route game, but they possessed similar inquisitive, searching minds. Eric said that Wilko would occasionally visit him at the semi-detached house he rented near Roundhay Park, and that they would talk about the game. Wilko would even join Eric and his son Raphael for a kickabout in the garden as Eric's wife Isabelle prepared a bite to eat. Wilko had more brains and hidden depth than most pundits would credit him for. Eric certainly thought so.

Eric made it clear he respected Wilko for the way he treated him from the start, and was grateful to him for his undiluted support and belief that he could bring an extra dimension to a functional Leeds team. Eric's words confirm he was glad to be on board with a man who had time for him and understood his distinctive qualities. Cantona said of their first meeting, 'He invited me to watch the match between Leeds United and Notts County. Our conversation lasted a little more than an hour. Certainly, no contract had yet been signed, but we knew quite well that a mutual adventure would soon be bringing us together. There would be no question of a trial period. My examination would take place on the field. Perhaps even in the next match at Oldham, if I felt that I was ready.

'Howard Wilkinson had been very clear with me from the first training sessions ... he was convinced that I could rapidly impose myself on Leeds United, but he also let me understand that he didn't want to push me too quickly. English clubs, it is true, display a certain distrust of foreign players. Their football is made out of aerial duels, of hard running and of tackles, which cannot be endured unless a player's physical condition is almost perfect.

'The British establishment also thinks that while a footballer who comes from the south of Europe may have irreproachable technical skills they do not believe that his body will be able to stand up to the strains of the northern [European] football. And here again, with the advantage of the time that has passed, I can better appreciate the judgement and opinions of Michel

Platini and Gérard Houllier, who helped me cross the Channel. They knew quite well that my heart and my legs were made to get on with British football.'

Wilko would also show his perception and appreciation at the skills of the genius he had brought, saying, 'His instinctive vision and instinctive passing skills were exquisite. Eric lifted the proceedings to a higher level with a series of devastating flicks and passes.'

Yet, despite the initial love-in, it would all end in tears nine months after the big man arrived. Wilko and Cantona would eventually disagree on the style of football to be played at Elland Road. Wilko wanted the direct, quick, lay-off approach that had brought the title back to continue; Eric wanted a more thoughtful, adventurous, imaginative style. Put simply, Cantona did not want the ball lashed long to the head of big Lee Chapman; Wilko, despite his acknowledgement that Cantona brought something exquisitely different to the party, did. In the end, the leopard could not quite bring itself to change its spots; the long ball game had brought success for Wilko so, in the final analysis, why fix something that wasn't broken? It was a shortsighted view, but at least Wilko had the guts to make his own call, even though it would mean letting the best player of his long footballing career slip through his fingers.

The highlight of Cantona's brief spell at Leeds? Legend-wise, it was undoubtedly his speech from the balcony of Leeds Town Hall to celebrate their league title win in 1992. Eric muttered the now immortal words, 'I am very happy. Thank you very much. Why I love you, I don't know why, but I love you.'

And his best game for the Elland Road outfit? Cantona has no doubts – the 3-0 win over Chelsea at Elland Road in April 1992. He had come on as a sub for Rod Wallace, scored the first goal and Eric was certainly not modest about his impact that day and the build-up to it, 'I had been winning the confidence of Wilkinson and the other players at Elland Road were becoming accustomed to my kind of play. The day would soon arrive for one of my most inspired moments, an incident that would remain engraved in the memory of the Leeds supporters.

'This day came at Elland Road on 11 April 1992. We were playing against Chelsea. It is difficult to describe the out-of-the-ordinary goal that I scored on that day. In three touches, I deceived the defenders who were coming to tackle me, without the ball touching the ground and then finally placed the ball in the far corner of the net. About ten minutes remained and, throughout the whole of that time, the fans stood up in the stands, singing and chanting. It was a very moving and extraordinary experience.'

He would also score a hat-trick for the club in their 4-3 win over Liverpool in the Charity Shield in the traditional pre-season curtain raiser for the 1992/93 season – and bring Leeds back from the dead in a European Cup first-round match against Stuttgart at Elland Road. They had lost the first leg 3-0, but Cantona turned the match around to inspire Leeds to a 4-1 win. Leeds were out on the away goals ruling but won a reprieve when it was discovered the Germans had fielded too many foreign players. Leeds would win the replayed tie 2-1 against Stuttgart, but exited the competition in the next round against Glasgow Rangers. Their league form was also indifferent and Eric's tenure was coming to an end.

The split with Wilko would be acrimonious – inevitable given the stubborn, proud nature of both men. Despite Leeds' poor form, Cantona had been delivering the goods, scoring 11 goals in 20 matches in all competitions, but he was finding it difficult to communicate with Wilko. Cantona explained it like this, 'There were problems. I began to have increasing difficulty in decoding the language used by my manager. When I say "decoding" that means understanding what Wilkinson was trying to get at. His comments were strange and rather incoherent, in my opinion. One moment he would tell me that he wants me to know that I owe everything to him, that I am only a Frenchman lost in the English league and, at other times, he would say to me that without me the team is nothing and that I am the essential part.

'"You put him in the shade," Leeds supporters told me after my departure. I can't believe that this was the reason. However, it became more and more clear that he wanted to get rid of me.' Wilkinson explained the problem diffrerently, saying that Cantona did not accept his authority and that he must be the only boss. 'To justify his version of events, he had to let me go to one of his greatest rivals for a sum which was far lower than my value....' Wilko eventually replaced the talismatic Frenchman with Carl Shutt.

The ensuing war of words was as sad as it was unpleasant. And so were the following 12 months. Yes, the Leeds fans had certainly taken Cantona to their hearts – yet they would soon be spitting and jeering at him when he turned out against them in the red shirt of their most hated rivals, Manchester United. His reign at Elland Road – and the adulation the Tykes' fans felt for Eric at his peak – is perhaps best described by author Rick Broadbent in his book, *Looking for Eric*. He describes the night Cantona led Leeds to that incredible 4-1 thrashing of Stuttgart, saying, 'The return leg was an epic encounter to rival the magical nights of the Revie era. This was football as the beautiful game. For Cantona the artist, who said he could not renounce beauty, this was the masterpiece. For Cantona the footballer, who said sublime moments of sporting beauty could provide glimpses of eternity, this was the game that will live for ever. It was billed as "Mission Impossible". No British side had ever come back from a three-goal deficit in Europe; but Leeds had the will and belief....'

And so the stage was finally set for Eric's date with destiny at Old Trafford. Legend has it that Ferguson signed Cantona as a spur of the moment act. Leeds Managing Director, Bill Fotherby, had apparently telephoned to ask Manchester United chairman Martin Edwards if Denis Irwin would be available for a move, and that, sitting across from him, Ferguson had scrawled on a piece of paper, 'Ask him if Cantona is for sale.' The piece of paper bit is true, as is the fact that Fotherby rang back later that day to confirm that Eric was, indeed, available.

But a source close to Sir Alex tells me that Ferguson had been on the case for months, that this was hardly a last-minute move dreamed up from nowhere. The United manager had been interested when Cantona turned up at Sheffield Wednesday, and he knew all about the man who had been a nightmare to manage in France. Indeed, he had already earmarked Eric Cantona for a starring role at Old Trafford, and he wanted to pit his managerial skills up against the man who would play the George Best role to his Busby. It would be the ultimate test and Ferguson was keen to bring it on when Fotherby gave the all-clear.

The wheels had actually been put in motion, I am told, weeks before when Gérard Houllier had secretly telephoned Ferguson to say that all was not well with Cantona at Leeds and that a bid to Howard Wilkinson might prove fruitful. Ferguson, the clever old dog he is, bided his time – he did not want to pay over the odds. He knew that if Cantona was perceived as the perennial problem boy he could snatch him on the cheap.

At the end of the day, Wilko was just mighty relieved to get his million quid back and get shot of a man he could no longer fathom, let alone manage. The early promise of their liaison had gone out of the window when Leeds had started to lose – they would finish 17th (three places above relegation) at the end of the season in the newly-formed Premier League.

So it was that on Thursday, 26 November 1992, Eric Cantona finally came home, for the ridiculously small fee of £1.2 million. He did not move for the money – indeed, he told his agent to negotiate the deal based around the same money he was on at Leeds. Ferguson will never forget that day; it would be the day that would help transform him from being just another manager at United into a legend. The signing of Cantona was the last piece in his own personal jigsaw. Ferguson would later comment on how Cantona had thrilled him by 'walking in as though he owned the bloody place' and that, while some players found Old Trafford and the United aura too much, Cantona was at the very head of the queue of those who 'simply belonged' from day one.

Now Ferguson would get his chance to manage the footballer he had longed to work with, to prove he could handle his own Best, where Busby had tried and failed with old Georgie-boy. It would be a journey scattered with danger, worry and problems; but also joy, wonder and glory.

On his arrival, Cantona said, 'I love to win, I love football, I love the pass, the move, the joy and I have to find that to be content. For Manchester United, it is the same. We have the same vision of football and victory. If you have 11 workmen, you will never win. If you have 11 artists, you will never win. It is important that the team complements each other and we have that.'

Ferguson, the fiery, demonstrative Scot, would gel with Cantona, the fiery, demonstrative Frenchman. It would mean the manager giving ground, allowing slack he would not previously have entertained, to get the best out of Eric. Like Busby with Best, he would treat Eric differently to the rest of the staff. That bull of a striker, Mark Hughes, would sum it up like this in his autobiography, *Hughsie*: 'Alex Ferguson didn't exactly rewrite the rule book but he treated him differently and explained to the rest of us that he was a special player requiring special treatment.'

Unlike Busby with Best, he would succeed and get the best out of his man not only in his peak years, but beyond. The softly-softly approach would be the making of the both of them and would arguably be the greatest commendation of Ferguson, the manager of men.

8

Heaven and Hell

'Ooh aah Cantona ... ooh aah Cantona.'
TERRACE CHANT, 1993

'I feel close to the rebelliousness and vigour of the youth here. Perhaps
time will separate us, but nobody can deny that here, behind the windows of
Manchester, there is an insane love of football, of celebration and of music.'
ERIC CANTONA, 1996

As they say in *Reservoir Dogs*, 'Let's go to work...' Let's get to the very heart of Cantona the footballer, and the extraordinary incident by which he will always be remembered. If Best's mischievous side is forever allied to the birds and the booze, Robbo to the ravaging injuries, Eric will invariably be linked to that night of kung fu fighting at Crystal Palace in January 1995. It was the turning point, the defining moment of his career. His subsequent nine-month ban cost United the League and Cup; indeed, it left them trophy-less at a time when the team was arguably strong enough to win everything; perhaps even the strongest in Ferguson's entire reign at Old Trafford.

Yet it did bring an unlikely bonus. For the first time in his career, Cantona found a man who would back him when most others were saying, 'Get rid of him'. In Alex Ferguson, he came across the only manager he had ever played under who would

117

hunt him down and plead with him to remain a part of his football club. Whether you believe he deserved Ferguson's mercy dash to Paris or not, the fact remains that Ferguson put his own reputation on the line for the mercurial Frenchman.

And, a full 12 years on, what do we now make of that night with the benefit of hindsight? Talking to United and Palace *aficionados*, I have unearthed some surprising facts, and views on the events of 25 January 1995. I am assured by one Palace insider that Matthew Simmons, the 20-year-old self-employed glazier and 'victim' of Cantona's attack, was not the loyal fan of the club as he was usually portrayed. Indeed, I am told his 'first love' was not Palace, but Fulham, and that he swiftly returned to Craven Cottage after he was given a life ban from Selhurst Park for his part in the run-in with Cantona.

The facts surrounding the incident have become clouded over time with club bias, emotion and moral outrage, so it is perhaps useful to remind ourselves what actually happened that night. All hell broke lose just after 9.00pm. Eric was sent off, four minutes into the second half of United's Premiership match against Palace – which ended 1-1 – for kicking out at defender Richard Shaw. As Cantona made his way from the pitch, Simmons rushed down the stands to taunt him. Cantona was enraged; he responded with his kung fu kick and then exchanged punches with Simmons. As a result, he was banned from football for eight months by the FA, although with a one-month suspension from United it effectively worked out to be a nine-month enforced break.

No player had ever attacked a fan in English football before. It remains arguably the most memorable/famous/infamous footballing image of the 20th century. Certainly, with the kick captured by the cameras, it is one of the most vivid images I can ever recall. Football writer Brian Oliver stated in the

Observer, 'There was a fascination in this Hollywood moment that goes into the dark world of "the glamour of violence"... Cantona's kick was unquestionably glamorous, because it was Cantona (dressed all in black), because it was Manchester United, because it had never happened before, because it was so shocking.'

Simmons would claim that all he said to Cantona – in true Leslie Phillips-stiff-upper-lip-style English – was along the lines of, 'Off, off, off! Go on, Cantona, that's an early bath for you.' Eric would say it was a much more racist attack, more along the lines of, 'Fuck off back to France, you French motherfucker....'

Simmons remains adamant that Cantona lied. 'For God's sake, you can't say a worse thing about anyone [than what he alleges I said], can you? What he did in saying that was totally unjustified. The man is filth. How can he accuse me of saying such a thing? Where has this allegation against me come from? From him. It ruined my life. And that is why it is inexcusable.'

Believe what you will, but to many Frenchmen, the latter comments about their mother, or any family members, would be like a red rag to a bull – just ask the brilliant Zinedine Zidane. In fact, the similarities between Zidane's sending off in the World Cup Final of 2006 and Eric's at Palace bear more consideration later.

Simmons would become one of the most recognised and hated men in Britain; he lost his job, family members ignored him and reporters pursued him. The threats against him would continue for years, but Simmons believes he was unfairly castigated. He said, 'I was in the wrong place at the wrong time. It's easier to go down the aisles and along the gangways to get to where you want to go. I was on my way to the toilet when I saw him approaching. Not much of an excuse, I know, but sometimes the truth is the simplest of things. Being where

I was probably wasn't the wisest thing. But it is not a criminal offence and certainly does not mean I should be hung, drawn and quartered.'

United loyalist Martin Creasy begs to differ. He told me, 'When Eric launched his assault on that Palace moron, I must have been the only United fan still in my seat in stunned disbelief, wondering if this would be the last we would ever see of the greatest United genius since George Best. United fans all around me were too busy jumping up and celebrating Eric's revenge in an incident some in the press would sneeringly label 'THE SHIT HITS THE FAN' to share my immediate concerns. People go on about cutting out racism in football. Total hypocrisy. If Eric had been English, would he have taken the level of crap he did – especially from the press? Of course not.'

Palace fans also had their views and, for the first time in print, here is a full, unexpurgated commentary from one of them, a prominent supporter, someone who has loyally supported the club for over 30 years, and who will certainly never forget.

Even 12 years after the event, the fears persist and the resentment still runs deep among some, as the Palace fan explained, 'Just to be absolutely certain, though, Frank, I really don't want my name attached to this under any circumstances. Not even a credit at the end please. It's a blow to the ego but, after reminding myself of all the aggro Matthew Simmons went through, I can't take any chances with my kids.'

Having been assured of anonymity, the fan went on to tell me, 'Cantona was the violent thug who saved his single most famous kick not for the ball he caressed so brilliantly, but for a member of the opposition crowd. Eric Cantona's assault on Matthew Simmons remains a milestone in the life of every Palace fan who was there ... and the many who weren't. His ensuing court case and almost-endearingly daft press conference entertained a news-hungry nation. And the catastrophic effect on United's title bid – and ultimately their Cup ambitions – engineered a rough kind of justice for all.

'If only the story stopped there … It was a mere few months later that the fates drew Palace and the Red Devils together for an FA Cup semi-final at Villa Park. Past encounters between the clubs had always held something of a David and Goliath flavour, and a general acceptance by Eagles fans that, by and large, we'd lose. And an almost avuncular benevolence from the United faithful, seemingly happy to see us in the top flight bearing the guaranteed gift of six points.

'This time, the mood was different. Yet, in spite of the animosity, I confess my own recollection of the trip is of a fantastic atmosphere, a cracking game we almost won, and booming chants of "Ooh aah Cantona" from the Holte End, which our wags effectively rebuffed with choruses of "Au revoir, Cantona", plus an accompanying goodbye wave. The only United lads we saw on the lookout for trouble were a mob who crossed at a junction 100 yards ahead an hour before kick-off. Naturally, we avoided them and chatted excitedly with the real fans in the famous red-and-white. Regrettably, other Palace followers were not so lucky.

'It wasn't until the next morning that I learned of Walsall, the pub battle, and the death of Paul Nixon. Many who were there, or who knew those involved, appear to have little doubt that an attack by United hooligans was the catalyst for the loss of Paul's life.

'Is it any wonder that the glitter of the Cup suddenly faded for Palace and all connected with them? That so many decided against a return trip to Villa Park days later? Or, even, that the Palace players then capitulated so meekly in the most surreal atmosphere ever to grace an FA Cup semi-final replay?

'Eric Cantona struck out in a blind rage following his dismissal at Selhurst. Of that there is no doubt. It was a calamitous error of judgement.

'Richard Shaw, the defender fouled by "the King" to earn his sending-off, was a steady crowd favourite. A dreadlocked trier whose close marking and determination were far more his trademark than any dirtiness or soccer ability. Quite what he did that night to send United's supremely-talented number 7 into such a frenzy is hard to imagine. But what came next was inexcusable, breaching accepted boundaries and risking the safety of both players and fans.

'Of course, the United publicity machine quickly and effectively pinned the blame on someone else, painting Simmons as a racist who had spouted anti-French vitriol at the innocent star. Others claimed the entire crowd were an animalistic bunch who created a hellish atmosphere bound to provoke trouble. Hardly likely. Selhurst to this day remains a stadium where the atmosphere is frequently tepid at best. Despite efforts to ignite the fanbase, the vast majority remains not only silent but, for the most part, virtually inanimate – especially in the genteel 1920s Old Stand, backdrop for that night's Main Event. Meanwhile, Simmons, despite reports of some ill-judged political affiliations in his past, would hardly qualify as Hitler youth. In any case, nothing uttered as fuming Cantona hustled past could justify a professional sportsman literally "crossing the line" in that way.

'While Cantona's flying kick merely grazed Matthew Simmons, it left an indelible scar on the face of football – and on the reputation of the Frenchman himself. The truly astonishing thing about the whole episode is that he was allowed to escape so lightly. Had a Palace player attempted such "vigilantism", fans would genuinely have anticipated a life ban.

And had any opponent lashed out a few miles up the road at Millwall, the concept of legal retribution would have been entirely moot. He would never have made it to the dressing room alive.

'So yes, Palace fans like me will always remember Cantona. But not as football royalty. He's not Prince Eric, the legendary talisman for one of the world's most famous teams. Not even Duke Eric, the twinkle-toed outlaw with the turned-up collar whose football ability was matched only by his on-field arrogance and innate lack of charm. For me, it's plain old Eric ... the man who would be King, were it not for that unfortunate little business a few miles south of the Thames.'

Most commentators would rail against Cantona, describing his assault as 'shameful'. There were a couple of notable dissenters, Jimmy Greaves in the *Sun* and Richard Williams in the *Independent on Sunday*. Greavsie wrote, 'We've heard a lot about Cantona's responsibilities. What about analysing the responsibility of Simmons and every foul-mouthed yob who thinks his £10 admission gives him the right to say what he likes to a man? ... to abuse, taunt, spit and behave in a way that would get you locked up if you repeated it in the high street.'

And Williams rightly believed that 'Cantona had the excuse of genuine provocation'. Simmons was subsequently convicted of provoking the incident.

David Beckham admitted he could understand, if not condone, Eric's outburst. He said, 'All great players have an edge to their character and to their football. That edge is what makes them more than ordinary. And if you go through a whole career with that quality, you're bound to have trouble with the authorities sooner or later.

'I think it [the kick] was just an instinctive reaction, a natural thing to do. Anybody getting that sort of abuse in the street would have reacted in the same way ... I'm not saying Eric was right, but you have to remember that, in any other circumstances, if someone was screaming that stuff at another person, you'd be surprised if there wasn't trouble.'

The referee that night, Alan Wilkie, remembers the build-up and the explosion, saying, 'I did not feel there was going to be a problem until Cantona went down after a challenge. As we left the pitch for half-time, he said, "No yellow cards!" When we were waiting in the tunnel for the restart, he said it again and [Alex] Ferguson confronted me and said, "Why don't you just do your fucking job!"

'The build-up to Cantona's sending-off went like this – Peter Schmeichel kicked the ball into the Palace half and when Richard Shaw turned to run, Cantona attempted to kick him. I gave him a straight red card.

'Cantona is dark-haired and that evening his eyes seemed almost black. With [United's] black strip and the dark night, he looked menacing. Now he had the look of the wounded hero. He gave me the feeling that there was an inevitability about a collision occurring. And now it had, I sensed Cantona wished it had not. Then he looked straight through me, turned and put his collar down. That meant, "My game is over." He walked off and stood by Ferguson, who would not acknowledge him. So Cantona moved towards the tunnel.

'All of a sudden, players were rushing over there. I manoeuvred myself in between players and crowd, trying to calm it down. Brian McClair was very helpful. He said, "Alan, blow the whistle and everything will settle." I restarted the match. The whole episode lasted 92 seconds but it seemed like 92 days.'

Wilkie believes Cantona should have been given a life ban for the assault. He said he would never forget the night, including unpleasant scenes in the dressing room after the match. Wilkie said, 'That room is so small we called it a closet and it was chaotic in there. We had a visit from Mr Ferguson and it was short and sweet.

'He was removed quite speedily by the senior policeman on duty. Let's say his behaviour was less than complimentary towards me – he was claiming it was all my fault, everything. If players have a problem about being verbally abused, they should try being a ref. Why can't they control themselves for 90 minutes? It's a passionate game and referees get as wound up and excited as players.

'I have no idea what the chap in the crowd said to Cantona. Obviously, it wasn't very complimentary and it provoked him at a moment of weakness. When it happened I felt he should have been banned for life and I still feel the same way.'

In the pictures of the assault, a woman near Simmons was noticeably looking shocked. Cathy Churchman had been sitting with her 15-year-old son, Steven, and daughter, Laura, 12, in front-row seats that night. She told the *Observer*'s Jamie Jackson, 'That kick changed my life. Because I was so close – his boot skimmed my coat and was inches from my face – I did interviews with newspapers, I was on television. I received call after call inviting me to shows such as *Kilroy*, which I turned down.

'I started doing sponsorship work with the club after Ron Noades [then Palace chairman] wrote to say he hoped the experience would not deter me from supporting the team. I made numerous friends among the players and [various] managers. My husband works in IT and he was in contact with people from all over the world. Some of his colleagues in America were saying, "Your wife is becoming more famous than Princess Di." And we all know how little they go in for football over there.'

Her son Steven explained why, in some pictures, it appeared that Cathy had been laughing at what Simmons was saying to Cantona. He said, 'We'd been having a laugh with the guy next to us. He'd phoned in sick for work that day. When Cantona was sent off, he was saying, "Oh God, I hope I'm not on *Match of the Day* or my boss will go mad." My mum was laughing at this guy, not at what Simmons was saying. We weren't taking that much notice of Cantona. Then Simmons came from 12 or 13 rows back just as Cantona passes. I haven't got a clue what he shouted, so I don't know how all these people rows back say they remember.'

As well as the eight-month ban from the FA, Cantona was sentenced to two weeks in prison, which was reduced on appeal to 120 hours' community service for the attack. He was also fined £20,000. It was during a news conference after the appeal that he would cryptically refer to the British press as 'a flock of seagulls following the trawler....'

For his part, Simmons would later say, 'By kicking me, Cantona showed a complete lack of professionalism and self-discipline. Everyone has lost their temper, myself included. The abuse that I got after the event – from Ferguson, from Cantona himself and the media – is inexcusable.'

Ferguson would claim to not have seen the incident and that it was only later that night when he watched the video of the match that the full impact of Cantona's extraordinary attack hit him. His claim to have missed the kick was backed up by Palace boss Alan Smith, who expressed astonishment when Ferguson told him an hour after the match that the whole thing was being overblown. Smith said, 'I remember Alex Ferguson coming in and saying he didn't think there was much wrong in what had happened. Alex being the intimidating figure he is, I just nodded and said nothing, which was ridiculous. If a mate of mine had trotted out that line, tried to defend the indefensible, I'd have laughed in his face and said, "You what?"'

Iain Dowie, a Palace striker back then, added, 'It was certainly a frightening game. You could see the lad run all the way down, say something to Cantona and get really close. Next there was a reaction and – bang! – it all kicked off. It was a sad day for football.'

That sentiment was shared by some who believed Cantona's kick was a terrible example for young children. In 1997, Wales national rugby coach Kevin Bowring harped back to the incident as a prime example of how sporting violence was being imitated by susceptible schoolchildren. He claimed the 'amateur ethos' of fair play and sportsmanship was vanishing as school coaches found themselves under increasing pressure to win matches at all costs, and kids copied their heroes' sometimes foul tactics to achieve it. Mr Bowring said the 'Corinthian spirit' was disappearing, partly due to bad behaviour on the pitch. 'In football, you have Eric Cantona fighting spectators, while Gazza is a wife-beater.'

Naturally enough, there was a mixed reaction among the public to Cantona's lunge – again breaking down fairly evenly on the lines of 'shameful' on one side, while on the other some had sympathy for Eric, arguing he was provoked beyond the call of duty because of the alleged racist element of Simmons' outburst.

Alex Paylor, writing for the online United fanzine *Red 11*, came down emphatically on the side of Cantona, saying, 'So poor Matthew Simmons was just the unsuspecting victim of Cantona's temper? Well, of course he was. I mean, it's part and parcel of the game, isn't it, having some lout rush from his seat to the front of the stands, yelling obscenities and racist remarks at a player? Footballers should be used to this kind of abuse, right? Well, let me remind you such behaviour is a criminal offence, and Simmons was convicted. Do you really think what he did is acceptable? In an ideal world, Cantona would have just ignored the moron. But in an ideal world, there wouldn't be a place for the likes of such bigots as Matthew Simmons either.'

Duleep Allirajah, writing in *Spiked*, made the point that the occasion was akin to football's equivalent of the JFK assassination, and asked for some sense of proportion to be brought to the proceedings. 'We can all remember precisely what we were doing on 25 January 1995 when Cantona lunged feet-first at Matthew Simmons. I wasn't at Selhurst Park that night but driving home listening to the match on the car radio. Judging by the frothing indignation of the radio commentators, you would have thought that the Pope had been gang-raped by aliens.

'I, too, was appalled, though not by Cantona's actions but by the unctuous moralising that followed. Maybe it's the company I keep, but most people I know thought that Cantona's flying kick was hilarious and well worth the admission price alone – and so, too, did some spectators, judging by the expressions of delight on their faces in newspaper photographs.

'Yet the ensuing inquest was relentlessly po-faced. I remember listening to a Radio Five Live phone-in debate on the subject between indignant "rent-a-pulpit" moralists calling for Cantona to be banned for life, and Manchester United fans whining about the intolerable provocation that Cantona had endured.

'Irritated by both camps, I phoned in to Radio Five myself. My point was that the actions of both Cantona and Matthew Simmons were, in their own ways, justifiable. Simmons was only doing his duty as a Palace fan by hurling abuse at an opponent, while Cantona was simply responding as any reasonable man might do when told to "Fuck off back to France, you French motherfucker!" (You need to replace 'France' with your own homeland here – though, admittedly, "Fuck off back to Bexhill, you East Sussex motherfucker" doesn't quite have the same cachet.)'

Up in Scotland, the University of Stirling even carried out a thought-provoking media research study into violence in sport, focusing particularly on the Cantona–Simmons incident. Again, there was a mixed reaction. The majority of those involved felt little sympathy for Eric while recognising that he was provoked. These are some of the findings from some of the culturally diverse research panels: 'Both the gay groups felt that most people were subjected to violent abuse at some stage in their public and private lives and had to ignore it. One noted, "If nurses have to tolerate it ... [and] other members of the public have to tolerate it, [so] why can't professional people who are in the public eye?" (Gay white man, 30–39, Manchester.) Cantona was perceived as resorting to violence without exploring other ways of dealing with the situation, which was unacceptable.

'The Scottish Pakistani group argued that while they could relate to being subjected to verbal abuse, Cantona was wrong, and that while provoked, his actions were not justified. However, members of the English Pakistani group thought differently. For them, in the face of extreme racial abuse, violence might be acceptable in the last resort. Most felt, however, that due to the fact it was seen on television, he had to be seen to be punished.

'Significantly, in all the working-class groups, members of which admitted to involvement in violent incidents, a clear-cut moral position was adopted. They felt that because of Cantona's high media profile, and because children looked up to footballers as role models, he had to be punished. In addition, these group members believed that, as football players are handsomely paid for their work, they should be prepared to accept verbal abuse from supporters.

'Both Pakistani groups viewed Cantona as a victim of verbal abuse, while the Scottish middle-class group, although having little sympathy for him, thought that he was a victim of English media coverage and a general dislike of the French. "The English media hate Cantona and he's French, and the English hate the French." (Middle-class white man, 18–29, Glasgow.)

'The media were also criticised by the West African group who thought extensive television coverage had led to an over-reaction from the public. Many in the group opposed the media's line: "I felt that the media was trying to tell me that it was really bad but yet I rejected it. It isn't that bad...."(West African man, Glasgow.)

'Most in this group saw Cantona as a victim of racism, and while they did not condone his action, they understood that people could be pushed to violence.'

The racism card would give credence to the idea mooted after the 2006 World Cup Final that Cantona's indiscretion was akin in many respects to that of Zinedine Zidane when he was sent off against Italy. Admittedly, the stakes and the tension were considerably higher with a world crown at stake, but there are several similarities over what happened and why. Zidane had put France ahead from the spot in the opening minutes but was then dismissed after slamming his head into Marco Materazzi's chest during the tense second period of extra time, which ended 1-1. It would prove to be Zidane's last act as a professional player and, with the French missing his prowess in the ensuing penalty shootout, Italy went on to claim the World Cup title.

Zidane gave an interview on French television channel TF1, and the words could have come from Cantona that night at Palace. Zidane admitted to having a dark side and said, 'I'm a human being and it has to be accepted, but I always try to be true to who I am.'

In 2004, he had said, 'I have a need to play intensely every day, to fight every match hard.' Similar to Eric, he was brought up in Marseille and, as a French Algerian, had had to battle for all that came his way. After his sending off, Zidane would not apologise but, again, in a way reminiscent of Eric, would add, 'I wouldn't change a thing. It's my destiny and I have to accept it. I believe in myself and in a higher power. Now a new, more private, life starts. I will go to Algeria and find my roots again.'

Gilbert Collard, one of France's most celebrated defence lawyers, publicly backed the shamed captain, claiming he had acted in honour. 'Of course it was wrong, but it was explained, if not justified, by honour.' Similarly, Eric, speaking ten years after the Palace game, would imply that he had acted correctly, saying, 'You have to allow yourself to lose control from time to time.'

Despite his dismissal, Zidane was awarded the prestigious Golden Ball award after journalists voted him the best player in the tournament.

Ten years after the incident, Palace would warn United fans they would be banned from Selhurst Park if they arrived planning to mark the anniversary of the kung fu kick by wearing Cantona masks. Palace stadium manager Kevin Corner said, 'If they wear them inside Selhurst Park, they will be immediately rejected on safety grounds. And no fans wearing Cantona masks will be allowed entry to the stadium.'

United fans had declared the return to Selhurst Park in 2005 as 'Cantona Day' and one contributor to United fanzine, *Red*

Issue, defiantly warned that many United fans would still wear the masks. He said, 'I will be wearing a mask and many other United fans will be as well. It is not against the law so who are they to say what we can and cannot do?'

In the *Daily Mirror*, the entertaining Tony Parsons marked the anniversary by saying, 'It is ten years since Eric Cantona launched the kung fu kick that shocked a nation. And when Manchester United returned to Crystal Palace on Saturday, the question that has haunted sports fans for a decade was being asked once more. Namely, should Eric just have given him a right-hander?

'Cantona's flying, side-thrust kick, although undoubtedly gloriously photogenic, didn't actually seem to inflict much damage on his foul-mouthed tormentor. As far as I can tell, Eric's opponent didn't even need a Nurofen. Matthew Simmons, the recipient of Cantona's boot, says he has truly suffered over the last decade but his suffering seems to have been exclusively of the mental kind.

'Getting kicked by Cantona didn't actually seem to hurt very much ... "The whole thing has ruined my life," says dumb bastard Simmons, as if he wasn't the instigator of the entire affair. But what Simmons has never said is, "Ouch, Eric, that really, really hurt!"

'It was a great-looking kick – it had height and reach, although Eric neglected to protect his testicles, which they teach you in Kung Fu For Beginners, Lesson Number One. But the kick didn't do any damage to anything apart from reputations. A big strong lad like Eric Cantona ... would have been better advised to punch him in the cake-hole.

'The tenth anniversary of Cantona's kung fu kick made me wonder why we don't teach boxing in State schools any more, why we don't love and respect this sport the way we should and the way it deserves. If Eric Cantona had given that foul-mouthed yob one stiff jab then he would no doubt have scattered his teeth all over south London.'

Back in 1995, the damage to Simmons' health, both physical and mental, was the least of Sir Alex Ferguson's worries. He was in no doubt that United as a club suffered badly as a consequence of the fall-out from that traumatic night. At the start of 1995, things had been looking good – he had just been awarded the CBE in the New Year's Honours; he had bought Andy Cole for £7 million from Newcastle United; and United looked on their way to a third Premier League title. But United would lose the plot after 25 January and failure to win at West Ham on the last day of the season and failing to beat Everton in the FA Cup Final meant that the trophy cabinet at Old Trafford was empty for the first time in five years.

Ferguson would grind his teeth on the *Cantona Speaks* video and complain, 'I think it's summed up in the three games we had in a row at home [between 15 March and 17 April]. We drew 0-0 with Chelsea, 0-0 with Tottenham and 0-0 with Leeds United. Having only lost the League by one point, no one's going to tell me or even attempt to convince me that he would not have made one goal or scored a goal in one of those three games.'

There was much speculation that Cantona would leave English football when his ban finished – Inter Milan were especially keen to secure his signature – but Alex Ferguson persuaded him to stay in Manchester and Cantona was once again inspirational. As we have said, Ferguson's work in travelling to Paris to track down the King in exile and to persuade him his future was still at Old Trafford was one of the key moves of his time as manager at Old Trafford.

Ferguson had a bit of work to do when he arrived in the

French capital. It is not always remembered that Cantona actually put in a transfer request in the summer of 1995, following an outcry to the news that he had taken part in a practice match against Rochdale. Although it was held behind closed doors at United's training ground, it appeared to breach the terms of the suspension, and the FA opened an inquiry. Ferguson convinced him all would turn out well if they both stayed solid to their belief in Manchester United – that the club was on the way to becoming the best in the world once again.

Richard Williams of the *Guardian* explained it in this typically elegant way, 'By asking for a move, he was making a stand not against the club but against English football. He went off to Paris, apparently intending to talk to the representatives of other clubs. That spring he had received a £4.2m offer from Massimo Moratti, then recently installed as president of Internazionale. Instead, he signed a new contract to stay at Old Trafford, worth £3 million over three years. But it was assumed Moratti's offer was on his mind when, in exasperation, he put in his request.

'Sir Alex Ferguson flew to Paris, where he sweet-talked Cantona back to the club. In truth, however, Cantona knew that in England he had found a place where his talent could find its fullest expression. In Italy, it would all have been very different. In the Premiership, Cantona's touch and vision shone. In Serie A he would not have stood out to such a degree, if at all. The directness of his play would have gone down well there, but his low boiling point would have betrayed him, perhaps fatally.

'Even facing England's relatively straightforward defenders, he lost his rag every now and then. In Italy, he would have been driven to a state of permanent distraction by the repertoire of sophisticated methods – some of them legitimate – in general use. Cantona saw all that, and stayed put.'

It is an interesting point of view – basically, that while Eric was riding high in England he could not cut it in Europe; and not only that he could not cut it, but also that he knew that. That he stayed for reasons of self-preservation.

Cantona himself would admit a debt to United and Ferguson at the time, saying, 'I value truth, honesty, respect for one another, sincerity, compassion and understanding. These qualities are found at United.

'They have believed in me and there is no greater source of confidence and inspiration for a player than the knowledge that people believe in you.'

Ferguson definitely made that summer trip to France in 1995 out of self-preservation. He had seen with his own eyes the effect Cantona had had on his team, turning them from also-rans into winners, and proving to be the last piece of the jigsaw that brought the League Championship back to Old Trafford. He was not going to allow his favourite piece of jewellery be flogged off as cheaply as that.

After his arrival at Old Trafford in 1992, Cantona had quickly settled into the team, not only scoring goals galore but also creating chances for the other players. For the next two years, United went on an amazing run, winning the inaugural Premiership in 1993 (that first Championship title in 26 years) and then the Double in 1994, with Cantona's two penalties helping them to a 4-0 win over Chelsea in the FA Cup Final.

When Eric arrived in 1992, United were lying sixth in the Premiership, nine points behind surprise leaders Norwich City and struggling to get goals – they had only scored 18 in 17 matches. That was all about to change. Cantona made his début in the 2-1 Manchester derby win over City on 6 December and his first goal came in a 1-1 draw at Chelsea on 19 December. A week later, on Boxing Day, United launched an amazing comeback away to Sheffield Wednesday, ending up 3-3 after being 3-0 down with 20 minutes to go. Cantona got the final goal and the Red Devils were on their way to an unprecedented domination of English football. That gritty comeback had proved to them that – with Eric on board and their renowned resilience – they could beat anyone. It was a defining moment for the club after 26 years of hurt.

The next couple of weeks saw a 5-0 win over Coventry and a 4-1 thrashing of Tottenham – Cantona had taken United to the top of the table, a slot that would generally be theirs throughout his five years, apart from a period during his nine-month ban. The fact remains that the 1994/95 campaign – which took the brunt of his ban – was the only one of Cantona's five seasons at United in which United failed to win the Premiership, or any other trophy; that, in black and white, sums up the effect the Frenchman had on the club. His influence as a single player on a team was never matched – either before his era, by the likes of Best, or after his reign, by the likes of Rooney, although you could argue Keane came close.

Cantona hit nine goals in 22 Premiership games in that first season, and he would drag the club to even greater heights in his second, scoring 25 goals in 48 matches and bringing United their first Double. There had even been hopes of a first Treble in the English game – but Aston Villa thoroughly outplayed them at Wembley in the League Cup final to win 3-1. His two penalties against Chelsea helped United to that comfortable 4-0 triumph in the FA Cup Final to secure the Double. Then came the icing on the cake – Cantona was named Footballer of the Year by the PFA, and captain of the French national side by new manager Aimé Jacquet. Yes, Eric was certainly on top of the world in the summer of 1994, yet a few months later, it would feel like it was all crashing down around him in the darkness of Selhurst Park. Life was always good or bad, up or down; there would be no grey areas in the remarkable existence of Eric Cantona, *enfant terrible*, and footballer extraordinaire.

9

Rebel with a Cause

*'I'm so proud the fans still sing my name, but I fear tomorrow they will stop.
I fear it because I love it. And everything you love, you fear you will lose.'*
ERIC CANTONA, 2004

'I think the rest of us are painting by numbers.'
MARK HUGHES, 1993

Cantona would return to action for United on 1 October 1995. The king of drama, he would invariably return in a spotlight appropriate to his presence on the beautiful game's stage. No small-time, behind-closed-doors comeback in the reserves for Cantona – no, he was propelled back into the front-line trenches by Ferguson, against Liverpool at Old Trafford.

United had started the season with a 3-1 loss at Aston Villa, a result that prompted the most famous clanger ever by TV pundit Alan Hansen. The former Liverpool centre-half-turned-*Match of the Day*-analyst brashly showed off his new 'skills' by dismissing a United shorn of the likes of Paul Ince, Andrei Kanchelskis and Mark Hughes – all shown the exit door in the closed season by Ferguson – and now reliant on a bunch of youngsters who had come through the Old Trafford academy ranks.

Midfielder Ince was sold to Inter Milan for £7.5 million; long-serving striker Hughes joined Chelsea for £1.5 million; and unsettled Russian winger Kanchelskis (United's leading scorer the previous season) was sold to Everton for £5 million. Ferguson was heavily criticised for these sales, especially when they lost at Villa. Hansen led the chorus of doubters; he was not convinced that Paul Scholes, David Beckham, the Neville brothers, Lee Sharpe and Nicky Butt were up to it. Ferguson had made a mistake, he affirmed, getting rid of experience and giving youth a go.

What Hansen did not know – maybe he should have, given he was now a professional pundit – was the quality of the youngsters assembled before him. He certainly had not done his homework. That initial loss at Villa Park would be the only one 'the kids' would suffer in the Premiership until Eric's return on 1 October. They won five and drew one of their top-flight encounters and, by the season's end, Hansen's words came back to haunt him as 'Fergie's Fledglings' helped United overhaul Newcastle United's ten-point lead at the top of the table.

Inevitably, Cantona was the star of the show on his return, scoring the late point-saver from the penalty spot after two goals from Robbie Fowler had cancelled out Nicky Butt's second-minute opener. After his goal, he swung nonchalantly around the left-hand goal post, as if an actor taking his bow to a rapt audience. Cantona would become the conductor of the orchestra, the man behind the rise and rise of 'the kids'. He would teach them by experience and nurture them. His positive influence on them is, I believe, one of the greatest and, surprisingly, little-heralded achievements of his reign.

Without Cantona, would 'the kids' have come on as quickly? I think not. I asked United fanatic Martin Creasy what he thought about the subject. He told me, 'I remember waiting to meet some mates for an Old Trafford game around Christmas 1995 when the team weren't sparking. I wasn't the only one that day who thought we might finish as low as sixth! But it was Eric more than anyone who galvanised the young stormtroopers over the coming weeks and months to what would finish in a glorious double – and even better by beating Liverpool in the final.

'He was not just a leader on the pitch – he can also take credit for inspiring that new generation of United stars – the most stunning collection of young talent since the Busby Babes. It was no coincidence that the emergence of Beckham, Scholes, Butt, the Neville brothers and even Giggs happened while Eric was in his pomp. They could learn at the feet of the master. Not just new tricks, new skills and new techniques for striking a football, but, just as importantly, the dedication to training, practising, developing and honing skills. They could also learn there were times when a solitary determination was needed. If you want to take shots from free kicks, preached the Frenchman, you can't just rely on inspiration on the day. It takes practice – hours of practice, when other players have long since headed through the gates in their expensive cars. David Beckham and Paul Scholes have acknowledged the contribution that Cantona made in their spectacular progress – and all those young players felt the same.'

That first season back he would take the game by the scruff of its neck and drag United and 'the kids', his kids, over the finishing line. At Christmas 1995, the Red Devils were ten points behind Kevin Keegan's Newcastle. Yet by early March, Cantona's efforts had helped reduce the deficit to four points and the big Frenchman really came into his own when the clubs met at St James's Park on 4 March 1996. The pressure was at its most intense and Cantona responded as though out for a stroll in the park, scoring the only goal of a match that left the United of Manchester just one point behind the United of Newcastle.

It was a turning point, as much a psychological one as a physical one. The Toon were now a demoralised, haunted army while United, with Cantona rampant, went from strength to strength. The effect as Cantona and Ferguson chiselled away at Newcastle's massive points advantage is best summarised, of course, by Keegan's outburst at Elland Road on Sky TV on 30 April 1996. While Cantona had steered United towards the summit, Ferguson had helped wind up the Geordies by claiming that teams like Leeds would not try as hard against them as they did against Manchester United. Interviewed after his team's 1-0 win at Leeds on that night, Keegan blew a fuse. With tears of frustration in his eyes, he said, 'When you do that with footballers like he said about Leeds ... I've kept really quiet, but I'll tell you something, he went down in my estimation when he said that ... we have not resorted to that. But I'll tell ya ... you can tell him now if you're watching it... we're still fighting for this title, and he's got to go to Middlesbrough and get something, and ... and I tell you honestly, I'd love it if we beat them ... love it.'

Unfortunately for Keegan, United did go to Middlesbrough and get something – a 3-0 win – with Cantona again pulling the strings. With one game of the season remaining, Manchester United led the Premiership by three points, and the title was on its way back to Old Trafford after that barren season coinciding with Cantona's ban. Newcastle's hunt for a first title since 1927 would continue as they recorded a 1-1 draw with Tottenham.

A week later, Manchester United became the first team to complete a second League Championship/FA Cup double when Cantona's 85th-minute goal gave them a 1-0 win over Liverpool in the FA Cup Final. In his post-match interview, Cantona, enigmatic as ever, said, 'You know, that's life. Up and down.'

But it couldn't really get any better for the man from France who had never previously found a footballing home. Or could it? Here he was, king of Old Trafford after close on four excellent years, four years that had brought trophies and kudos galore. His redemption from his 'crime' at Selhurst Park was complete. Yet within 12 months – by May 1997 – the King would be gone.

In his final season at Old Trafford, United would retain the league title, meaning Cantona had won four in five years. Again, United would not succeed in Europe and Cantona would walk away at the age of 30, announcing he was retiring from football. Shortly afterwards, he would become captain of the French National Beach Football team and say that he planned a career in acting. It was a total shock to all at Old Trafford – especially the fans who continued to idolise him. He had effectively gone without saying goodbye, muttering darkly about the ever-increasing commercial grip on football. He did not like the way some at the club saw him purely as a marketable commodity – that the club was cashing in on sales of shirts with his name on them.

Was he actually consumed with resentment brought on by greed? Some top-liners at United believe so to this day. One insider told me, 'Eric was harping on about leaving because he did not want to be a marketing ploy and did not want money to be made off his back, but that seemed to be just a front. He was actually just peeved that he wasn't taking a big enough cut from the sales. If he was that bothered about it all, why did he put his name to a range of shirts to be sold at the megastore in 2004 and 2005?'

Cantona had played in a total of 185 games for United, scoring 82 goals. He had won four Premiership titles, two FA Cups and four Charity Shields. He was sent off five times while at the club.

The news of his retirement did not shock those who knew

him across the Channel. Rolland Courbis, coach at Olympique Marseille, said he believed Eric Cantona's decision to quit football was the correct one. 'The decision is typical of the man,' he said. 'Unlike certain players, he is not waiting until he is past his peak to quit. He will not stick around for that one season too long, he is quitting at the top.'

Guy Roux, still coach of Auxerre, said he was 'not sure' Cantona would stick to his decision. 'Big stars like to bring the curtain down several times. I am sure he will have a few encores, and I'm well used to surprises with Cantona.'

Alex Ferguson paid his tribute by saying, 'He conveyed a regal authority and the place was in a frenzy every time he touched the ball. I was struck by his insistence on making the easy pass whenever possible, a characteristic that showed itself as a great strength of his game in his time with us.

'Nobody had more imagination when it came to spotting the opportunity for an improbable and devastating pass or more technical dexterity in threading the ball through crowding defenders. But like all truly exceptional creative players, Cantona did something extravagant only when it was necessary.

'No one should have any doubt about the contribution made by Eric Cantona. He brought priceless style and presence to the team. He was the best Christmas present I was ever given. I had resolved that I would ignore all past attempts to present him as an *enfant terrible* and judge him on what he was like in his dealings with me. He was not, I soon discovered, the overwhelmingly confident person many perceived him to be. He needed nourishing. Like most players he needed to be told he was special. He gave a great deal of himself to the game.'

United fans would never really get over his departure – even today they sing his name at every match. This poignant tribute from United fan Paul Busby, from Manchester, summed up the general feeling of shock and loss felt by the supporters at the time: 'Cantona signed for United in November 1992 and, that night, I gave the news to my father who was clinging to life in a Manchester hospital. I told him that with Eric, we would finally win the league after our 26-year wait. Those were the last words I ever spoke to my father. Later that night, he died. Eric kept my promise, not once but four times. Thank you, Eric.'

Peter Hargreaves, also of Manchester, had this to say: 'The premature retirement of Eric Cantona is a sad blow to everybody connected with Manchester United, be they an official, a player or a mere supporter like myself. Not since the days of Denis Law has any single player been the subject of such hero worship and idolatry. Like Law, he was his own man; he did things his way or not at all. Like Law, he was a tempestuous, occasionally violent person. And, like Law, he was a genius and I loved him.

'I have been watching Manchester United for over 40 years and, in that time, I have been fortunate enough to see some of the greatest players of all time play in the beloved red shirt; I number Eric Cantona among the best.

'As a mere supporter, I can offer Cantona very little, other, that is, than my thanks for what he has done for Manchester United and what he has given to me by way of his contribution as a player. I maintain my own best-ever Manchester United team, it includes players from five decades. Eric Cantona is in that team and that is the highest praise that I can give to the man.'

A fan from Scandinavia pointed out that Cantona had left at Whitsun, saying, 'Today is Whitsun, on which day Christians celebrate the rising of Jesus from Earth to the heavens. Not being religious myself, for me, from now on, Whitsun will always be the day that Eric left us. We may get a replacement, may even win the European Cup, but for those of us who suffered the barren years, and then witnessed the coming of Le Dieu, Eric Cantona will always be our Saviour.

'Thanks for the memories, thanks for the triumphs, thanks for the brilliance, thanks for the fighting spirit, thanks for being UNITED through and through.'

Yet away from Old Trafford, some football fans applauded Eric's decision. On the BBC's Sports Talk website, Kieran, from England, said, 'Eric Cantona retired at the top because he wanted to be remembered as a class act (recently voted Man United greatest-ever player) and not a player who lost his touch. Ian Rush went on to play Division Three football, which has perhaps spoilt his reputation.'

And Brian Malone from Ireland concurred, 'There's nothing worse than seeing an old has-been plying his trade in the Premiership just to pick up his salary at the end of the week. Eric Cantona is the best example. He stunned the footballing world by retiring at his peak. He refused to allow his legacy be tainted by becoming ordinary. What a legend!'

Most journalists were in agreement that Cantona had delivered the goods in his four-and-a-half-year spell at United. Steve Curry, writing in the *Daily Mail* in December 2002, marked the 10th anniversary of Eric's United début by saying, 'It is ten years ago today that a 26-year-old Cantona, tall, straight-backed and with his collar characteristically turned up, made his début for United ... United found a man dedicated to his work. His application amazed Ferguson and, when Cantona asked for the assistance of two players at the end of his first training session to give him additional practice, the manager admits he was taken aback. It was a habit from which the club still benefit today....'

Curry went on to describe the hold Eric had over the club at the peak of his popularity. 'Cantona felt he had become a pawn in the game of the merchandising department. There is no doubt the replica shirts, Cantona mugs and anything else with his name on it, sold like hot cakes. It indicated afresh that he had become a greater United icon than any of his predecessors – Bobby Charlton, Denis Law and George Best included.'

The money row – again. Three months after his departure, United would put out a statement saying that Eric would not get a penny from the amount he was demanding in the ongoing squabble over image-rights royalties. United said he had newly claimed he was owed a £750,000 share from the sale of souvenir items bearing his name by the club, but that he had been paid in full when he quit in the May. It was an unsavoury dispute and, some critics would contend, typical of United through the ages; they had never easily parted with money – even some of the survivors of the Munich air disaster had been forced to battle for compensation.

Now Eric was being labelled a mercenary – and, in a new twist, his ageing mother Eleonore decided to speak out on his behalf. She said, 'I do not understand how there can be a row with Manchester United. He loves the club and he loves the spectators. He was the master who gave the young players their voice. I am certain he will return to Old Trafford next month to say goodbye to the fans.

'Eric is not interested in money. It is not what makes him tick. He does not live in a castle and does not pursue a life of materialism. The heart rules his life. That is the most important thing to him. If someone says he is being greedy, it is false.'

Her words rang true. While at Old Trafford, Eric would live in a semi-detached house in Boothstown, an average suburb of Manchester, similar to the property he had rented in Roundhay prior to his move from Leeds. He did not appear money-motivated, but he made his stand because he believed the club owed him cash from souvenirs sold off at the megastore.

United, rather haughtily, then put out another statement saying they had thrown out what remained of merchandise bearing Cantona's name prior to a deadline set between the club and his advisers. Clearly something was amiss and it would be four long years before he returned to Old Trafford in a high-profile capacity. He turned out for a United XI in Ryan Giggs' testimonial against Celtic in August 2001, coming on as a 73rd-minute substitute.

By that time, the Frenchman had been voted the best player ever to put on a United shirt by the club's fans and Giggs was grateful to him, saying, 'I asked Eric to come over and play whatever part he wanted in the game. He came over and it was great to see Eric play here again.'

When looking back over Eric's United career, the theme of failure in Europe refuses to go away – and it could even be argued that that blind spot was another key part of his decision to quit in 1997. Certainly the 1996/97 season's failure to reach the final of the Champions League hit Eric hard. The return semi-final leg at Borussia Dortmund on 9 April left him devastated according to United insiders. Cantona, Ferguson and Keane knew they had let slip a major chance to reach the final and lift the Cup for the first time since 1968.

It would be Dortmund who would go on to be crowned champions – they were a typical, functional German machine without the flair of United or Real Madrid, but were expertly marshalled by Ottmar Hiztfeld. United lost 1-0 – 2-0 on aggregate – and Cantona was heartbroken after the frustrating defeat. *Mail on Sunday* journalist Andy Bucklow believes the failure against Dortmund was a definite factor in Cantona's decision to quit. He told me, 'Dortmund were yet another unfancied continental team unfazed by Eric. All-conquering at home as Eric was, to some he was a busted flush when faced with breaching the cuter defences which lay in wait beyond Dover. Eric seemed to know it himself and, one month after the Dortmund disaster, as captain, he lifted the Premiership trophy after a 2-0 win over West Ham then disappeared as suddenly as he had arrived.

'He had contributed enormously to slaking the 25-year thirst of success-starved Old Trafford. But mere glory wasn't enough for Eric. And ultimate glory now seemed out of reach for, despite the latest title triumph, United were entering a period of mini transition and would win nothing the following season.

'Eric didn't do transition but perhaps, more importantly, he couldn't accept that he could no longer live up to standards which agonisingly fell just short when it really mattered.

'Success at his adopted home had gone hand in hand with his frustration at team-mates, and even more at himself, for being unable to make anything more than a fleeting impact on licking up the continental cream. Eric's slim Euro highlights package in this respect included a face-saving equaliser in a 3-3 draw at Old Trafford against the might of Galatasaray, an away goal at Fenerbahce and, perhaps his finest hour a month before the Dortmund débâcle, scoring the second in a memorable 4-0 dismantling of a classy pre-Mourinho Porto side. On this night, the young players seemed to come of age as United swept away one of the best teams in Europe. Their time would come, but Eric decided his time was up.'

Cantona also knew that foreign teams would try to get him sent off – they were well aware of his temperament. It meant he worked hard to keep himself in check, which took something away from his spark and natural flair, particularly in the European away games. Of course, it would not always save him from himself. His crime sheet in Europe included a bad night at the office in Turkey. After a night of misery and frustration for under-achieving United in the self-proclaimed hell of Galatasaray, the niggling, time-wasting Turks drove Cantona to such distraction that he was sent off in the mayhem that followed the final whistle after comments made to the referee. He would be banned for four European matches in a throwback to his disciplinary problems in previous years in France.

Other pundits point out that, at the time, United – and Cantona – were also hindered by the foreign players rule in force at the time. It allowed only three foreign players plus two 'assimilated' ones who had come through their youth set-up in any team. As Andy Bucklow eloquently explained to me, 'Eric's football brain was clearly one step ahead of the Premiership defenders of the day, although thankfully not out of sync with quality team-mates such as Keane, Giggs, Hughes and Kanchelskis. The problem with this little lot though was that, in the early days of the newly formatted Champions League, all – along with the likes of Peter Schmeichel and Denis Irwin – were subject to the now defunct foreigners restriction rule which prohibited United and, by definition, Eric, from ever living up to their potential.

'I've always maintained that that 1994 side, which also contained the likes of Bruce, Pallister, Ince and a still interested Lee Sharpe, was better than the one which eventually lifted the trophy in 1999. Eric was the subtle icing on a very rich cake. Yet that side never even got a sniff of a quarter-final.

'Despite the intensity and power, adhesed with not a little skill, it was still early days for United back at Europe's top table despite the Cup Winners' Cup triumph three years earlier. With the restrictions, Fergie was like a boxer contesting for a heavyweight title with one hand behind his back. Six Englishmen had to be in the team, so who to drop? Certainly not Eric.'

Former England boss Glenn Hoddle also weighed in on the debate, arguing United were in better European shape once Cantona had been replaced by Teddy Sheringham. Hoddle said at the time, 'I watched Teddy in the Charity Shield [his first match for United in 1997] and it looked to me as if he'd been playing for United for six years rather than a few minutes. I think his signing is an added bonus for the club in terms of their European prospects.

'Eric did a lot of great things for United but he wasn't playing international football for France; he didn't have the same experience. Teddy was picking up in the European Championship and playing extremely well in England's World Cup qualifying games. In a sense, the Champions League is a step down from that and Teddy has the ability and the confidence to shine in such company.' Hoddle would be proved spectacularly correct when Sheringham went on to grab that last-gasp equaliser against Bayern Munich in the 1999 European Cup Final, the prelude to Ole Gunnar Solskjær's remarkable winner.

It is also an interesting comment of Hoddle's regarding Eric's international career – that he did not play as well for United in Europe owing to the early end to his playing days for his country. He made 43 appearances for France, scoring 19 goals, but his career ended in 1994 when he was just 27.

It had looked as though he was set for legendary status with France after they failed to qualify for the 1994 World Cup in the USA. Gérard Houllier resigned as boss with Aimé Jacquet taking over. Jacquet began to rebuild the team for Euro '96 and appointed Cantona as the captain, a position he held until the Selhurst Park incident in January 1995. The kung fu kick would cost him more than just the domestic honours United missed out on that season. His nine-month suspension also prevented him from playing in international matches and, by the time he was back in business, he could not get back in the team. He had been replaced as the team's playmaker by a certain Zinedine Zidane, and would never again be selected for the national squad. It meant he lost out on three years of vital international football experience, experience that, as Hoddle suggests, clearly could have contributed to his problems when adapting to European football with United.

Mentioning his kung fu attack again is probably as good a time as any to examine his full 'crime sheet'. Of course, there were other incidents on the domestic front, most of them before the 1995 kung fu attack at Selhurst Park. They certainly make grim reading.

In February 1993, he was fined £1,000 for spitting at a Leeds fan on his first visit back to Elland Road.

In March 1994, Eric was sent off for stamping on Swindon midfielder John Moncur. Three days later, he was dismissed again at Arsenal for two bookable offences. The episodes at Swindon and Arsenal would earn him a five-match ban.

Then, in August 1994, Cantona was given an early bath for fouling Rangers defender Steven Pressley in a pre-season friendly, his fourth red card in nine months. Even after the kung fu attack he could not stay out of trouble – a few weeks after the incident, he was caught up in a row with an ITN reporter who had tracked him to Guadeloupe, where he was on holiday with his family. It was alleged Cantona tried a repeat show on the reporter of the lunge he had first exacted on Simmons.

While in no way condoning his actions, they did come as part of the parcel that made up this extraordinary man and footballer. If you took away the edge, you took away some of his performance, but clearly he was out of order resorting to kung fu kicks – however detestable the victim – or stamping on opponents.

Ferguson points to the other side of Cantona – the one who helped the kids, the one who was a perfect trainer, the one who was a fine captain of Manchester United – to counter the negatives. But wasn't it a gamble to appoint Cantona as skipper because of his disciplinary lapses? Ferguson gives short shrift to that one, saying, 'Eric was an excellent captain because he had the presence and stature to do it. I believe It was his suspension which helped to change his outlook. It was a terrible thing to happen to the lad and it took a lot of courage to come back and become the player he was after it. I had no qualms about appointing Eric, and he fully justified the appointment with his leadership and example.'

Nine years after the King had gone, Ferguson also had this tribute for Cantona, the footballer supreme and his best-ever signing, 'If you look at us signing Eric Cantona for £1 million – and I think this is probably the best way to do it – and how much Andriy Shevchenko is going for – £35 million – you have to ask yourself this: is Shevchenko 35 times better than Cantona?

'I sometimes watch videos of Cantona now and we probably didn't realise just how good he was. We thought he was great, we thought he was the best player ever, but it is only when you look back at videos of what he did, that you think, "Bloody hell!" Then you think, he cost us £1 million.'

When I look back on the reign of Cantona – the number seven who will for ever be in my consciousness with that proud, tall, straight-backed poise of his, and his collar characteristically turned up bearing down on goal – I can certainly see what Ferguson is getting at. How the big Frenchman ultimately brought much more to United than perhaps any other player ever. How he catapulted them back into the big-time through his own aura of invincibility. How he finally came home after years of wandering and searching. In Ferguson, he found an unlikely soul-mate – it made it all the more remarkable when he walked away for good in 1997.

Even then, I believe Cantona made the correct decision. He was an intelligent man; he knew he and United had gone as far as they could. He left with his reputation intact, and his departure opened the door for the arrival of Sheringham and eventual European glory.

What to make of his life after United? Typically, he would wander down a couple of perverse avenues – acting and beach football. Money-wise, he didn't need to do anything, but he remained a free spirit and went where the muse took him.

This is how one film magazine succinctly summed up Cantona's acting career in 2003: 'Eric Cantona – the Frenchman left Manchester United at the age of 30 to launch a film career. The tough guy was more convincing as a boxer in *Les Enfants du Marais* than as an ambassador in *Elizabeth*. Last heard of putting on a fat-suit to play a 25-stone policeman in *The Overeater*.'

In fact, Cantona had been involved in 13 movies by 2006 – his most recent that year being in the French gangster film, *Le Deuxième Souffle*. His most famous role to date was as a typically brooding French nobleman in the British film about the early life of Elizabeth I. He was cast in the role by Working Title Films, which made *Four Weddings and a Funeral*. Producer Tim Bevan would defend Cantona's involvement, saying, 'This is not a joke – we think he can act.'

Eric also won praise for his part in Nike's spectacular advert campaign for the 2002 World Cup Finals. Cantona was cast as the all-powerful ringmaster behind a tournament that was a footballing version of sudden death. Set on a huge container ship, 24 of the game's biggest names were drawn together for the Secret Tournament, a three-on-three competition where there was only one rule – first goal wins. The players were split into eight teams and Cantona had the perfect view as he commandeered the tournament. The advert, directed by Terry Gilliam of Monty Python fame, was a massive success and Cantona earned good reviews for his role.

London's *Evening Standard* theatre critic Matthew Norman believed Cantona would have been ideal for a role in *The Shining*, but was also complimentary about his acting skills. He wrote in 1999, 'Considering some of his more opaque philosophical reflections, it might have been assumed that Eric Cantona's film career would begin and end with a role as an extra in a remake of *One Flew Over the Cuckoo's Nest*. But no, M Cantona's cinematic ambitions go far deeper and, after a bit part in *Elizabeth*, his portrayal of a small-town boxer with a big temper in *Les Enfants du Marais*, a film doing good box office in France, has been well received.'

GQ editor Dylan Jones summed up the appeal of Cantona the man, the footballer, the actor, the philosopher as well as anyone when writing a piece for the *Mail on Sunday* in 2006. According to Jones, Eric was more than just a mere footballer – how, in a sense, it was inevitable that he would try acting when he quit United. He was very much a man of the people, not just a man limited to a footballing appeal. Trying to explain the attraction of football, the former Manchester City fan turned to Cantona and his influence for help. Jones wrote, 'But most importantly, for the Premiership, for me, for the footballing fraternity as a whole, there was Eric. King Eric. Not only did Cantona play a talismanic role in the revival of Manchester United as a footballing powerhouse, he also performed the same function for the Premiership itself.

'Eric got me to games again, got me off the sofa and into Old Trafford. I woke up one morning and thought, "Christ, how did that happen?" I realised all I cared about was Eric. How could you not love a man who stoically turned his collar up every time he walked on to the pitch, who launched 'that' kung fu kick against 'that' Crystal Palace oik, who said the most ridiculous things ... like, "I don't play against a particular team; I play against the idea of losing..." "I didn't study; I live ....You can't study these things, life teaches them to you. You don't find them in a book. I've read a lot of Socrates on page three of the *Sun*." And, my favourite, "I am God." And so, almost by default, I became a surrogate Manchester United fan.'

So, what of the future? Well, he's still involved with his acting and the beach football – he is a promoter for the sport and is desperate for his France team, made up of former professionals and coached by himself, to usurp the Brazilians as the undisputed world champions. In November 2006, he led the team to third place in the World Cup in Brazil.

But here's the burning question, the one United fans continue to ask as Ferguson's reign moves towards its inevitable end ... will Eric the King ever return to reign again at Old Trafford? As manager maybe? As far as Cantona is concerned, 'Maybe one day I will go back to United, but for the moment I have too many interesting things going on, what with beach soccer and the cinema.'

By November 2006, Eric had admitted that the idea was becoming more attractive to him by the day. Members of his French beach soccer team certainly believed he was growing increasingly astute as a coach, and he himself admitted his team talks were based on those once given to himself by Ferguson. In other words, he had learned well from the combustible Scot, who had this to say on the subject of Cantona the football manager: 'I think Eric would do very well in the job. He is single-minded ... I'm sure he would be a great manager. I've always thought he had the capabilities to be a great coach in the English game.'

It's a fair recommendation, and imagine this scenario: it is 27 January 2015 – and Eric Cantona, manager of Man United, leads out his team at Selhurst Park for a Premiership match, 20 years to the day since his infamous kung fu attack on Matthew Simmons. Now that would be some finale to the story ... wouldn't it? And who would ever bet against the enigmatic Monsieur Cantona when it comes to surprise endings? Not me....

10

When Football was King

*'All I ever wanted to do was kick a football about.
It didn't enter my head to do anything else.'*
DAVID BECKHAM, 2000

'I have a camera up my backside almost 24 hours a day.'
DAVID BECKHAM, 2000

Washed up, dismissed as a has-been (and, in some cruel and obviously unwarranted cases, a never-was) and scrambling about desperately to establish some sort of viable legacy to a career that promised so much but ultimately fizzled out in pathos. OK, enough of Tony Blair ... but, joking aside, David Beckham's footballing lifetime should never have ended up this way, should it? I am confident that given the benefit of time and a more rational reappraisal, Beckham will not be treated nearly as harshly as he was as this book headed for the printers in 2007.

Let's be honest – this was a man who *did* his bit, who actually *did* earn his place in the pantheon of United greats and wearers of the coveted number 7 shirt. At United, he won *six* Premiership titles, two FA Cup winners' medals and, of course, played a major role in the lifting of the European Cup in 1999 when – due to the bans on Paul Scholes and Roy Keane – he stepped gamely into their central midfield space against Bayern Munich in Barcelona. He would also, memorably, win Spain's La Liga title with Real Madrid before leaving for LA in 2007.

By May 2007, he had also won 94 England caps, 58 as captain of his country, and played in the final stages of three World Cups and two European Championships. He would also make an unexpected comeback as England stuttered in their Euro 2008 qualifying campaign. And, when he finally quit Manchester for Madrid, Real were willing to pay £25 million for his services.

Lampooned as a numbskull, a man ruled by his wife, a foolish clothes-horse, a swaggerer who was more interested in showing off the money he and his wife gleefully made from the Beckham brand than enhancing his footballing career, the real Beckham was none of these. In reality, away from the headlines and the image pumped up by an incessant media frenzy, David Beckham was actually a rather fine footballer, with a lovely right peg, and certainly a model professional. He was also a decent, likeable man, someone who coped admirably with a daily press intrusion that made the claustrophobia exhibited in the movie *The Truman Show* look like a carefree walk in the park.

Similar to Eric Cantona, the man from whom he would inherit the number 7 shirt, he knew the benefits of hard work on the training ground. Even before the arrival of the King, he would spend hours alone putting in crosses and trying out free kicks. He would also be the first to admit he was no natural genius, that he was a product of the long, lonely hours he committed to fine-tuning his end product. At his peak, he was the best crosser of the ball in world football and the most talented dead-ball exponent.

He was also actually a rather modest man, far from the big-head the media would portray, but he did have his values and opinions indoctrinated from a working-class upbringing in East London – he was hardly the ventriloquist's dummy of his wife Victoria, aka 'Posh' – although she could at times influence him towards her way of thinking. He himself could be stubborn and steadfast when needed.

In short, he was not the village idiot he was often depicted as being – although I would concede that when it came to the biggest decisions of his footballing career, Beckham could act rashly, without enough prior thought about the likely negative outcomes. He would shoot from the hip and pay a rough price in the twilight of his career.

Yet, in earlier days, David Beckham did his duty for his country, both as player and skipper. Again, when the record books are rewritten, we may find he hardly deserved the generally critical abuse that followed him when he was booted out of the England camp after the disappointment of World Cup 2006. It's too easy to forget how this man personally dragged England to the World Cup of 2002 when all seemed lost at Old Trafford against Greece, geeing up demoralised troops and leading them to Japan and South Korea with *that* wonder goal.

This is a man who became the most famous footballer on earth – arguably, at the peak of his popularity in 2002, even the most famous person on the planet. Now that is surely a remarkable achievement – a game lad from East London transformed into the world's number-one icon.

Undoubtedly, he made mistakes – there were the outlandish fashion statements he made accompanying his wife; the desire to show off his bling; the apparent need to be the centre of attention … and when he put his foot in it, it was always a massive foot.

No, Beckham never did anything without the accompanying headlines. His problem was he seemed to get sucked into believing his own publicity, and maybe he did listen a little too much to Victoria who, with her days in the Spice Girls, was much the more experienced and streetwise of the two when it came to celebrity, dealing with the press and keeping up the right image for the Beckham brand she would rigorously promote and defend.

He was no fool, but he did not have the vision to see that he would never get the better of Ferguson, his Old Trafford taskmaster and a seasoned and determined fighter. With a little more subtlety and manoeuvring, he could have ended his days at Old Trafford and the legacy would probably have needed no finessing at the end of his career. More success would surely have followed.

Yet the Beckhams, of course, did not do subtlety. He decided to take his grievance over the boot Fergie kicked into his face into the public domain. He decided to wear his hair pulled back with an Alice band to show off the full glory of the stitches and bruising, and to look all poutingly hurt when the paparazzi gathered to capture the startling pictures that greeted us across our breakfast tables that unforgettable Monday morning in 2003.

It probably seemed sweet revenge in the spur of the moment, yet it would be the ultimate ammunition for Ferguson to sack him. He was convinced Beckham had let the pop star lifestyle go to his head; now he knew for sure. Ferguson did not want it publicly perceived that he was squeezing out the golden boy of Old Trafford. Yet, to an extent, it seems that was just what he had been doing for a couple of years building up to Beckham's departure to Madrid in the summer of 2003.

For the last few months of his United career, I am told by a senior United insider that Ferguson did not speak to Beckham unless he absolutely had to. He was sick of the boy; he wanted rid but, being the clever Glaswegian, he knew the deed had to be done with care. He drove Beckham to the brink by ignoring him, dropping him for key matches and making him feel unwanted.

By the summer of 2003, he had had a bellyful of Ferguson's antics and told his agent that, yes, he would be open to a move to Real Madrid. With more clarity, he may have realised that the best route would have been to back down with the United boss, subtly alter his hectic lifestyle and to keep the peace, but that would have taken some superhuman effort. Ferguson was pushing him to the brink and Beckham could take no more.

In falling out with Ferguson – by not backing down over his celebrity lifestyle – and moving to Madrid, he would pay dearly. The rows with the boss cost him his place at United, and his choice of Madrid instead of Barcelona brought an unhappy spell to the back end of his career. In turn, his impotence at Real led to his downfall with England. He was not playing well in his third season at the Bernabeu and that form was replicated at the World Cup in Germany. Beckham could not simply turn it on like a tap as some could; he needed a run of games to settle his form. He had always been like that. Here was a man who also needed security and to feel loved – he lacked both from 2003 in Manchester, and then in the alien culture of Madrid.

Interesting to think that Beckham's decision to move to Madrid in the summer of 2003 would also change the very hierarchy at the top of European football. He made the mistake of thinking he was about to join a team of world-beaters, that he would seal his legacy with La Liga trophies and European Cups galore. The move no doubt appealed to his ego – David

Beckham, *galactico*, one of the best in the world playing with the best in the world.

He turned down the offer to join a hungry Barcelona without a moment's thought – instead opting for a fat, slothful Madrid, packed with men who did not apparently have the same burning desire for glory. He plumped for a team already in decline, a team who permitted the one real gem in its collection to be snaffled away from under its very nose. It was particularly bad business to allow the one tiger Madrid had in their tank – the inimitable and brilliant holding midfielder Claude Makelele – to move to Chelsea for £14 million.

But again, Beckham did not have the wider vision to look beyond the gloss and the bling; he was entranced by the lifestyle with the likes of Zidane, Figo and Ronaldo on offer at Madrid. His snub to Barça opened the door to the Catalan signing of Ronaldinho and the rest, as they say, is history.

On paper at least, Beckham's lean years in Madrid should never have happened. This was football's golden boy and the last years of his career should have been the icing on an already spectacular cake. When he joined Madrid at the tender age of 28, the world was literally at his pampered feet. He had worn the magical number 7 shirt in the most successful United squad ever, captained the England team in a World Cup tournament and signed a multi-million pound deal with one of football's most legendary football clubs, Real Madrid. He was also one of the world's most photographed men, and was never out of the gossip columns, magazines or sports pages. He had been a United great and was still the main man for England. Yet, three years later, he was being depicted in the press as a busted flush. Just how did this come to pass?

Let's begin at the beginning. The story starts when David

Robert Joseph Beckham was born in the nondescript borough of Leytonstone in East London on 2 May 1975 to working-class parents Ted, a gas engineer, and Sandra, a hairdresser. They would later move to nearby Chingford and Ted, a footie fanatic, would become the biggest influence on Beckham's drive towards pro football as he helped develop his skills. Ted himself was a useful amateur player and he would drill into his son the need to keep working at his own game. He was a forceful taskmaster; a hard, but inspiring Svengali to the young Beckham. David would say of him, 'My dad would tell me if I'd done well, but if I'd done badly he'd definitely tell me I'd done badly. He certainly never told me I was the best. What I was told was to work hard at it, and that's what I did.'

Ted would have him out on the local football pitch for hours, concentrating on improving his game, building up his skills and his stamina; David was also a strong cross-country runner at this time, regularly finishing first in his age group in the Essex cross-country championships, and this would help him develop physically.

Ted was undoubtedly a domineering father and all-encompassing influence. As my psychoanalyst friend says, 'In some ways, he typified the men David would work with, particularly Ferguson. Tough, demanding, no-nonsense men, who would only accept the best from people. It perhaps explains why, in 2003, David would finally rebel against Ferguson and leave Manchester United. After all, he had been close to strong men most of his life and now he had had enough.'

The following quote backs up that theory. It is from Ted, telling his boy to keep his feet on the ground shortly after he had signed as a trainee, but it could as easily have been from Ferguson: 'You may have signed for Man United, but you haven't done anything yet. When you've played for the first team, then we can talk about you having achieved something. Until then, don't start thinking you've made it.'

Ted would also bring another key influence to bear; he was a Manchester United supporter and was determined his son would also be a red. He needn't have worried – he was a convert by the age of five when he went to see United in action for the first time, bedecked in his United tracksuit and looking forward to seeing his heroes of the time, Steve Coppell being the main one. That was on 6 September 1980, when United ground out a 0-0 draw at Tottenham. A year later, the young Beckham was United's mascot against West Ham.

By the time he was ten, the boy Beckham's bedroom wall would be covered with posters of his United heroes. Bryan Robson was his favourite; Beckham would admit he admired the former United captain's never-say-die attitude and his dynamic, box-to-box style. Later, he would also idolise Glenn Hoddle for his extraordinary skills, the way he could make the ball work for him, his free kicks and subtlety. In his glory years at United, Beckham's game would be a photofit mix of both men's best qualities – the stamina and graft of the tireless Robson, allied with the pinpoint dexterity of Hoddle's craft.

Even at ten, David knew United were the only team for him. He told his father as much and Ted, in particularly loyal tones, explained he would back him and follow him wherever he ended up. Beckham owed a major debt to his father and would repay it when he made the big-time, paying off his parents' mortgage and looking after them financially.

United were first alerted by Beckham in 1986 when he was just 11 years old. David had become skills champion for his age group at the Bobby Charlton Soccer Schools. That success gave him the chance to attend a two-week trip during which he would train with FC Barcelona at the Camp Nou stadium – but, even more prestigious and important, were United legend Charlton's words to the effect that David was the best 11-year-old he had seen in his six years of running the school.

Shortly afterwards, United sent their London scout Malcolm Fidgeon to watch him playing for Waltham Forest U12s and he was invited for a trial at Old Trafford. For the next three years, he would continue to make progress in the Essex Sunday League, alternating it with trips up to United for more trial games and to watch training. United wanted him to be part of their set-up from an early age and were delighted to secure his signature on a two-year schoolboy deal on his 13th birthday.

When he reached 16, David Beckham was faced with his first major footballing decision. Unlike the one that would blight his career in 2003, he made the right one at the outset of his footballing life, choosing to sign for United instead of his local team, Tottenham Hotspur. He left home and signed as a trainee at Old Trafford on 8 July 1991.

Alex Ferguson was nearly five years into his stewardship as United boss when David arrived fresh-faced and keen to prove he had what it takes. The slumbering giants of Old Trafford were at last starting to awake after years in the wilderness. The dour Dave Sexton had gone in 1981 with the hedonistic Ron Atkinson following him out of the door five years later.

After a rocky start, the Ferguson years – and winning ethos – were finally starting to kick in. David arrived at a Manchester United on the brink of a return to the good times under the fiery Scot. The year before, they had won the FA Cup and, in David's first season as a trainee, they would also win the European Cup Winners' Cup.

The boy certainly appeared to have his work cut out if he was going to make it big at Old Trafford. He and his father never had any doubts he was good enough, and he would get an early chance to prove it. In 1992, Manchester United won the FA Youth Cup with their finest crop of youngsters since the Babes of the late 1950s. David was a key player in a team that also included Gary Neville, Paul Scholes and Ryan Giggs – scoring in the second-leg of the final against Crystal Palace.

Yet while David and dad Ted knew he had the skill to make it big, they both worried about whether he had what it took physically. Despite the hours of training and stamina building, he had arrived at United if not a weakling then certainly no Charles Atlas.

Eric Harrison, who coached and cajoled David and the boys who would become knows as 'Fergie's Fledglings' admitted everyone was relieved when the boy suddenly shot up in size. He said, 'I told David when he was 16 that, if he continued his progress, he would definitely play in our first team. I was a little worried because, physically, he was behind everybody else, and didn't have the strength. Then he shot up 6 inches overnight, at 16 going on 17. He had worries himself if he would make it.'

Eight years later, in 2000, Steve McClaren, back then United's assistant to Ferguson, would comment on just how much effort David put into his fitness training when he revealed, 'I remember a year ago, giving him a rest of a week, ten days, when we were rotating the squad just after Christmas. The day he returned to training was the fitness test day. He had had ten days of doing practically nothing, as he admitted, which was what we wanted. He came and did the "bleep" test (a commonly used fitness gauge in which players run over a set distance, wait for the bleep, then run back with the distance between bleeps becoming gradually shorter) and we had to tell him to stop because he was the only one left standing and he would have kept running and running.'

Yes, even in 1992, David was profiting from a growing mental and physical strength, a combination that would prove beneficial in the next 11 years of glory. Chris Casper was another of the babes under Harrison's guidance. He did not make it big like Beckham – a series of cruel injuries would effectively wreck his career at the young age of 26. He himself became a coach and went on to manage Bury FC, and he also believes David deserves credit for the way in which he battled to the top.

Casper said, 'As a 16-year-old, Eric Harrison gave us a work ethic and discipline that came from Sir Alex at the top. They would never let you stand still. Take David Beckham – of course, he's got talent, but he worked so hard at his game. He deserves everything he's got.'

That glory run in the Youth Cup had a sweet spin-off for David. Ferguson decided he was ready for his senior team début on 23 September 1992, when he came on as a substitute for Andrei Kanchelskis in the League Cup clash at Brighton. Since the Youth Cup triumph, he had been training regularly with the first team and playing for the reserves. Ferguson knew he had a bunch of brilliant kids on the books and had great hopes they would come through in a couple of years. In the interim, he had decided to introduce them gradually to life among his first team so that the eventual permanent inclusion would not be too much of a shock.

David took another step to his destiny when he signed as a professional on 23 January 1993, and made his first full appearance in September 1994 against Port Vale, again in the League Cup. It would be the first of his 311 games for United, in which he scored 74 goals and won an astonishing 11 medals. His début duly followed in December with his first goal for United, in the 4-0 Champions League win over Turkish side Galatasaray.

In early 1995, David would be at the receiving end of what would turn out to be the first of several attempts by Ferguson to keep his feet on the ground. He decided that David needed some hardening up and sent the golden boy on loan to Preston North End. I asked a senior United insider about this in 2006 and was told, 'David was nearly in tears, believing his dream was over before it had properly got off the ground.'

He even told his dad Ted, 'Dad, the boss wants me to go out on loan to Preston ... I don't know whether they hate me ... I think they want to get rid of me. He [Ferguson] said it would do me good and make me stronger. He said I could go there just for games and keep training with United in the week.'

To his credit, David took it well. He decided to live and train in Preston to show his new team-mates he was no big-time Charlie. He scored on his début against Doncaster and manager Gary Peters made it clear he wanted the boy to stay. Ferguson ordered David back to Old Trafford after he had completed just five games.

Peters said, 'He did really well for us and I was sorry to see him go. He was a great pro from the first day and quickly won over the trust and affection of the other lads. We could have gone great guns if we had kept him in our side for a full season, but Alex pulled the plug just as he was settling in.' Ferguson's 'on-the-record' explanation for the early recall was that David was needed to fill in because United were short of players for their next match against Leeds.

At least the North End fans of the time were able to say they had seen the biggest name in world football play for them – even if David could never lay claim to being of the same quality as Sir Tom Finney, the genius with whom Preston will eternally be associated.

The Beckham era at Old Trafford was imminent. After the 0-

0 draw at home against Leeds on 17 April 1995 – the match for which he was recalled – United were unable to hold off Blackburn in the battle for the Premiership. They lost their hold on that trophy after drawing 1-1 at West Ham in their final league match of the season, and also had the indignity of losing control of the FA Cup – the second part of the Double they had secured the previous season – when Everton beat them 1-0 at in the Final at Wembley.

Ferguson decided the time was now right for his revolution, a changing of the old guard for the new. He sold off Kanchelskis, Ince and Hughes – and brought Beckham, Butt, the Neville brothers and Paul Scholes into his senior team. It was the true dawning of the age of the Ferguson babes.

David would reward him by scoring his first Premiership goal in the first match of the 1995/96 season, the 3-1 loss at Villa Park that prompted *Match of the Day* pundit Alan Hansen's 'kids win nothing' soundbite. The United team that day was: Peter Schmeichel; Paul Parker, Gary Neville, Gary Pallister, Denis Irwin; Phil Neville, Roy Keane, Nicky Butt, Lee Sharpe; Paul Scholes and Brian McClair. David came on as a 45th-minute sub, scoring his goal eight minutes from time. It was the first of eight he would score that season as United regained the Double – the Premiership and FA Cup – they had lost the previous May, and his form and creativity firmly established him in the first team. It was also the first time any English club had won the Double twice.

David was the leading light of the new breed of English footballer. He didn't drink, he didn't do drugs, he was clean-living and he lived for football. Stats anoraks would work out that he covered over eight miles a game during a match; fitness was king for the new kids on the block. Gone were the days at United when Best and McGrath could turn out after downing a skinful the night before. This new outlook coincided brilliantly with the hard-working, no-surrender ethos of Ferguson, and would propel David and Manchester United to unparalleled glory in the English game.

David would soon link up with the returning prodigal son – Cantona was back from his nine-month ban in October 1995 – and his build-up work with the Frenchman would take the team to the very top again after the previous nightmare season.

The FA Cup Final of 1996 was the epitome of the changing nature of domestic football and how fitness and clean living would be the key to glory. It would prove to be a Wembley showdown between two sets of whippersnappers, but with only one inevitable conclusion. Lined up on one side were the so-called 'Spice Boys' of Liverpool. They included the Scouse scallywags, Robbie Fowler and Steve McManaman, and the rakish Jason McAteer and Jamie Redknapp. They liked a laugh, a drink and a good time. Good for them ... but they were up against the new boys of United – Beckham, Scholes et al – fit and raring to go for the full 90. At the end of the day, the Scousers would be most remembered for their ludicrous white suits – and for being fun-loving fops who had been out-thought and outfought.

David led the charge, testing keeper David 'Calamity' James after five minutes with a rasping shot. Eighty minutes on – and with still plenty of fuel in the old tank – David would provide the corner from which a revitalised Cantona volleyed home past the helpless, hapless James. Like a king among his loyal young cohorts, Cantona led the celebrations for his goal and the subsequent victory march around all corners of Wembley. Nine months after Alan Hansen's words of warning, United, far from winning nothing with kids, had lifted the two biggest domestic trophies.

Beckham would become a household name three months later – beginning the 1996/97 season with his wonder goal, the one from the halfway line, against Wimbledon at Selhurst Park. It was one of the three goals for which he will for ever be remembered; the other two being for England against Greece, in a World Cup qualifier in 2001, and Argentina, from the penalty spot in the World Cup of 2002.

That goal away at Wimbledon will always be a firm favourite of United fans. The Red Devils were 2-0 up when David spotted that Dons' keeper Neil Sullivan was standing a long way off his goal-line. With beauty and ease, David lifted a shot from the halfway line over Sullivan and into the net. It was a goal that would have left even Pelé blushing with pride. Not bad for a kid from the East End. It truly launched David into the big time – everyone was now talking about the blond Cockney kid playing for Man U.

United would go on to win the league again in the 1996/97 season – David's second Premiership winner's medal in consecutive seasons since breaking into the side, and he would also win the Young Player of the Year award. He had also been fast-tracked into the England team, making his début against Moldova in September 1996 under the 'tutelage' of new national boss Glenn Hoddle.

But he and United would finish trophy-less the following season – if you discount the season-opening FA Charity Shield win over Chelsea – with Arsenal beating them to the league crown and rubbing it in by also securing the Double by winning the FA Cup. That season had started with David finally taking on the number 7 shirt after Cantona had retired three months earlier. He had previously worn the number 10 shirt, and, before that, number 24. David scored 11 goals and earned six yellow cards for his endeavours – and, although low at winning nothing, he did finish a barren campaign on a high by scoring United's final goal of the season. It came after 58 minutes and was the third in the 3-0 Premiership win over Leeds at Old Trafford on 4 May 1998.

At the start of that campaign, Cantona had passed the captain's armband on to Roy Keane but disaster had struck for United – ironically, in the away Premiership match at Leeds on 27 September 1997 – when Keane suffered a terrible setback. The cruciate knee injury he picked up in a clash with Leeds' Alf Inge Haaland would sideline the new skipper for the whole season and be a major factor in United losing out to the Gunners in the battle for the league title. Of course, the run-in with Haaland would have a particularly bitter taste for Keane – the Norwegian had called him a cheat as he lay injured on the pitch and, five years later, Roy would put his professional reputation on the line by getting even with him in a Manchester derby after Haaland had moved to United's neighbours, City.

That 1997/98 campaign would certainly be one of heartache for David, too, not just in terms of finishing second to Arsenal, but also in the summer when he was sent off for England against Argentina. We will discuss his international career more fully later, but suffice it to say that when he returned to Manchester United for pre-season training for the 1998/99 season, he was at his lowest ebb. He would be vilified at grounds all over the country for the sending off, cited by Hoddle as the reason for England's premature departure – and was still down after a season without a trophy.

But after his darkest hour, David would soon be on Cloud 9 again as he and United switched into top gear and went on to capture an unprecedented Treble in 1999. It would be his – and United's – finest moment, and cemented his place as one of the club's all-time greats and a player truly worthy of that number 7 shirt. It was an achievement in itself, providing him with the glittering legacy he mistakenly believed he had forfeited by blotting his copy book when infamously sent off in the World Cup.

11

Zero to Hero

'That was rock bottom because the whole experience hit me ...
I had not cried like I did then since I was a child. For a good ten
minutes I just lost it.'
DAVID BECKHAM ON HIS SENDING OFF FOR ENGLAND
AGAINST ARGENTINA, 1998

'It was as if something supernatural had happened.'
GARY NEVILLE ON THE NIGHT UNITED WON THE EUROPEAN CUP AND
THE TREBLE BY BEATING BAYERN MUNICH IN BARCELONA, 1999

As we have previously noted, Eric Cantona quit Manchester
United on 18 May 1997. Five weeks later – 27 June 1997
– Teddy Sheringham would walk through the door Eric had
closed behind him. His signing was no off-the-cuff rebound
move by Ferguson to ease the pain of Cantona's departure. No,
it was a carefully thought-out part of a masterplan by the
United boss, who was now approaching the peak of his
powers. I am told Sheringham would even have arrived if
Cantona had not departed because Ferguson was determined
to build the second great team of his reign – a team that could
win the European Cup.

As we also noted, Eric could not make it happen in Europe for
United. Ferguson believed that Sheringham could. The old
campaigner had already shown with England and co-star Alan
Shearer in Euro '96 that he was a clever, ingenious player. He
lacked pace, but more than made up for it with the speed in his

brain. Like Cantona and, later, Paul Scholes – and even Wayne Rooney – he had the uncanny knack of seeing the pass and the flow of play that would result seconds before it crystallised.

Ferguson, to his great credit, appreciated that vision and had no hesitation in handing over a cheque for £3.5 million for Sheringham – a considerable outlay for a 31-year-old – when Eric handed in his notice. Given the unenviable task and massive expectations of filling Cantona's boots, the Londoner, not surprisingly, initially struggled. But you could see in glimpses why Ferguson rated him, and how his massive experience in European and world football could influence United, by taking a look at the team he selected against Monaco in the European Cup quarter-final second leg on 18 March 1998. It read: Van Der Gouw; G Neville, Irwin, Johnsen, P Neville; Beckham, Butt, Scholes; Cole, Sheringham, Solskjær. Ferguson was clearly trying to bring a little more guile and craft to his side; the battle-hardy, brilliant 1994 first team had been dismantled and replaced with the kids from the youth set-up and a few deft imports including Sheringham. United would go out on away goals to Monaco, but the skeleton of the new, possibly greatest-ever United side was rapidly being fleshed out.

Into this new mix, David Beckham would play a vital role. His all-action game plus his pinpoint crosses and dangerous set-piece contributions would provide ammunition for Sheringham, Cole and Solskjær – and vital goals from himself.

During the summer of 1998, Ferguson would carry out more fine-tuning as he braced himself for a mighty European assault by splashing out a combined total of £27.5million on Jaap Stam, Jesper Blomqvist and Dwight Yorke. All three would – along with Sheringham – go on to play a key part in United's European Cup win in Barcelona the following May.

But another, and just as vitally important, factor in the Treble year and Ferguson's annus mirabilis were the inspirational form and battling qualities shown by David Beckham after he returned from that hellish summer of 1998. The season that followed would be David's best as he transformed from boy into man and became the ultimate hero from a previous almighty zero. The new season could not have got off to a worse start for him. He arrived back at United after a traumatic World Cup '98 in France – his sending-off in the second-round loss to Argentina casting him as the villain responsible for his country's early exit and a barrage of abuse and hatred headed his way at football grounds all over the country. The golden boy was at his lowest ebb, his mood not helped by a campaign of vilification in national newspapers and a Beckham effigy being strung up on a lamp-post outside a pub in East London.

Ferguson made it clear that he had the full support of everyone at United. Like a loyal father to his prodigal son, he told him, 'Get yourself back here, where people love you and support you. You can have your say back to the rest of them after the season begins.'

David, still just 23, would prove to his manager and everyone in England that he had grit and guts in abundance as he knuckled down at United and simply got on with his job – although United could not have got off to a worse start to their season of triple destiny, losing the Charity Shield 3-0 to arch rivals Arsenal. In their first league match, United were still not functioning well; they drew 2-2 with Leicester, but at least David had the satisfaction of scoring one of the goals with a trademark free kick.

Roy Keane was back in the side after his lengthy absence and, inevitably, it took him time to find his feet. United were chugging along like a vintage motor with a blocked exhaust pipe – it showed as they crashed 3-0 again to Arsenal, this time at Highbury, on 20 September 1998. Stam, Blomqvist and Yorke were still acclimatising and it did not help when Nicky Butt was sent off. United then went on a 12-match unbeaten run in all competitions and, by Christmas, were firing on all cylinders.

In Europe, they had drawn 2-2 away at Bayern and 3-3 away at Barcelona – ironic, considering how both Bayern and the Camp Nou, home of Barça, would later play such a remarkable part of their first European Cup win since 1968 – as they marched into the next stage. The Andy Cole–Dwight Yorke partnership was beginning to make hay and Stam was rapidly establishing himself as a mountainous one-man defence; he was impossible to pass.

And David? He was the jewel in the crown as 1998 became 1999. From 3 January 1999, United would play 31 matches in all competitions and lose none of them. It was a remarkable record and there were some high-scoring victories including an 8-1 win at Nottingham Forest and a 6-2 win at Leicester. On 24 January 1999, United would also beat Liverpool 2-1 in an FA Cup fourth-round clash at Old Trafford, a tie worthy of mention because it would prove a fine taster of what would later come at the Camp Nou. With two minutes left, the Red Devils were still trailing 1-0 to a third-minute Michael Owen goal – yet in the 88th minute, David set up Dwight Yorke from a free kick and sub Solskjær won the tie with the 90 minutes up with a fine shot. Sound familiar?

David would show how he had matured by ignoring the explosive potential caused by a reunion with Diego Simeone in the European Cup quarter-final two-legger against Inter Milan. United progressed 3-1 on aggregate and David kept out of trouble – indeed, he swapped shirts with the Argentinian after the second leg, and now has it framed on a wall at his English home in Hertfordshire. David also had the great personal satisfaction of setting up Dwight Yorke for both goals in the 2-0 first leg win over Inter and Simeone.

Keane would then steal the limelight by driving United into the European Cup Final with that astonishing one-man show against Juventus in Turin, but David would have the final say – taking Keane's role – against Bayern. United had been forced to come back from 2-0 down against Juventus in the second leg after drawing the first 1-1 at Old Trafford. Keane gave his finest performance in a United shirt to drag his team to a 3-2 win, with David setting him up for United's first goal. David's accurate corner was forcibly headed home by the Irishman after 24 minutes.

It set up a tantalising end-of-season run-in for David and United. In the space of ten days, they could win – or lose – three trophies. For David, it would mean three fairytales; in the first match, he would score United's first goal as they came back from 1-0 down to beat Spurs 2-1 at Old Trafford on 16 May 1999, and clinch the Premiership crown. A week later, he pulled the strings in central midfield in the 2-0 FA Cup Final win over Newcastle.

Initially starting on the right wing, he moved inside after Keane fell victim to another injury on just 11 minutes. David's fine performance went a long way to keeping him in the role four days later when Ferguson had to reorganise his team for the match against Bayern, with both Keane and Scholes unavailable because of suspension. Inevitably perhaps, in the FA Cup Final, David even set up the second goal, netted by Scholes.

A few days later, David would sum up his feelings about the European Cup and Treble win like this: 'That night in the Nou Camp was the greatest feeling I have known on a football pitch. We had already won the league and the FA Cup and the day before the European Cup Final, the manager told me I was playing central midfield as I had done for most of the FA Cup Final. If I am honest, I prefer playing in the middle.'

Maybe, but it was never his best position. At his peak, David Beckham was the best right-sided midfielder in the world – he wasn't a winger, he was never fast enough to be one – in terms of the crosses he supplied. He did not hit the same heights in the centre; he could not tackle well and did not have Keane's ability to dictate the flow of the match. It perhaps helps explain why, for most of that night in Barcelona, United were second best to a typically resilient German footballing machine.

United did not have the balance Keane and Scholes would have brought, nor the fiery determination to win at all costs. That they still emerged victorious is further testament to the application and determination of David Beckham and the rest of the team that night. They never gave in. Fair enough, they were a tad lucky, but fortune is said to favour the brave.

David admitted he did not feel much sympathy for the Germans as injury-time goals from Sheringham and Solskjær killed off their dream. Lothar Matthäus had been walking around the pitch clenching his fists in triumph at his Bayern fans and, as David says, 'I even saw the trophy up in the stands with Bayern Munich ribbons already on it. It was an unbelievable sight. I was almost sick.'

That feeling would quickly pass as David set up both goals from inswinging corners – another massive milestone in his comeback from the dire low of summer 1998. In most of the pictures of the celebrations after the match, David is pictured directly to the right of Ferguson, hugging the man who had brought him to this stage, and it would be the closest the two men would ever get. That night, David paid Ferguson back for all his faith in him; thereafter, there was only one way to go, and that was downwards. It was the beginning of the end for the two men who had both played such a key role in fashioning Manchester United to their greatest-ever year of success.

David summed up the season of his life like this: 'It started with me not sure about whether I'd make it through to the following May in one piece. It ended up being the most incredible season any of us – maybe any footballer playing in this country – will ever experience.'

David had even chosen the suits United would wear for the day of the European Cup Final. From being out on a lonely ledge at the start of the season, he ended it as the man whom Ferguson even trusted to make sure his men looked the part for the biggest night of his and their footballing careers. David did not let his boss down away from the pitch; United looked suave and smart in the outfits he had asked Donatella Versace to come up with on the big day. As he said, they 'looked the business'.

With their business completed for the 1998/99 season after that night's work in the Camp Nou, David and United faced a predictable problem as they entered the new millennium – exactly where did they go from here? It was not an easy question to answer, but, in hindsight, he would never fly as high again. Then again, none of the side or the management team would – including boss Ferguson and skipper Keane.

Yet there would be one more honour – again at the highest level. In recognition of his efforts for United – particularly for the two injury-time corners that helped secure the European Cup – he was named runner-up to Rivaldo in 1999's European Footballer of the Year and FIFA World Player of the Year awards.

The following season would not be as memorable, although David did win another Premiership medal with United. The media would ask whether he was allowing his celebrity status to go to his head after his marriage to Victoria 'Posh Spice' Adams and he was sent off while playing for United for the first time in the ill-fated trip to Brazil for the so-called World Club Championship in January 2000.

United had pulled out of that season's FA Cup to take part in the inaugural event – it would prove a disastrous decision as they stumbled home without success. David was red-carded in the match against Mexican outfit Necaxa for a studs-up challenge on Jose Milian. If there were any consolation for David, it appeared in Ferguson's defence of David over the dismissal – it was solid proof that, at that time at least, the duo was still a rock-solid partnership. Ferguson claimed there was nothing wrong with David's challenge and barked, 'The reaction of the Mexican players got him sent off. The referee reacted to the Mexican players and that's disappointing. It was a 50-50 ball and they both had their feet in the air. But the Mexican players tried to get him sent off and the referee has reacted to that.'

The fact Ferguson was talking bullshit was irrelevant – it was a dangerous studs-up challenge that merited a red card – at least he still felt able to defend his man. David and United would win the Premiership again in the 2000/01 season, but by now his relationship with Ferguson was starting to deteriorate.

There would be other compensations, though. He was voted the BBC Sports Personality of the Year for 2001 and, once again, finished runner-up, this time to Luis Figo of Portugal, for the FIFA World Player of the Year award.

The next season would be a bad one for David – and Ferguson. United would win nothing and David's campaign would finish early at the end of another Argentinian's boot. On 10 April 2002, David was injured in the Champions League match against Deportivo La Coruña, breaking the second metatarsal bone in his left foot.

It was the first time most football fans had ever heard of the particular injury, but it brought special interest at home and abroad as the press speculated about its long-term impact as England and Argentina were due to meet in the group stages of that summer's World Cup. One consolation for David was that he put pen to paper on a new deal in May designed to keep him at Manchester United for another three years.

Ferguson had also put his foot in it that season – announcing it would be his last, only to change his mind halfway through. It had an effect on the players, throwing them off course and their form suffered. Arsenal won the Premiership and FA Cup double, Middlesbrough knocked United out of the FA Cup in the fourth round and, with David watching with an injured foot from the stands, the team crashed out of the European Cup. They lost on the away goals rule to Bayer Leverkusen after finishing 2-2 at Old Trafford and 1-1 in Germany.

That defeat was certainly a crushing one for Ferguson. He knew the Germans – apart from the brilliant Michael Ballack – were eminently beatable and he sat grim-faced at Hampden Park as Real Madrid beat Bayer 2-1 in the final. A week earlier, Sylvain Wiltord scored Arsenal's goal as they celebrated taking the Premiership title off their Manchester rivals in a 1-0 win at Old Trafford, marking the final nail in the coffin in what had been a dreadful season for United.

It was May 2002 and Ferguson was an angry man. His dream had been to see his United win the European Cup again in his native Glasgow – and he had had to swallow his pride as Real instead lifted the trophy, for a ninth time. He looked around his empire and saw decay and a lack of hunger. Even David Beckham, the boy to whom he had been a second father, the boy he had nurtured from 13 years old into a world-class player, the boy he knew was similar to himself in that his love for Manchester United FC was the mainstay of his life did not escape scrutiny.

Ferguson looked at David that summer as he headed to Japan for the World Cup of 2002 and seemed unhappy. David spoke about Ferguson's unhappiness with his England situation in this way: 'I had the feeling he wasn't too happy, generally about the extra responsibility – and the extra attention – that came with me captaining England.'

Despite signing his new contract, within 12 months David Beckham would be gone. His last season at Old Trafford started badly and got steadily worse. Ferguson would welcome him back from the World Cup by stressing how important a 100 per cent effort from him would be for a successful campaign. Especially *this* season; it provided the United manager with one more promised land finish if all went well, for the European Cup Final of 2003 would be played out at Old Trafford. How Ferguson dreamed of taking the unrelenting applause that winning the trophy in front of his own supporters would bring. It was the ultimate dream, the ultimate way to eclipse Sir Matt Busby's one European Cup win and his own singular success.

The problem was, it was never really on the cards, and Ferguson must take a major portion of the blame for that. In the end, AC Milan would claim the trophy in Manchester after beating their Italian rivals Juventus 3-2 on penalties after the match had ended 0-0.

Following an injury early in the season, David was unable to regain his place in the United starting line-up, with Ferguson instead preferring to play Ole Gunnar Solskjær on the right side of midfield.

David's relationship with his manager deteriorated further on 15 February 2003 when, in the changing room following a defeat to Arsenal, Ferguson kicked the boot that struck David over the eye, causing a cut that required stitches. Bookies quickly offered odds on which of the men would be the first to leave the club. In reality, it was never in doubt; United were never going to sack Ferguson at the time. He would survive and David would be forced out to join Real Madrid on 1 July 2003.

David's final act of defiance to Ferguson would be to refuse to move to Barcelona. The United manager believed it would be less of a blow as Barça were not then rated as serious a rival as Madrid. How times change – and quickly – in the magical world of football.

In the event, David's exit would be catastrophic for Ferguson, David and Manchester United. Ferguson would lose the man who supplied the ammunition for Ruud van Nistelrooy's goals, with the result that United would struggle desperately for two seasons. David would not be a major success in the latter years of his career, and Madrid would supplant United as the biggest club in the world in commercial terms.

On the day his transfer was completed, Real shirts bearing his name sold out within hours. David would take the number 23 shirt (he was a big fan of the basketball legend Michael Jordan who had worn the same number) at the Santiago Bernabeu as club skipper Raúl González had the right to wear number 7 written into his contract.

The Beckham era was over at United and it would not be long before the pundits even started to question his right to be an automatic choice for England. His form would be indifferent at Real and he would find it hard to step up a gear for England. He seemed lethargic at Euro 2004 and was not the same player by the time of World Cup 2006.

Yet, as with United, he had given England good service and his playing days with the national team should be remembered fondly, rather than with a cynical sneer.

It had always been his dream to play for England as a young trainee coming through the United ranks; to play and captain

187

the national side was a dream come true and, at the peak of his game, in 2001 he carried the English team to the following year's World Cup. He had made his first start in England colours on 1 September 1996, in the 3-0 World Cup qualifying match win in Moldova.

New boss Glenn Hoddle – who had replaced Terry Venables after Euro '96 – gave him that first cap and chose him for all of England's qualifiers for the 1998 World Cup. But then, when the action started in France, Hoddle appeared to get cold feet about his rising right-sided star, accusing him of 'not being focused'. He left him out of England's first two matches, but picked him for their third match against Colombia. David rewarded him by scoring from a long-range free kick in a 2-0 victory. Later, David would reveal that he believed Hoddle had dropped him because he had spent a day off sunbathing with Victoria rather than joining up with the rest of the squad's communal activities.

In his controversial World Cup diary, Hoddle wrote, 'I wanted him to make clear he understood the decision, say he was disappointed but that he was ready and willing when called upon.' Hoddle would also humiliate him in front of the other players during training in France – asking him to perform a particular trick and then saying he wasn't talented enough to do it.

In the second round, of course, David would be sent off against Argentina for violent conduct after appearing to kick out at Simeone. Hoddle would ignore him as he made the long walk to the dressing room and later would imply that England's defeat was David's fault, that with 11 against 11, England would have come through. He was probably right, but it was poor man-management. The match finished 2-2 with England eliminated in the penalty shootout.

Many supporters and journalists also blamed David and the

Daily Mirror printed a dartboard with his picture in the middle. Six years later, David would admit, 'For all that I've put that time behind me now, some of it still haunts me; my face as a dartboard, the effigy hanging from a lamp-post, the staged interviews with supporters. "Beckham's a disgrace to his country ... He should never play for England again."'

It would be two years before the abuse finally abated. England would be knocked out of Euro 2000 at the group stage and, during the 3-2 defeat by Portugal, some fans would taunt him, screaming, 'We hope your kid dies of cancer.' It was undoubtedly the turning point. David responded with a one-fingered gesture but the editors of the daily papers knew enough was enough. The vilification had to end and they asked their readers to stop abusing David and his family.

On 15 November 2000, David's rehabilitation was complete. Kevin Keegan had walked out of the England manager's job after his team had lost the final match at Wembley 1-0 to the Germans, and Peter Taylor was drafted in as caretaker boss. He brought in some young players and made David his captain. It was a job he would keep under new incumbent Sven-Göran Eriksson, a job he admitted was his single proudest achievement in football.

David and the Swede would initially combine brilliantly. They would lead England to a 5-1 World Cup qualifying win in Germany and a 2-2 draw with Greece at Old Trafford that secured England's place in the World Cup of 2002. England had needed to win or draw that match against the Greeks on 6 October 2001 to qualify outright for the World Cup, but were trailing 2-1 with the clock ticking and they were not performing well.

A difficult play-off against the Ukraine loomed when David secured his place as one of England's greatest performers in the eye of intense pressure. Having failed with five previous long-range free kicks, he secured qualification for Japan and South Korea with a fabulous goal in the 93rd minute – unleashing an unstoppable right-foot strike, just as news filtered through of Group 9 rivals Germany's failure to beat Finland.

Teddy Sheringham had shaped up to take the free kick after he was fouled ten yards outside the box, but David had shoved him aside, telling him it was his. That was the measure of his new-found confidence as an England player; how far he had come in the three years since his sending off against Argentina. As Martin Keown jumped on him after the wonder goal against the Greeks, it was easy to understand why he told David, 'That's amazing! That's amazing! That's why you're the man!'

There would be one other goal for England neither he, nor we, would ever forget. It came in the World Cup of 2002 in the group stage – and would bring 'closure' to David's greatest agony of 1998. The opponents were, once again, the Argentinians, but this time David stayed on the field and put them out of the competition before the knockout stages. He sent them home in disgrace – just as they had done to England, and David – four years previously.

It was the sweetest of karmas, or, as David himself put it, 'Everything else I've done in my life, everything that's ever happened to me, it's all been heading towards this.' His revenge came with a penalty goal in the 44th minute to give England a 1-0 win in the Group F match.

His nemesis Simeone had made as if to shake his hand as David stepped forward to take the spot kick, but he was having none of it, striking the ball emphatically past goalkeeper Pablo Cavallero. To add a little extra irony, both David and Simeone would begin the second half as captains of their countries after Juan Sebastian Veron had been substituted at the interval.

Afterwards, David said it was 'just unbelievable' adding, 'The

nerves, the pressure and four years of memories just fell away
... I couldn't have wished the burden away. I had to live
through it. What had happened in 1998 had done a lot to
make me the person I'd become, captaining my country at
another World Cup in 2002. But with one kick it was all off my
shoulders for good.

'It was a fantastic feeling – probably the sweetest moment of
my whole career. It is a victory for the whole nation. When you
play one of the best teams in the world, to score the goal that
wins the game is very special.

'It puts the ghosts of France '98 to rest once and for all. I have
always said I have never been nervous, but I was definitely
nervous getting ready to take that. I just ran up and hit it as
hard as I can and hoped for the best.'

He also admitted he had known Simeone was trying to wind
him up yet again by attempting to shake his hand prior to the
spot kick, but that he had been wise to him. David added,
'There were a few antics going on before I took it. The
goalkeeper was telling me where I was going to put the ball and
Simeone tried to shake my hand. I didn't shake his hand then,
but made sure I did at the end.'

Of course, there were less joyous moments to come as the
years rolled by, including the quarter-final loss to Brazil in the
same competition and an ultimately disappointing Euro 2004
and World Cup 2006. But weighing it all up, David Beckham's
international career was better than most. I asked Nick
Chapman of *Sun Sport* if that was a fair assessment. He said it
undoubtedly was and told me of his own fond memories of
David Beckham, the man who would have died for England,
beginning with the night he earned the captain's armband for
the first time.

Chapman told me, 'My wife thought I was mad, verging on

the certifiable. My friends agreed. And I was beginning to have serious doubts myself. But in November 2000, I decided to ignore the abuse and travel across to Turin for a meaningless friendly international between Italy and managerless, clueless, rudderless England.

'Two games earlier, I had been at the game that was to see the closure of the famous old Wembley Stadium – an abject 1-0 World Cup qualifying defeat to Germany that saw the end of Kevin Keegan's managerial career. I then travelled to Helsinki to watch England under caretaker-boss Howard Wilkinson bore the world to tears with a 0-0 draw against Finland.

'So why, one month later, would I choose a midweek trip to northern Italy to watch a friendly? The answer is two-fold – Peter Taylor … and David Beckham. And it was a trip I will never forget. Forget the fact I managed to beat the pre-match alcohol ban and enjoy a couple of bottles of decent Italian wine with my pasta. Forget the fact Gennaro Gattuso chose this game to announce his own arrival on the international scene with a barely deserved winner for the Italians. Forget also that this was David Beckham's 37th appearance for his country. Because Italy 1-England 0 on 15 November 2000 at the Stadio delle Alpi in Turin was the day Peter Taylor upset the establishment by giving promising young England players their chance – and the day a fresh-faced, energetic David Beckham was first handed the captain's armband. And for that, the whole nation should thank Peter Taylor.

'It signalled the start of a magnificent era for English inter-national football, an era in which England were finally talked of again in the same breath as world greats like Brazil and Argentina. It was an era in which England, probably for the first time since Bobby Moore and Bobby Charlton, possessed one of the world's truly great international talents.

'David Beckham will be a topic of much heated debate among England fans for as long as we are alive. Was he that good a player? Was he the right choice as captain? Did he deserve the accolades and adulation that came his way?

'The answer is simple – yes, yes and yes. David Beckham took the reins of a side that was sinking fast, both in terms of on-pitch achievement and off-pitch image. We were in danger of becoming a European also-ran. I will always believe it was Beckham and not the arrival of Sven-Göran Eriksson that dramatically turned it all around.

'Beckham exuded confidence, he clearly had the support and real affection of his international team-mates and – most important of all to those risking bankruptcy to follow a hapless team on its miserable travels around the globe – he played, talked and acted like he was one of us.

'David Beckham was a supporter lucky enough to wear a shirt. No one on the terraces pumped out his chest with pride more than Beckham whenever the national anthem was sung. No one on the terraces celebrated an England goal more emotionally and no one on the terraces hurt more after a defeat. We had seen wholehearted captains in the recent past, of course – Alan Shearer, Martin Keown, Sol Campbell, Tony Adams, Paul Ince – they all wore the shirt with pride and all treated the armband with respect. But Beckham was just plain different. He played with boyish enthusiasm, he spoke to the media with an honest, naïve approach and always seemed to understand how privileged he was to hold such an honourable position.

'England won seven of their next eight internationals with Beckham as captain – the only exception a meaningless pre-season friendly against the Dutch at White Hart Lane. But it was David's tenth game as skipper that will go down in history as his greatest personal achievement. Those of us who were there, and the millions watching on television, know full well the scoreline should have read: David Beckham 2-Greece 2.

'Never before have I witnessed a competitive international match so dominated by one player. How fitting that David should score the last-minute free kick equaliser at Old Trafford that earned England an undeserved draw – and a place at the 2002 World Cup Finals in Japan and South Korea.

'Sadly, Japan saw the start of the problems that were to blight Beckham's England future and unfairly take the gloss off an incredible career. Shortly before the tournament, on 10 April 2002, Beckham introduced English football to the word "metatarsal". None of us had heard of this bone until Aldo Duscher stood on Beckham's foot during a Champions League match between Manchester United and Deportivo La Coruña, breaking a metatarsal. We were to hear of little else for years.

'Despite clearly lacking fitness – something that was to be Beckham's undoing in the unbelievable heat and humidity of Japan – Eriksson decided he couldn't travel to the World Cup Finals without his inspirational skipper. An understandable, if ultimately unsuccessful gamble.

'Those of us lucky enough to have been in Japan will readily testify to the difficulties of playing in such extraordinary conditions. Maybe we should be grateful England played bitter rivals Argentina inside the controlled environment of the Sapporo Dome. It was the game that finally saw us beat the South Americans again in a competitive fixture.

'It was also the game that saw David gain personal revenge for one of the most miserable chapters of his own career. Four years earlier, at France '98, David was infamously sent off against Argentina for a tame if ill-advised flick of the boot at

Diego Simeone – a game England eventually lost on penalties to go out. That incident made David public enemy number one in England.

'Four years on and his 44th-minute penalty winner against the Argentines was the perfect reply for the now undisputed hero of English football. Unfortunately, the only direction an undisputed hero can go is down. England's campaign quickly wilted in the Japanese heat. The awful 0-0 draw with Nigeria in Osaka remains one of the worst England performances I have seen.

'Euro 2004 in Portugal was another tale of what might have been – or more accurately "what should have been" in the eyes of the huge English support. More than 60,000 of us travelled to Portugal for the tournament and all of us were left with a bitter taste in the mouth at the nature of our elimination – another penalty defeat, to Portugal, in a game most of us feel we should have won.

'It was symbolic of David's gradual decline that his was one of the missed penalties – his second costly spot-kick miss of the tournament. By now, Beckham's domestic career was also in upheaval, where a seemingly magnificent move to Real Madrid was quickly faltering with the loss of his first-team place amid numerous managerial changes.

'And so we moved on to Germany 2006. The big debate was not whether Beckham deserved to retain the captaincy but whether he deserved to be in the squad at all. As ever, Eriksson stayed loyal to his captain. By now, many were questioning whether it was Beckham rather than Eriksson who was running the show.

'Germany 2006 was a disaster, both for Beckham and for England. The man who, four years earlier, had dragged England into the Japan finals was a shadow of his former self. No more surging runs, no more beaming smiles, no more inspiration.

But Beckham was still the man behind the rebirth of English football when all had seemed lost. Thanks, Becks.'

Elegantly, eloquently put by one of England's biggest, and most loyal, fans.

There would be a curtain call for Becks under the new Fabio Capello regime – with the Italian calling him up for his 100th cap against the French in Paris on 26 March, 2008. Beckham would put in the effort but, despite the golden boots and the well-earned acclaim both on and off the terraces, it was clear that his best days were now behind him. England lost 1-0, but Beckham at least had a barrowful of fond memories – and the knowledge he had joined the all-too-small elite club of England centurions – on the long flight back to LA.

Having examined David's club and international careers, now it's time for the final ride on the Beckham journey – to Spain, to his home life, his scandals, his bust-ups and his future. Fasten your seatbelts; whatever your final view on Beckham, travelling with the world's most famous sportsman of his generation is anything but dull.

12

Posh, Dosh and Losing It

'We're pregnant'
VICTORIA BECKHAM TO DAVID THE NIGHT BEFORE
THE ARGENTINA MATCH, 1998

'I love the States. I love the patriotism, the way of life.'
DAVID BECKHAM, 2004

'My wife picked me out of a football sticker book. And I chose her off the telly.'
DAVID BECKHAM, 2004

'I had absolutely no intention of ever leaving United.'
DAVID BECKHAM, 2004

'He's just like Muhammad Ali – the greatest and the prettiest.'
PHOTOGRAPHER DAVID LACHAPELLE, 2006

In his entertaining autobiography, *My Side*, David Beckham lists his achievements at the back of the book. Before noting down the European Cup, Premiership and FA Cup triumphs, he makes a list of his most 'notable moments'. From a cynical point of view, you could imply, therefore, that being the 'first solo male on front cover of *Marie Claire*' in June 2002 maybe means more subconsciously to David than his club achievements, otherwise they would surely have been added at the back of the data section, rather than the front.

For information purposes, and to get another take on the man's psyche, I should tell you that his other 'notable moments' include: first sportsman on front cover of *The Face* (July 2001);

meeting Tony Blair (May 2002); meeting Nelson Mandela (May 2003); and being awarded the OBE for his efforts both on and off the pitch (November 2003).

Of course, the very fact that such a section exists – and that David took time out to create it – along with the wording on the OBE award (for efforts both on *and off* the pitch) suggests that the boy places great importance, and no doubt takes great personal pleasure, in the way he became a *celebrity* footballer.

And he does. David Beckham was the world's first footballer truly to embrace celebrity; he loved the red carpet treatment and the parties. OK, George Best was the first celebrity footballer, but that was forced upon him; he did not seek it, neither did he enjoy the press being at his gate all hours. It helped to force him to retreat inside his shell years before he may have chosen to go there.

David, however, loved being a media star – at least, while the going was good. He positively bathed in the headlines about himself and craved the limelight like a crack addict would need his drug fix.

Looking at his career from a detached standpoint, you could also argue that the beginning of the end actually arrived that seemingly magical summer of 1999, when he married his Spice Girl, Victoria. Just two months after United's jaw-dropping victory over Bayern Munich in Barcelona, he was posing for *OK!* magazine on a mocked-up velvet throne in a crazy, excessively hedonistic wedding, with a reported £2 million fee from the magazine in his back pocket. It was a wedding his mentor Sir Alex Ferguson would not attend, his public excuse being that he had another family occasion to attend on the same day.

It was hardly Ferguson's scene, hardly what he expected from the men he entrusted and whom he saw as standard-bearers of his own character – mirrors of himself. Just as Busby had been unable to relate to the ballyhoo surrounding Best, so Ferguson could not, did not want to, have anything to do with the celebrity circus that was rapidly surrounding his star player.

Ferguson would privately contend that his relationship with Beckham changed the day he met Victoria. There is some truth in the argument that, after years of control by Ferguson, he merely, and quite rightly, finally gained the confidence to mouth what he had long been thinking.

My view is that David would still have one day fallen out with Ferguson given both men's large egos and stubbornness – that a parting of the ways was inevitable. I believe that the advent of Victoria increased David's confidence and brought that ultimate bust-up to the fore earlier than would have happened if David had been alone.

David certainly had a feminine side that contrasts markedly with Ferguson. The Scot was carved out of the granite of Govan, a tough Glasgwegian enclave where men were men and brought home a working wage while women made your tea and did your ironing.

David was not from that ideological background. True, his father Ted was a dominant, powerful force in his life, but he also had a strong mother figure in Sandra, and two strong-willed sisters, Lynne and Joanne. That feminine side would come to the fore in the way he loved to dress up and expend an enormous amount of energy on his appearance even before he met Victoria; his hair and grooming had to be just right.

Going back to his school years, there's another pointer to David the not-so-stereotypical footballer. Yes, he loved helping Sandra out at mealtimes and, at secondary school, he chose Home Economics as one of his O-level options – 'cooking, basically', as he is not ashamed to admit. By the age of 13, he was preparing the family's meals while Sandra was spending the day at the hair salon and, if she was cutting hair at home, would be a good boy and make tea and biscuits for the clients. It is hardly your John Terry-style of footballer, all clenched fists and screaming at your team-mates to match your effort.

Dig back a bit further, and you find Beckham the choir boy; he loved singing and sang a solo in the primary school choir. Then there is the constant bursting into tears at a moment's notice – when he signed as an amateur for United; when he won the European Cup; and when he was sitting on the bench in Germany in the World Cup of 2006, after getting injured against the Portuguese. He knew then that the game was up for Beckham the leader of men at international level, and his emotions were all too clear for everyone to see.

There is also the clear attraction to the good life, even before he met Posh. For example, at the age of 13, when Spurs offered him a six-year deal, far from thinking of the exciting footballing career that lay ahead, Beckham's rather unusual thought process took him to this point: 'A thought flashed through my mind ... by the time I'm 18, I could be driving a Porsche.' It is hardly the thought that would have entered Georgie Best's thoughts as he climbed aboard the Belfast ferry for Manchester at the tender age of 15.

No, here was a boy who would be at ease with fame and embarking on the road that would lead to it. In November 1996 he whiled away a dull night watching TV with best friend and team-mate Gary Neville in a Tbilisi hotel room, on the eve of England's match against Georgia in a World Cup qualifier.

A video of the Spice Girls unfolded on the screen and Beckham's fate was ordained. He was infatuated by 'the posh one ... the one with the bob. The one with the legs.' He told a typically stoical Neville that he had to meet her, that he wanted her.

Fair play to him – she was a looker, easily the best of the

diverse bunch that made up the rest of the group. He was also impressed by the fact that the Spice Girls were 'the biggest thing on the planet'. Without knowing it at the time, that dull, rainy night in Georgia would prove a key moment in his life; it would in one fell swoop bring him a beautiful girl and the celebrity lifestyle to go with it. This was Brand Beckham in its embryonic form.

It would emerge that she, too, was a Londoner, that she had, in fact, been born and bred just down the road from Leytonstone. She was a Goff's Oak girl and she, too, had long nurtured a plan to become a star. She had attended dance and acting schools as a youngster and was a woman who had a tough, determined edge behind that pretty face and long legs. She would become David's mentor as he entered the world of celebrity, gently transforming him from an outwardly macho footballer into one of the world's most eligible, stylish and famous men. She would, in short, help him to become an icon. The final irony, of course, would be that he would ultimately become a bigger, more saleable name – and brand – than Victoria herself. Eventually, she would need him more than he needed her.

It hadn't looked that way when they first dated – this girl was certainly different to the ones he had previously been out with, including the down-to-earth Mancunian Deana, with whom he had spent three years. Posh was a different kettle of fish – she was beautiful but a star, she was high maintenance and he needed to give her his full attention. She was, inevitably, as needy as him for the limelight, for the comforting knowledge that she was worthy and worthwhile, that she was a valid human being.

Clearly, when he started dating her, his life would change dramatically. The very distances involved in what was initially a long-distance romance – as they snatched love in between her touring with the Spice Girls and him playing for United – cannot have enhanced the lifestyle of a pro footballer. He was stuck in his car on endless round-trips to spend time with her rather than unwinding and relaxing inbetween games. He would later claim that he felt the driving was beneficial as it gave him peace and a chance to think.

There was also the initial problem that she was already in a relationship with a boyfriend, Stuart. None of it could have been conducive to a clear head while he was trying to establish himself as a United name. But there was no stopping him, no time for reflection, because, as he admitted, 'I knew straight away I was crazy for Victoria.'

In fairness, they were ideally matched given their respective upbringings, they were both from the Essex/East London area and they both shared a burning ambition to be famous and loved. He proposed on 24 January1998, after they had been together for six months. Then, the night before the World Cup match against Argentina in 1998, she rang him on his mobile, uttering the immortal words, 'We're pregnant.' Their first son Brooklyn would be born on 4 March 1999.

Their love for each other was touching, if maybe a little cloying. My psychoanalyst friend puts it like this: 'You could argue that they were – indeed, that they are – co-dependent. That they need each other to be there all the time if they are to thrive and survive. That perhaps they depend upon each other too much to boost each other's esteem. It is an addiction within itself.'

It's a convincing point of view, undoubtedly. Whatever the nature of their love match, it was complete after that amazing Treble of 1999 when, as David himself put it, the 'prince' married his 'princess' on 4 July 1999. Independence day for some, but certainly not for Ferguson.

The wedding was, inevitably, a fairly crass, bling-enhanced media circus at a castle in Ireland. The couple had already splashed out a fortune on what would become their main home in Sawbridgeworth, Hertfordshire – Beckingham Palace, to some – but they wanted a bash that no one would ever forget and so travelled to Luttrellstown for a ceremony conducted by the Bishop of Cork. It was all rather OTT in an über-Hollywood/Las Vegas sort of way. As they became man and wife, a single dove was released as a symbol of their love, which some observers found a little too ostentatious to be taken seriously. The BBC reported it in this way: 'All 236 guests at the reception had to wear a security tag – even the couple's baby son Brooklyn. Just 29 close family and friends, including fellow Spice Girls Mel G, Mel C and Emma, witnessed the ceremony, which was conducted by Bishop of Cork, Paul Colton.

'Posh Spice – one of the architects of the "girl power" philosophy – stuck to her principles and did not pledge to "obey" the Manchester United player. The new Mr and Mrs Beckham both shed tears after exchanging vows.'

Indeed they did ... while some commentators were shedding tears of laughter at the excesses, including the identical thrones and the specially commissioned David and Victoria coat-of-arms.

The BBC report continued, 'The couple, famed for their expensive tastes, had their party outfits designed by Antonio Berardi. No expense was spared for the reception, reported to have cost £500,000, and a total of 437 staff were required for the whole day.

'Wedding guests were greeted with a glass of rose champagne from Laurent Perrier. An 18-piece orchestra was playing specially rehearsed numbers, including a Spice Girls medley. At 20.00 BST, the guests sat down in one of the marquees erected in the grounds for a meal, created by chef Jason Reynolds, which included David Beckham's favourite dessert, sticky toffee pudding.'

The payoff, when it came, was a stunner. 'The couple will not be getting any presents. They have asked for shopping vouchers instead.' It sort of summed up the thinking of the newly crowned Prince and Princess of celebrity culture. Here they were, two of the richest people in the UK and they were asking for shopping vouchers as gifts! It was remarkable; terrifically poor taste but symptomatic of their characters and nature. Any deeper-thinking individuals would have surely allowed their guests to bring along something they deemed suitable rather than trying to influence their choice of gifts – or, if they had insisted on shopping vouchers, then at least have them donated to people who truly needed a few bits and pieces from M&S or C&A. The wealthy Beckhams were hardly in that category. It was a stunning own-goal that summed up the tackiness of the wedding.

Sir Alex Ferguson kept well away. He did not enjoy having a celebrity footballer on his books; his mission had always been motivated by the team being the be all and end all. Now here was one of his men dominating the front pages of the tabloids as well as the back.

Problems started to appear when Ferguson learned David had planned an extended honeymoon. I am told by an insider that Beckham had set up an extra two days away in the south of France via United chairman Martin Edwards and that, when Ferguson learned of the arrangement, he went ballistic.

The end result was that he bollocked David down the phone and ordered him back to pre-season training ... with the reserves. Ferguson had taught him a lesson but, with hindsight, he would surely regret the decision. Was this the right way for

Ferguson to deal with the man who had, after all, helped him to his own greatest triumph in Barcelona just a couple of months earlier? I think not.

Then there was the question of David's involvement with England. He clearly put a great deal into representing his country and enjoyed it. That would, of course, amplify over the years as David became captain of the national team. Would this detract from his club form?

The allegiances of Ferguson, a proud Scot, were hardly likely to include a soft spot for the England team and it would be natural for him to expect Beckham to put club before country. My feeling was that the media icon and national treasure was committed to both causes and I cannot see that he ever undervalued United.

Others, however, would question his priorities. Ian McGarry, writing in the *Daily Mail* in November 2001, said, 'When he speaks of the hunger to succeed, there is a heavy hint that it is the prospect of lifting the World Cup next summer in an England jersey which really fires his imagination, rather than yet more glory for Manchester United.

'At United, especially, the men who have won everything may simply have already acquired a taste for a different kind of achievement. Never mind Europe ... does Beckham dream more of thumping home a World Cup Final winner – perhaps against Argentina?'

David would add to the debate when he said that the wonder goal against Greece was 'in his mind every minute of the day'.

By 2001, Ferguson was becoming increasingly fuelled by his own particular holy grail – to win the European Cup for a second time. McGarry put it this way: 'The Old Trafford manager is guilty of a similar passion in his obsession with the Champions League and there is little doubt that he would trade three domestic trophies (and maybe even his own grandmother) to win the European Cup....' I am sure that David would also have been delighted with a second European Cup medal – as well as a World Cup winner's one.

The spats between manager and player would intensify from 2001 to 2003, to the point where either one man had to back down, or one had to leave. Neither took a step back from the situation to think, 'Well, maybe I could make a peace offering.' The spats did neither of their reputations any good.

There had been an earlier high-profile incident in February 2000, when Ferguson dropped David publicly over a babysitting dispute. His son Brooklyn had been poorly and he left a message on United assistant manager Steve McClaren's phone, explaining the situation, and stayed at his London home for an extra day to care for the boy.

The way the bust-up developed on this one between David and Ferguson was typical of most of their fall-outs. Ferguson would think David was trying to pull a fast one by going behind his back, while Beckham did not, at the time at least, see that his manager could take it the wrong way.

McClaren did not get the message; at least, he did not reply to it and, by the time David returned to United's Carrington training HQ one day late on Friday, 18 February, Ferguson was fuming. He bollocked him in front of the first-team squad, told him to go and train with the reserves and then the two had another set-to in Ferguson's office. David explained what had happened with his son, but Ferguson would have none of it. I am told he accused David of going off the rails – of putting his celebrity lifestyle before Manchester United.

What really tipped Ferguson over the edge was a picture splashed across the tabloids of Victoria attending a charity bash the very night David was caring for Brooklyn. David claimed that by that time, the boy was recovering a little, but Ferguson simply sneered at him with the killer words, 'You were babysitting while your wife was out gallivanting.' The last word particularly hit a chord with David, the clear dislike and disrespect his manager harboured for his wife.

Ferguson told him he had his priorities wrong after David had explained he believed his first priority was to his family. Ferguson is alleged to have said, 'Your responsibilities are here at the club, not at home with your son.' Years on, and with a little more wisdom and compassion, I am sure, at least I would hope, that Ferguson would not continue that line of argument. I have no doubt at all that if his wife Cathy were taken ill he would be away from Old Trafford like a shot. And he knows it.

For his part, David would surely now handle the situation differently. He would make sure he contacted his manager and try to sort it out in a more mature manner.

As far as the public was concerned, loyalties were split. Some fans, such as Andy Labrow, of Manchester, believed Ferguson had called it right, 'It is not for us to judge where Mr Beckham puts his priorities. However, considering the amount of money he is paid, he must accept any consequences for anything less than 100 per cent commitment.' As did Seb Johnson, of London, 'Alex Ferguson was right to drop Beckham, as it would not be good for team spirit if he picked a player who missed training, whatever the reason.'

Others believed David had been right to look after his son and that Ferguson was the bad guy, including Matt Simpson, from Manchester, 'Family is a very important part of life. Clearly, his son is very important to him. If that means Beckham (or anyone else) has to miss training (or a morning off work), then so be it. You only get one chance of family life, so enjoy it you must, otherwise you will live to regret it. I'm surprised Ferguson

207

didn't show some compassion for extenuating circumstances, but it doesn't surprise me he didn't.'

Niki Sims of London also had sympathy for Beckham, 'Surely Beckham has his priorities set right and, if by looking after his sick baby son he is left out of the team, then someone should tell Ferguson to check his priorities. Beckham is in the fortunate position to be able to give up working if he so chooses, but his priority of family first should not even come into question.'

Ferguson would also ignore the TV pundits who called him 'prehistoric' over his stance. He also had to deal with mischievous fans willing to put the boot in on Beckham and co, who rang in to get the boss fuming by telling him they had seen David at Manchester airport boarding a flight to Barcelona, or to London and creating rumours that he would leave for a top European side if the money was right.

It was nonsense on a spectacular scale. Beckham was United through and through and, by 2002, he hardly needed to engineer a move to bring in more readies. In May of that year, he had signed his new three-year contract, following months of negotiations with the club, mostly concerning extra payments for his image rights. The readies from the new deal – £90,000 a week – plus his contracts with advertisers outside the game made him the highest-paid player in the world at the time, earning £11 million a year.

The new deal was made up of £70,000 a week in basic pay and £20,000 in 'image rights' – and represented a 300 per cent salary increase. Beckham's comments at the time hardly seem those of a man intent on getting out of Manchester: 'The club has bent over backwards to be fair in their dealings with me and I always knew that Manchester United were the only club I ever wanted to play for.

'Sir Alex Ferguson had made it very clear that he wanted me

to be an important part of the club's future and his word was good enough for me. The bond between myself and the club and the fans is stronger than ever before. All the players at Manchester United feel that special bond and there is not a day passes when I do not feel very lucky and privileged to be part of such a fantastic club.'

He was so loyal to the club that he signed a deal that would, if it went the distance, have committed him until the age of 30. But could he survive a manager he alleged in his autobiography was 'short-tempered and miserable ... ' and a manager who did not like his lifestyle, his wife or his obsession with England? As David also concedes, 'Maybe my manager at Manchester United would have preferred me to have found a nice, quiet girl who'd stay indoors, clean the house, change the nappies and have my dinner ready in the evening.'

It was a tragedy for Manchester United FC that its two main men were heading for a parting because they could not patch up their differences, or at least have given the other the benefit of the doubt. Ferguson, as the manager, is most culpable for the departure of David Beckham in this sense, although David, clearly, could have chosen to deal differently with a man from a different era, a man with a different set of morals and a different hinterland. Ferguson was an old campaigner who, if pampered and pandered to, would possibly have given David a little more ground and freedom. He did, after all, with Eric Cantona. But while Cantona laughed with him, perhaps Ferguson felt Beckham was laughing *at* him by adhering to such an outrageously lavish lifestyle. David's father Ted summed it all up by saying, 'It's ridiculous that all this happens just because Fergie doesn't like him any more.'

The end of the road for the duo effectively came after the 2-0 FA Cup fifth-round home loss to Arsenal in February 2003 –

although it would be just a little longer before David exited for Madrid. Ferguson blamed David for one of the goals, claiming he had not back-tracked enough. I am told that in the dressing room he pointed a finger at David and told him he was 'fuckin'' useless'. Ferguson then kicked out in frustration and he connected with a boot, which was launched into the air and hit David above the left eye. I am also reliably informed that it was, indeed, an accident. I can accept that; even in his playing days, Ferguson would have struggled to hit a target so accurately. The end result was that David stormed angrily away from Old Trafford and the two men had reached an impasse that would prove impossible to overcome.

To his credit, David, at last, tried to find common ground and a way to let bygones be bygones, dismissing the incident as something or nothing in public, and attempting to absolve Ferguson of blame. David said, 'I want to assure all Manchester United fans that there is complete harmony and focus as we prepare for the Juventus game [the following Wednesday in the Champions League at Old Trafford]. The dressing room incident was just one of those things – it's all in the past now.'

But, even until the bitter end, Ferguson would not give an inch. He denied David had needed stitches for the wound, although they were apparent in the pictures that appeared in the day's newspapers, and laughed off the injury as 'a graze', also refusing to apologise for his angry outburst. Ferguson did say, 'Contrary to reports, David Beckham did not have two stitches – it was a graze which was dealt with by the doctor. It was a freakish incident. If I tried it a hundred or a million times it couldn't happen again. If I could, I would have carried on playing! There is no problem and we move on. That is all there is to say.'

His words were ungracious, unrepentant and sat uneasily with

United's vast army of supporters. This was Ferguson at his worst; other key men – Jaap Stam, Ruud van Nistelrooy and even the mighty Roy Keane would suffer undignified exits at his hands.

It was hardly in the club's interests and the loss of these warriors and gifted men would certainly destabilise the club; they would lose ground on their rivals after being stripped of key assets. Ferguson would suffer the consequences after David's exit in the summer of 2003 when United entered a period of relative decline both at home and in Europe.

In the European Champions League quarter-final second leg against Real Madrid on 23 April 2003, David's real worth to United was never more needed. The days were drawing in on David's Old Trafford career, and it was not difficult to see why. Instead of playing him against Real, Ferguson, astonishingly, chose a half-fit Juan Veron in his place. United had lost the first leg 3-1 a fortnight earlier, and needed to be firing on all cylinders if they were to claw back the deficit. So, just how did Ferguson expect it to work out when he threw in Veron, who had been out injured for the previous seven weeks?

It seemed to be another chapter in the manager's doomed campaign to prove everyone, particularly the press, wrong about the Argentine on whom he had splashed out £28.1 million. A star for his country, he never managed to transfer his undoubted talent and skills on to the English stage after leaving Lazio in Italy. Sure, he was bought specifically to bring creativeness to United in Europe, but he was not match fit. It was folly to leave Beckham out for him.

The facts portray the reality of it all very clearly. United were losing 3-2 on the night after a Ronaldo hat-trick for Real. David did not come on as a substitute until 63 minutes – as a direct replacement for the out-of-sorts Veron. Within 21 minutes, David had scored twice, and United ran out 4-3 winners but lost

6-5 on aggregate. It made you think what could have been but for the manager's denying David a place against the club for whom Ferguson feared he wanted to sign, and the manager's determination to prove that Veron was one of his masterstrokes. He clearly was not; at that moment in time, David Beckham clearly was. Just look again at video footage of his first goal on the night, that fantastic trademark free kick from 20 yards out, if you need proof.

After the defeat, Ferguson explained he had not kept David out for Veron, but for Solskjær. Ferguson said, 'I saw it as quite a straightforward decision. Solskjær's form has been fantastic on the right-hand side. I don't regard Ole Gunnar Solskjær as a substitute any more – he deserved his place. He had three or four great attempts on goal and he provided a real threat for us, which is what he has been doing. When players hit that kind of form you can't just leave Solskjær out because he has been a substitute in the past.'

From 2003–06, he would make a series of baffling decisions with his tactics and team and only really reverted to the genius he once had been at the start of the 2006 season when he seemed finally to have found a new inner peace and resolve. During the puzzling two-and-a-half years before that, United were like a rocky ship foundering in rough seas.

On the night, Real Madrid coach Vicente del Bosque refused to get involved in Ferguson's decision to leave out David, even though it increased speculation that the golden boy was soon to join the Spanish giants. Diplomatically, he said, 'That's not something for me to comment on. It is up to Sir Alex Ferguson. He obviously thought there were other players better placed on the night to do better.'

David Beckham's last match for United would be in the 2-1 win at Everton on 11 May 2003. The Red Devils had clinched the title the week before with a 4-1 win over Charlton at Old Trafford. David, inevitably, had scored against the Addicks and then went on to sign off his United career at Goodison with another of his clinical free kicks from 20-odd yards after David Unsworth had brought down Solskjær just before the interval.

An ironic aside to the proceedings was that United sent on Laurent Blanc at half time for the final performance of his career – and his first moment of note was to enter the referee's notebook for fouling a young upstart in the Everton ranks by the name of Wayne Rooney. As one icon in David Beckham was about to exit Old Trafford, another in the making was coming through the Goodison ranks. They passed like ships in the night, little knowing they could have been sailing the same course if it had not all gone pear-shaped for David.

David signed an agreement to join Madrid on 18 June 2003, much against the wishes of Ferguson. United had attempted to offload him to Barcelona, but David was having none of it, making it clear Madrid was the only destination he would consider. The fee, considering he was only 28 and easily the most marketable footballer in the world, was a bargain £24.5 million – with just a measly £17 million up front. The length of his contract would be four years.

Peter Kenyon, now Chelsea boss but then chief executive of Manchester United, was the man who brokered the move. He said, 'While we are sad to see David go after so many great years at Old Trafford, we believe this is a good deal for the club, and we now look forward to building on the success of last season's Championship title. We wish David all the best in his new career in Spain and thank him for his fantastic contribution to the team's achievements in the last decade.'

A good deal for the club? In actual fact, it was a disastrous one. United – and Ruud van Nistelrooy in particular – would suffer on the field as his replacement Cristiano Ronaldo, inevitably, took time to bed in. And the Red Devils would also lose out drastically off the field as Madrid cashed in on the Beckham name. Kenyon's business acumen would again be questioned when he lost the opportunity to bring Ronaldinho to United after failing to agree on the transfer fee.

A summer holiday kept David from his new place of work until 2 July, when he was finally unveiled as the latest of the Real *galacticos* in a big-time ceremony at the club's basketball stadium. In attendance were 500 journalists from 25 countries; Kenyon and Ferguson had clearly handed Madrid a massive cash cow and they were determined to make the best of it. Beckham was handed the number 23 shirt by Madrid legend Alfredo di Stefano, and declared himself ready for action, admitting he 'couldn't wait' to get down to business.

'I have always loved football,' he said. 'Of course, I love my family. I have a wonderful life, but football is everything to me, and joining Real Madrid is a dream come true. I would like to say thank you to everyone for coming and joining me in my arrival. *Gracias* ... *hola* Madrid!'

Real president Florentino Perez added, 'Despite all that's going on, we're not going to lose sight of the fact that we are unveiling this great player. He is a great player who is going to become part of the club's great history. He is a man of our times and a symbol of modern-day stardom and what is certain is Real have signed Beckham because he's a great footballer and a very dedicated professional. His team spirit is unsurpassed and he is one of the best English players of all time and if only because of that he is with us. We love Beckham because he makes us the best team on and off the pitch.'

Even at the time you got the feeling that everyone who was somebody at Madrid was trying desperately not to mention

David's marketability. It was as if the subject was a no-go area, that if they did get too far into it, it would kill the dream. But the truth of it, even from the start, appeared to be that Real Madrid did not see David Beckham as being as good a footballer as we in England did. They were definitely attracted to the man's promotional abilities – and the money he could make them; they were not so sure about him being a true *galactico* in terms of pure talent. Although, of course, they were at pains in public at least, to ensure that this should not be seen as being the case.

So, what to make of David's spell in the Spanish capital? Two simple words – a mistake ... apart from that late La Liga title surge when he was still playing a bit-part role in the last months of his Real career. He ended up having major fall-outs with his wife over alleged dalliances with other women and regressed as a footballer. Let's be clear about this – David tried hard to fit in with the team, did his best to learn a bit of the language and was let down by team-mates who seemed unwilling to work hard for success, whose arrogance was so great they imagined it would simply be served up to them on a plate. He was still the consummate pro, working hard at his game and putting in the hours on the training field. His skipper at Madrid, Raul, was full of admiration for David, saying after a few months, 'Physically he is strong, he has started very well and has gained the respect of team-mates and fans. Work and quality, he's got both those traits.'

Yet David admitted it had not been easy fitting into new surroundings after 15 years at Manchester United; indeed, he conceded life at times had been 'intolerable'. David said, 'I had moved to a new environment and people didn't know me, were not used to me and how I am. In Manchester, I could go to the big shopping centre and walk around with my family with very few problems. That kind of thing is just not possible in Madrid. I cannot go out of my front door without things going crazy.

'It takes so much energy out of me. You even have to plan how to take a trip to the supermarket without being photographed. It can be tough. Last season, I had my family with me more than people thought. My wife was with me most of the time, except when Brooklyn was at his school in England. Now we have finally got Brooklyn in a school in Spain. I didn't send him at the start because of something Zinedine Zidane told me. He said his children were in school over there and for a few months TV people were filming them in the playground.

'I have always maintained that I will never put my children in that kind of situation. If we go over there as a family and that kind of thing happens, then I would take a long look at it again. My family is number one and my football number two – and that is the way it will always be. I am very protective of my boys. Life has been difficult at times.'

That was something of an understatement, although it was surely not that surprising that some football groupies would target him when he was initially alone for long periods in Madrid. Here he was, the world's most famous sportsman with the looks of Brad Pitt and the style, designer clothes and readies to go with it. One hanger-on who cashed in was his former personal assistant Rebecca Loos. In April 2004, the Spanish girl would claim to have had sex with him on several occasions – although David would deny it – and the result was that she lined herself up a career in the world of showbiz.

Loos had infiltrated the closely-knit Beckham inner circle by virtue of being the only employee in the Madrid office of David's agents at the time, SFX, who spoke English and Spanish fluently. She would cash in by selling her story to the *News of the World* and claiming she became an 'alternative wife' to David at a time when Victoria was spending a lot of time back in England trying to kick-start her by now failing career as a singer.

Loos would claim she and David had a four-month affair and was reported to have earned £100,000 from the tabloid, plus subsequent fees for TV appearances. Being part of the Beckham clique was clearly a money-spinner – and not just for the main man. A week after the claims by Loos, another woman, Malaysian-born Australian model Sarah Marbeck, claimed that she had twice slept with David. He dismissed this allegation and that by Loos as 'ludicrous'. Maybe they were, but things were clearly not going to plan for our David in Madrid.

In his first season, Real finished fourth in the league and were knocked out of the Champions League having got through to the last eight. In the second, they did better in the league – finishing second – but worse in Europe, exiting at the last-16 stage, a situation that would be mirrored exactly in David's third season at the Santiago Bernabeu. The days of wine and roses he had experienced at United were gone and, by December 2006, he was no more than a bit-part player in a new drama under the direction of tough Italian taskmaster Fabio Cappello. The irony was that, under Capello, he should have thrived. Throughout his career, David reacted best when pushed to the limit, yet the Italian seemed unwilling to give him a proper chance after learning he had signed for LA Galaxy in January 2007. Sure, he recalled Beckham to the team for the title run-in in April and May 2007, but it had the air of an apologetic curtain call rather than the season-long flourish it should have been. It was a great pity.

By 2007, it was revealed that while David was struggling to get into the Real Madrid team, he was still the highest-earning footballer in British football. He had amassed a personal fortune of £87 million, with the next highest being Michael Owen on £32 million. Was that final consolation enough for David Beckham, the man who lived for his football? The end of an era was on the horizon as far as his football career was concerned. He still had the looks and the charm to work as a model or an actor if he wanted, but this was a man with football running through his veins. There was also talk that he might return to England with his hometown club Spurs or to Celtic in Scotland. Either move might have brought a final challenge, but he was also interested in heading for America – and Los Angeles Galaxy. The problem with such a move was that it would be public acceptance that he was no longer Beckham the footballer, but Beckham the celebrity.

No matter, Beckham and wife Victoria had made their decision: LA it was to be. Beckham, now 31, agreed a five-year deal with Galaxy in January 2007, worth a cool £128 million. He said, 'I am proud to have played for two of the biggest clubs in football and I look forward to the new challenge of growing the world's most popular game in a country that is as passionate about its sport as my own.'

Galaxy, funnily enough, are owned by sports and entertainment giants AEG, who are also partners in Beckham's soccer academy in Los Angeles. But, all the talk of opening up the game in America could not hide the fact that Beckham's own game was up.

If only a peace could have been brokered with Ferguson – enabling him to return for a curtain call at Old Trafford. On Tuesday 13 March 2007, when I went to see the Red Devils take on a European XI for UNICEF, I got a glimpse of the affection with which he is still held at United. Beckham had been penciled in to play, but unfortunately was sidelined with an injury. Yet, when he appeared in the VIP section in the main stand, mayhem ensued at the ground. Celebrities nearby were almost falling over each other to snatch a picture of the boy on their camera phones and the applause was deafening when he spoke to United fans from the pitch at half-time. This man is still loved and revered at his natural home. He should never have left United; he should never have been allowed to leave.

Beckham's decision to move to LA is ultimately the natural, sad destination that had been gradually approaching over the years, the moment when the ageing process would limit his sporting ambition whilst his celebrity status would continue to burn brightly. It would suit the fairytale ending of this one-time Prince of football – as was being widely predicted – if he were to be knighted.

Arise Sir David ... and goodbye. But thanks always, mate, for those unforgettable memories of when your football was king ... and so were you, for United and England.

13

The Two Ronnys

'In my opinion, Manchester United is the greatest club in the world
and for that reason I picked them.'
CRISTIANO RONALDO, 2003

'He is waiting to be an icon. He would enhance any team,
any league anywhere.'
EUSEBIO, 2003

'Cristiano has everything needed to be one of the stars of world football.'
LUIZ FELIPE SCOLARI, MANAGER OF PORTUGAL, 2004

'George Best, he ain't....' That was the sceptical response of a certain foolish publishing type when I revealed that I was planning to include the boy from Madeira with the dazzling feet in United's Magnificent Sevens. In many ways, it was typical of the general view from journalist friends, footballing pundits and fans – but I have to say I believe it is a jaundiced, discriminatory and ill-thought-out assessment. I know Cristiano Ronaldo is a work in progress but I will stick my neck out right here and say I believe he could be the best of the lot. Yes, even as good as Georgie-boy when all aspects of his game finally gel.

Still laughing at that one? Well, Sir Bobby Robson agreed with me. He said, 'He has as much ability as George Best and could have an equally great career if he improves his marksmanship. He gets in great positions and should score another ten goals a season.'

Sir Alex Ferguson also agrees, 'There is no doubt Cristiano can become the best player in the world. He has everything, really, and in terms of players who can attack defenders at speed, no one in Europe comes close. There are some central midfield players like Kaka and Ronaldinho, who can attack from central areas and are very good at it. But they are world-class players anyway. Ronaldo is in that bracket now. He runs with the ball at such incredible speed it is not easy for defenders to handle him and his record for Portugal shows you exactly where he is going.'

And that neatly brings us to his work with the Portuguese national side ... in October 2006, at the still tender age of 21, he had already earned 41 full caps and had scored 12 times. To put that into perspective – and to bring a little more credence to our case for this boy becoming the best – George Best played 37 times for Northern Ireland, hitting the back of the net nine times. And that was not just by the age of 21 – it was by his retirement from the game.

Ronaldo has two attributes only one of our other Magnificent Sevens possessed – he has the size and strength of Cantona, but also the speed and close control even the Gallic genius could only dream of. He is a big man; it amazes me how he pulls some of his stunts on the pitch. Considering his size, he has remarkable close ball control, pace and a two-footed ability. His tricks are of the kind you would imagine could only be performed by a smaller guy like, say, Jinky Johnstone or Best himself. But Ronny – as he is affectionately known to the United faithful – stands at 6ft 2in and weighs in at something approaching 13st 7lb.

He is a phenomenon; he should not be able to weave and dazzle so elegantly given his size. But he does and he will surely only get better. He has the ability to become the best player in the world – yes, even better than Ronaldinho. Along with Wayne Rooney and Lionel Messi, he is one of the three most promising players on the planet. It is certainly to Sir Alex Ferguson's credit that he had the foresight – and bravery – to sign two of that magical trio.

Like both Rooney and Messi, Ronaldo would come from humble beginnings, but rather more humble than both ... his home made even the council house Rooney was brought up in Liverpool's Croxteth appear luxurious by comparison. It had more of the Cantona about it; just as Eric was brought up in a cave on the outskirts of Marseille, so Cristiano spent his early years in a tin shack in the hills of Funchal, the main city and capital of Madeira, an island that lies south of Portugal in the North Atlantic Ocean.

Funchal is a city of deep contrasts. It has the appearance and affluence of a cosmopolitan European capital – promenades and boulevards, majestic colonial architecture, statues, hotels and restaurants, open-air cafés and a cathedral, plazas and ceremonial soldiers. Yet only a few streets back, as the hills rise, agriculture begins – and so does the *favela*, the shanty town built up in the hills, on the edge of this otherwise beautiful city. Unlike, say, Rio, Funchal's *favela* was – indeed, still is – renowned as a safe place, with friendly locals on street corners selling fish and vegetables. It was a place where the young Ronaldo could feel at ease, forever playing with his football on the street in front of an increasingly-amazed mass of admirers. Some were, inevitably, not so awestruck; the older boys who would forever be chasing him and beating him up when he embarrassed them with his skills. Even then, the lad had guts; he refused to let them get to him and continued to produce his bag of tricks in the street.

It was certainly a surprise to me to learn that Cristiano

Ronaldo had been born in a shack in a shanty town. I had never imagined there being that side to Madeira – my conception was that it was a rich holiday island, resplendent with lush, tropical gardens and luxury hotels, and largely the abode of doddery pensioners seeking a peaceful refuge. But take the road up the hill away from the harbour and delve into the back streets and you will find the habitat in which the young Cristiano would learn his trade.

Inevitably, the rusted tin shack became a tourist attraction. Now it is has gone after being knocked down in May 2007. The bulldozers were sent in and all that remains now is a blank space. But, if you get on any tourist bus, the guide will still point it out and say, 'That is where the footballer Cristiano Ronaldo was born and grew up.' Why? Because Ronny is now officially the most famous person from Madeira. Ever. The tour bus operators also now point out another landmark forever associated with the United winger; after he returned to the city in 2005, he splashed out on a massive home overlooking the bay. The five-bedroom mansion is certainly a far cry from the now legendary shack in which he grew up.

Cristiano Ronaldo dos Santos Aveiro was born in Funchal on 5 February 1985. He grew up with a brother, Hugo, and two sisters, Katia and Elma. Katia, now a professional singer and seven years older than Cristiano, admitted that their childhood in such poverty was not easy, but that they were a close-knit family. She said, 'It was a very simple and humble time. We weren't born into a rich family, but nevertheless we were never hungry or without shoes on our feet and a roof above our heads. We had the essential things we needed to survive ... we had food, a small home and loving parents and family. It taught us to appreciate everything we now have.

'When Cristiano joined Sporting Lisbon we were – and we still are – a very close and united family. That is why, no matter where Cristiano goes, one of us will always live with him, until he gets married and starts his own family … even now that he lives in England, my mother Maria and sister Elma live with him so that they can support him and take care of him, as he is the baby of our family.'

Ronaldo's father, José Dinis Aveiro, named him after the late American president Ronald Reagan, not out of any political admiration, but because he loved the B-movie man's acting 'skills'. José was the kit man of the local team Andorinha, and Ronaldo played for the youth team at the age of eight on an artificial pitch. José said, 'The moment he touched a ball, I knew he was special.' Maritimo, one of the big clubs on the island, offered Andorinha £200 for his services, but instead, at the age of ten, he joined the island's biggest team, CD Nacional, for two years' worth of boots and jerseys.

He was the literal footballing prodigy and, within another two years, Ronaldo had quit Madeira after being lured by scouts from Sporting Lisbon, even though he was a fan of their city rivals Benfica, in the Portuguese capital 600 miles away. He went with criticism ringing in his ears from Nacional. The club never doubted his ability, but doubted he had the character to be a key part of a team. Antonio Mendosa, who was head coach of Nacional when Ronaldo was there, says, 'He didn't behave in class. He was just a kid, but he created problems. He was difficult to control.'

The baton of bringing him into line was passed to Sporting. There, he was nurtured through the youth teams and attended the same football academy that had produced Luis Figo.

Given Ronaldo's age and that he would inevitably suffer homesickness, Sporting perceptively paid for his mother to join him in Lisbon until he reached the age of 17. Once again, his grit and unwillingness to conform surfaced; at the age of 15, he threw a chair at a coach who was taking the mickey out of him for his Madeiran accent. His punishment was to be left out of a youth team trip. This was a boy with attitude, an attitude that could cost him his career before he had really started if he wasn't taught how to behave. Clearly he needed someone to take him under his wing and help him mature. Someone like Sir Alex Ferguson.

His antics did not go down well with Sporting, who expected their chosen boys to be grateful and compliant, given the enormous opportunities they were enjoying. Former Sporting coach, Octavio Machado, still refuses to forgive Ronaldo for his poor discipline at the time. 'It was ugly,' Machado said. 'Cristiano Ronaldo is a point of reference, but his youth did not justify those tantrums which could be very costly for the team if he took them on to the pitch.' Nonetheless, Ronaldo became the only player in Sporting's history to play for the U18, U21, B team and first team in one season.

He would sign pro forms for Sporting, marking his début with two goals in a 3-0 victory over Moreirense in 2002 and following it up with a fine display against Inter Milan in the Champions League third qualifying round. Wearing the number 28 shirt, he would play a total of only 25 matches in the Portuguese league – starting 11 of them – for the Lions in his first and only season in 2002/03, scoring three goals, before leaving the club for Manchester on 13 August 2003.

Upon his arrival, Sir Alex Ferguson would immediately hand him the coveted number 7 shirt vacated by David Beckham; he had no doubt his new recruit had the balls and guts to deal with the accolade of becoming a member of the club's elite Magnificent Sevens.

Ronaldo had caught the attention of the Old Trafford club's

scouts at the Toulon U20 tournament in the summer of 2002, but it was only after he starred in Sporting's 3-1 2003 pre-season friendly win over United that Ferguson decided to sign him. Ferguson would later reveal that, in the dressing room after the game, his players talked constantly about the young Ronaldo. Even on the plane journey back to Manchester, the United players pleaded with their boss to sign the young star. Ferguson even admitted that the last time his players eulogised about a player to that extent was just prior to him signing Eric Cantona. Other European giants, including AC Milan and Juventus, were also hovering but United acted quickest and, just a couple of weeks later, the Portuguese wonderboy was at Old Trafford.

Let's give some credit also to the much-maligned Carlos Queiroz here. The United assistant manager – known to disillusioned fans as 'Qantas' back in 2005 because his inconsistent team tactics left them baffled about who was coming and going in the side – had already tipped Ferguson the wink about Ronaldo. He promised the United boss that here was a kid who would not only fulfil his promise, but could go on to become the best player in the world. Fair dues to old Qantas, who also played a significant part in enabling Ronaldo to return to United after the World Cup 2006 bust-up with Wayne Rooney.

Former United skipper Roy Keane also liked what he saw during that friendly match in Lisbon. He said, 'I had heard one or two rumours about Ronaldo before the Lisbon game, but the quality really showed through that night. He is a big, strong lad and his movement was excellent. He really looked a hell of a player and we were talking about him so much afterwards.'

Former Liverpool manager Gérard Houllier would suffer a 'Man who failed to sign the Beatles' moment at the time. He had noted Ronaldo's form even when he was 16, but decided against signing him. I am told from a source at Liverpool that Houllier, currently manager of French side Lyon, had reservations about whether Ronaldo would settle abroad. Surely a little more research – the boy had left home at 12, after all – would have provided the answer. It certainly did for Ferguson two years later. It would prove a costly blunder for the Kop kings as, for the next four years, they searched far and wide to find a man capable of filling their troublesome right-wing spot, a problem that has persisted ever since. Houllier's successor Rafa Benitez would even try to overcome the deficiency by forcing his best player, Stevie Gerrard, to play there, rather than in his natural central-midfield role.

Back in 2003, Eusebio, arguably Portugal's greatest ever player, was also full of praise for Cristiano, again making it clear that the United boss was in no way gambling, even though the 18-year-old would cost a £12 million transfer fee – a world record fee for a teenager. Eusebio said, 'English fans love spectacular players like Alan Shearer – and that is exactly what United have signed in this young guy. Cristiano Ronaldo has magic in his boots and I'm delighted he has signed for Manchester United because that is my team in England. There are some things he does with a ball that make me touch my head and wonder how he did it.'

The Portuguese star's United début came on 16 August 2003 at Old Trafford in the Premiership clash against Bolton Wanderers. As he stepped from the bench in the 59th minute of the first home game of the season, Old Trafford rose to greet him. United were already 1-0 ahead but, within minutes, Ronaldo had won a penalty which Ruud van Nistelrooy duly converted. Displaying a dazzling array of step-overs and feints, he dribbled past Kevin Nolan and Nicky Hunt, creating chances and generally tormenting the Bolton defence. The fans warmed to him immediately, chanting, 'You've only come to see Ronaldo' at the away supporters.

After his scintillating début, Ronaldo was the talk of the town, and the papers immediately heralded him as the new George Best. The match ended in a 4-0 win to United and the headline 'SEVEN HEAVEN' was a common one in the next day's tabloids. Yet there was a secret side to Ronaldo emerging behind the scenes. A senior employee of United told me that, away from the football pitch, the boy is not nearly as confident as he appears on it. I am told that, even after that cracker of a début, he felt overwhelmed in the dressing room afterwards and that, in private, he asked Ferguson if he could lose the number 7 shirt and return to the more anonymous number 28 he had worn in Lisbon.

Ferguson, quite rightly in my mind, refused the request. For his faults – and he has them – the Manchester United manager also has few peers when it comes to dealing correctly with young players in their formative years. He knows exactly when to read the riot act or when it is time for an arm around the shoulder. Clearly, in Ronaldo's case at that time, he correctly recognised that here was a boy who needed building up, a boy who needed to know his manager believed in him and cared for him.

My psychoanalyst friend put this spin on it: 'Well, he was a lad of just 18, in a foreign country, an alien environment with few friends, and he was expected to fill the shirt of a man who was probably the most famous footballer on earth. How would you feel? Nervous and totally overwhelmed? He could turn it on on the pitch – that was his sanctuary – but off it, he would need all the help he could get. My view is that he was, and still is, a boy who is actually rather introverted and shy away from football.'

Sounds like Georgie Best, and Ronaldo himself would admit

all he really wanted was to be seen as a great footballer. He said, 'I am happiest in my life when I have the ball at my feet. I don't know how to explain it. It is as though the ball becomes a part of me. It is just a natural thing and something I find very difficult to control because much of my game is instinctive. I just don't think about it.'

Sir Alex was delighted with Ronaldo's début. He said, 'I think the fans have got a new hero to talk about tonight.'

Ronaldo had spoken before the match about his joy at joining the Red Devils. He said, 'When a club of the stature of Manchester United come in for you and want to sign you, you don't think twice. In my opinion, Manchester United is the greatest club in the world and, for that reason, I picked them.

'Lots of young players have triumphed at United, so why can't it happen to me? I'm not worried ... I'm young. It's an incentive to do the best I can. I'm living a dream I never want to wake up from. I knew United were tracking various Sporting players but I never figured I would be the one chosen. The Premier League is shown on Portuguese television so I know lots about English football. From what I have seen, I think that with work, hard work, I will be able to push for a first-team place. I think my game will suit the English way of playing. I am especially proud to be the first Portuguese player to join United.'

Again, the more humble side of Ronaldo could be seen if you read in between the lines, particularly when he talked about never figuring he would be the chosen one when United's scouts watched Sporting's players. There seemed to be more depth to the boy than he was originally – and in certain quarters, still is – credited.

Ronaldo added, 'It's a great joy to have signed for Manchester United but it's also a great responsibility. I am delighted to be here; Old Trafford is a big and famous stadium. The facilities here at Carrington are excellent and I have been received well by everyone. I hope to play and help the team achieve everything it wants.

'The number 7 shirt is an honour and a responsibility. I hope it brings me a lot of luck. I did not come to replace Beckham. I know that everyone will demand a lot of me, but we are different players. I've got to keep my feet on the ground and hopefully succeed. If I achieve half as much as he has in his career, it would be an achievement.'

And Ferguson explained why he had felt it appropriate to hand the number 7 shirt to the prodigious boy from Portugal, although it was an explanation that took some understanding. The United manager said, 'Ronaldo is young. Some famous players at this club have had the jersey. It wasn't a matter of who do we give the number 7 to, it was appropriate a young player like Ronaldo should take it.'

In his first season at the Theatre of Dreams, Ronaldo collected an FA Cup winner's medal courtesy of United's 3-0 drubbing of Millwall in the final at Cardiff in May 2004. He played a major role in the victory, nodding home the first goal from a cross by Gary Neville and giving full-back Robbie Ryan a nightmare afternoon at the office. Wearing gold boots, the Portuguese lived up to his billing, earning the Man of the Match award and this tribute from Gary Neville after United wrapped up their 11th FA Cup win: 'Ryan Giggs and Ruud van Nistelrooy produced some good moments for us, but Cristiano Ronaldo was particularly outstanding. I think Ronaldo can be one of the top footballers in the world. To come with the price tag on his head and at his age, he has been outstanding for us this season.'

Boss Ferguson added to the compliments after securing the 17th trophy of his reign. 'Yes, Ronaldo was outstanding. We need to look after him in the right way because he is going to be a great footballer.'

In that first season, Ronaldo made a total of 39 appearances in all competitions, scoring 6 goals. The fans loved him from the very start and voted him their Player of the Season, after he had been at the club just seven months. The following campaign, he would up the ante still further, making 50 appearances and grabbing 9 goals. Rooney would join him at Old Trafford by September 2004, but the season would prove barren in terms of medals as the Roman Abramovich-funded and José Mourinho-masterminded era dawned at Chelsea. There would be compensations for Ronaldo off the field as 2004 turned into 2005, even though he and United would end the season losing to Arsenal on penalties in the FA Cup Final.

Ronaldo had arrived at United on a basic salary of £25,000 a week, but his agent, Jorge Mendes, who also represents Mourinho, quickly built that up with a series of lucrative promotional deals. Contracts with Nike, Pepe Jeans and Suzuki Cars were set up and Ronaldo was voted the sexiest player in the Portuguese national team by *PortugalGay* magazine. He was soon also on the cover of the Portuguese version of *GQ* magazine.

On the surface, he could have lived, and still could live, the life of a playboy. But he has a deeper, more reflective side. It was that humane side that prompted him to help buy a house in Indonesia for a seven-year-old boy victim of the Boxing Day tsunami of 2004 and his father. The boy, called Martunis, had been spotted stranded alone by a British TV crew in a helicopter on a Banda Aceh beach drinking rain water. When they went to rescue him, he was found wearing a Portuguese football shirt ... with the name Ronaldo on the back. Ronaldo said, 'It really got to me – after seeing the pictures of the boy suffering, I was so touched.' Touched enough to donate enough money – and to encourage other members of the national squad to do so – to buy the boy a new home after he was reunited with his father.

Sky News' Ian Dovaston was the TV reporter who found Martunis. He said, 'It was clear to our Indonesian driver and helper that the boy had seen his mother and father swept away, did not know if they were alive or not, and had been wandering ever since. He had mosquito bites and was very thin.'

Dovaston explained that Martunis had survived for three weeks by living on berries, dry noodles and puddle water. Doctors who examined him said he was dehydrated and malnourished. Dovaston and his TV crew took him to the local Save the Children office and he was eventually reunited with his father – then came the warm-hearted intervention from Ronaldo, who also ensured the pair were VIP guests of his for a subsequent Portugal fixture.

Ronaldo would need all his strength to deal with major problems of his own during the 2005/06 season. In his third campaign at United, he would make 47 appearances and score 12 goals and it would end with the club winning the Carling Cup – but along the way would take in the death of his father, a training ground bust-up with Ruud van Nistelrooy, a controversial V-sign to Benfica fans after defeat in Lisbon and rape allegations in London.

Ronaldo was devastated when his father José Dinis died on 6 September 2005. He had been the catalyst to his career, encouraging and cajoling him to become the best in the world. Yet the 21-year-old still had the strength of mind to play in a World Cup qualifier against Russia a day later, a move that earned a tribute from Portugal coach Luiz Felipe Scolari. Ronaldo helped his team-mates earn a 0-0 draw in Moscow to leave Portugal one win from the finals. Scolari said, 'Cristiano had the support of the whole team in this important moment of his life. We are very proud of him.' Ronaldo admitted in private that he had turned out as a mark of respect for his father, who had lived his life for football and died at just 51 years of age.

Then, on 20 October 2005, Ronaldo was arrested over allegations that he'd raped a woman at the Sanderson Hotel, near Oxford Circus in central London. The woman claimed he had assaulted her in a penthouse suite after the club's match against Fulham two weeks earlier. Ronaldo supplied a DNA sample and was bailed as the Crown Prosecution Service decided whether there was sufficient evidence to charge him. Ronaldo immediately denied the claims – saying he was the victim of a 'stitch-up'. He claimed the woman had concocted the rape story when he refused to pay her for her company. The police eventually cleared him of the allegations after a seven-week investigation and, as an added bonus, on the day he received the news from the Crown Prosecution Service, he also agreed a two-year extension to his contract at Old Trafford that would tie him to the club until 2010 and double his weekly wage to £50,000. It brought this remark from Sir Alex Ferguson: 'This deal represents our faith in young players and Ronaldo will develop into a fantastic player.'

The nightmare publicity had been something he could have done without following his father's death. The rape allegation just did not sit with the easygoing character of the man or the way he treated the women in his life. Until the summer of 2006, he had lived with his mother and sister in a house at Woodford in Cheshire and one inside story I was given about Ronaldo seemed to sum up the man's relationship with women. After the FA Cup defeat by Arsenal in May 2005, United were drowning their sorrows at their hotel, the Vale of Glamorgan. Ronaldo had persuaded two girls from the luxury

234

hotel's leisure complex to join them during their 'celebration' meal. He couldn't stop chatting through a 'boring speech' by the boss and then asked the girls if they would like to carry on the night at a Cardiff club. They both smiled nervously at each other, and Ronaldo, picking up on their fears, pulled an older woman over to his side. 'It be OK,' he pleaded. 'This is my mum, and she come everywhere with me.'

Of course, he has been spotted with women as his fame has grown – pin-ups included. He once dated Miss Portugal, was close to the stunning model Jordana Jardel, sister of former Bolton striker Mario, and has also romanced Merche Romero, a Spanish TV anchorwoman working in Portugal, a divorcée and nine years his senior. But he remains for the most part a shy boy, still influenced by what his mother Maria and sisters think. His sister Katia says they will remain a constant in his life. She said, 'My mother is an essential part of his life as he turns to her for help in decisions he makes and with problems that he may have … in fact our mother is the essential part in all of our lives as she is always there for all of us, no matter what.

'There is no doubt that our mother is the master of her children, which is why she worries a lot about Cristiano, and the life he has decided to live … that is why, when there are rumours going around about him, we get very protective and upset, as we don't want to see him being hurt or his dream torn apart. We are a very close family and the more problems we face together, the stronger and closer we will continue to get!'

No doubt Maria would not have been pleased by the confrontation Cristiano had with Ruud van Nistelrooy back in January 2006. Sir Alex Ferguson was forced to step in and restore order after the training ground bust-up between the two. Tensions had been growing as the Dutchman voiced his anger at Ronaldo's 'showboating' over the previous couple of months. He claimed the Portuguese lad was greedy and not providing him with the service he had taken for granted when David Beckham was at the club.

It all came to a head in mid-January after United had lost 3-1 to Manchester City, with Ronaldo being sent off for lunging at Andy Cole. The previous month, Ronaldo had been dropped by United after being substituted in Lisbon during the Champions League defeat to Benfica, a match which saw him booed off by the local supporters after he raised a finger at them. It was also a match many consider as being Ronaldo's poorest performance for the club.

Van Nistelrooy was one of those seething at Ronaldo's loss of form and he let him know it at that fateful training session. Ferguson had to step in to sort things out; he was unhappy with van Nistelrooy and this episode marks the beginning of the end of the big striker's reign at the Theatre of Dreams.

Previously, I am also told by a United insider, Ronaldo had also had training ground bust-ups with Nicky Butt (before he left for Newcastle) and Alan Smith over his 'greediness', but that generally he is well liked by his United team-mates and a popular member of the dressing room.

Ronaldo was big enough, when asked about the incidents, to concede that he did need to become more of a team player, saying, 'I admit I did over-indulge on the tricks at times. I know the fans think I do it too much but I want them to know I am working on it. In the past, I have got over-excited and got carried away.'

Sir Alex Ferguson conceded in February 2006 that the previous year had been a tough one for his Portuguese whiz-kid but was also quick to stress that he had no doubt he would come through it, saying, 'He has had a troubled time. Eventually, he will come back all right. I'm sure of that. We didn't foresee what has happened to him and it's normal that a young player should need a rest. These days, it's hard for young players as we expect so much from them. You can forget how young they are. But the important thing is the long term and we're confident that he will be OK.'

And indeed he was. In tandem with Rooney, he inspired United to another trophy as they bulldozed Wigan 4-0 in the Carling Cup Final. Rooney grabbed a brace and Ronaldo the third goal. It appeared all was turning out fine again, that Ronaldo was settling down after a tumultuous year.

But appearances can be deceptive. The World Cup of 2006 was looming, and along with it subsequent months of vilification and accusations of cheating that would have tested the staying power of even the most battle-hardy of old pros, let alone a relatively new kid on the block.

14

The Boy Who Would Be King

*'Benfica know Ronaldo well, they know how to deal against his game,
so I think it is not so easy to get one of his penalties.'*
JOSÉ MOURINHO, DECEMBER 2006

*'For me, there is no doubt.
Today, Cristiano Ronaldo is better than Wayne Rooney for United.'*
EUSEBIO, DECEMBER 2006

*'The people in England criticise me for anything I do. They love that.
Since the World Cup, I have just tried to do my best.
If I'm criticised by somebody else, I really don't care.'*
CRISTIANO RONALDO, DECEMBER 2006

'Manchester United are a magnificent sporting institution. They have Sir Alex Ferguson, one of the greatest managers to prowl a dugout. They have Paul Scholes and Wayne Rooney, wonderful blends of technique and work-rate. And they also have Cristiano Ronaldo, a brilliant talent, one of the footballers of the season, but a player prone to cheating … [and] fraudulent antics … The widespread desire for someone to give Chelsea a run for their unbelievable money is tempered by disgust at the gamesmanship of United's number 7, the club's most famous shirt….'

Those damning words were how Henry Winter, one of Fleet Street's most eloquent football writers, began his match report after United beat Middlesbrough 2-1 at the Riverside at the start of December 2006. Winter claimed that Ronaldo 'collapsed after over-running the ball past [keeper] Mark Schwarzer' on 19 minutes and that the subsequent penalty, converted by Louis Saha, was unfair, immoral and illegal – as, consequently, was the win which took the Red Devils six points clear of Chelsea at the top of the Premiership.

Des Kelly, the *Daily Mail*'s fine sports columnist, was another who believed that the incident damned Ronaldo at a time when his football during the early part of his fourth season at Manchester United had been good enough to earn him the accolade of being the best footballer in Britain at the time. Kelly wrote, 'Ronaldo did not stumble accidentally; he did not leap selflessly out of the way of an advancing goalkeeper; he did not helplessly fall to earth. The player dived, pure and simple....The great sadness is Ronaldo had been arguably the player of the season so far.'

The 'Boro incident was just the latest in a catalogue of alleged 'diving' misdemeanours by the winger – 'crimes' which made him Public Enemy Number 1 to many followers of the Premiership. Ferguson himself would dismiss the incident, slapping Ronaldo on the back at the end of the match, saying, 'It looks as though the goalkeeper didn't touch him, but it's the intent … what could he do? He's going to be carted anyway – it's a penalty kick.' TV pundit Alan Hansen would back Ferguson up on this occasion, saying that Schwarzer had thrown Ronaldo off balance as he tried to get to the ball with his approach. Hansen concluded, 'Under the laws that a centre-forward lives by, he [Ronaldo] was guilty of no crime.'

'Boro boss Gareth Southgate, naturally enough, begged to differ – he had no doubt Ronaldo had tricked the referee. Asked if he thought he had cheated to win a penalty, he said, 'Yeah. It's very difficult for the referee, because it happened very quickly, but how many times are we going to see it? The lad's got a history of doing it.'

Four days later, the whole issue of Ronaldo staying on his feet exploded again. Ferguson, questioned before the Champions League match against Benfica, claimed it had been an opportunity the press had been waiting for since Ronaldo's infamous part in Wayne Rooney's sending off five months earlier in the World Cup quarter-final between England and Portugal – that Ronaldo was now being persecuted for his behaviour in that match. Ferguson said, 'I've looked at the penalty incident a million times and there is no way a player is going to give up an opportunity to score into an empty goal. For me, it's a clear penalty. But you [the press] have had it in the papers for the last three days, with comment pieces from everyone you can think of. I hope I'm wrong but I have a feeling it's the revenge of the English press. I think you've been waiting for months to do this.'

To give him his due, the United manager had, in the past, admitted that Ronaldo did sometimes go to ground too easily. But now he was claiming that was no longer the case and that, with such dynamic dribbling, there would inevitably be times when his man simply lost his balance. Ferguson fumed, 'We don't condone diving at this club. I've said that time and time again, and Cristiano is well aware of that. But if you're driving a car at 70mph and another car careers in front of you, what do you do? Brake or go right into the car?' He ended his tirade with a patronising pop at Gareth Southgate, saying, 'Gareth Southgate's very naïve, of course. He's just a young manager. We'll have to give him a chance to settle in.'

For all his mind games and barbs, Ferguson had a point. At that stage of the season, Ronaldo was the third most-fouled player in the Premiership. Ferguson added, 'We played Manchester City last season and there were two career-threatening challenges on him before he was sent off for his own frustration. The first thing that happened on Saturday was that he was hacked from behind and the referee [Chris Foy] did not book the player, which just encourages opponents to keep kicking him and kicking him. And what is more serious in our game – preventing the best players from playing, or going on for three days about a dive that isn't a dive?'

It was a fair comment. The rights and wrongs of Ronaldo's alleged theatricals had been debated furiously within the game since the start of 2004. Those first few months (the last of 2003) of his introduction to English football had been the honeymoon period, when there appeared a general consensus that here was a bright new talent who needed encouragement, not widespread disapproval. Then it all seemed to change. Defenders and fans of others clubs were getting mighty peeved that the Portuguese was leaving them on their backsides with shattered egos with his extravagant display of dazzling skills. Shades of the reaction he got back in the *favela* from the bully-boys who simply couldn't cope with his supreme ability on the ball.

From being initially lauded as a magician, the conjuror was accused by the media of being a cheat. The allegations would take shape over the following two years, peaking in the summer of 2006 when he was accused of deliberately getting his team-mate Wayne Rooney sent off in that combustible World Cup quarter-final, and in the 2006/07 season, rivals continually complained that he was a diver.

So what's the truth of it? Cynical professional or genius? Probably a bit of both by 2007, if we are honest. As Sir Bobby Charlton said, 'You can dislike him for some of the things he does, but what a talent!' That was an astute comment from one of the all-time greats. Ronaldo is undoubtedly a genius with those twinkling feet of his, but he is also not against resorting to the dark arts if it helps him to be a winner – the latter, of course, being a seemingly ingrained trait of players coming from the Continent to the Premiership. Having said that, I have no doubt it is a part of his game he will iron out as the years roll by. He is good enough to leave an opponent on his backside and change the course of a game without having to resort to tactics that may be the norm on the Continent, but that are certainly less tolerated in the British game.

And what would you rather have – a football match dominated by method or one engineered by unpredicatability and sheer demonic skill? Jeff Powell, of the *Daily Mail*, summed it up best with these words, also written after the Middlesbrough bust-up: 'It is about time this, his adopted country, started to be a little more grateful for this precious gift from our oldest ally. To condemn Ronaldo as a rank diver – as a desperate Gareth Southgate and others have presumed to do of late – is as gross an injustice as to dismiss Oscar Wilde as a pornographer. If he dabbles in the dark arts occasionally, it is only to give dramatic emphasis to his talent by way of buying himself a measure of protection from the mob. Ronaldo hurdles more tackles in a match than Red Rum jumped fences to win three Grand Nationals ... come on, England, give the boy a break.'

United's official mouthpiece, the club programme *United Review*, also put up a persuasive call for the boy to be backed rather than barracked. It had this to say about Ronaldo's 2006/07 contribution, just before the match at the Riverside, 'The boy from Madeira has grown in stature this season. Being a figure of vilification among opposition fans might have affected lesser characters, but Ronaldo has thrived ... Greatly improved decision-making, a more consistent end product ... have seen Ronaldo realise his mind-boggling potential and have marked him down as one of the best young talents in football.'

The club's view seems a fair assessment to me; indeed, there

243

was even a suggestion that Ronaldo's form and attitude was worthy of a national Player of the Year award, let alone just the one at Old Trafford. At that stage of the season, he was certainly United's brightest star, outshining Rooney and Co by a mile. So maybe the incident at Middlesbrough should be seen in that context – if you see it as a transgression, then it was a rare one in a season of great achievement and growing maturity after a nightmare summer.

Ah, that summer … let's take a closer look at the incident with Rooney in the World Cup quarter-final, an incident comparable with Beckham's sending off in 1998 against Argentina in France in terms of consequent vilification and abuse, and Cantona's treatment after his kung fu kick. Funny how often the United Magnificent Sevens have shared similar forms of backlash throughout their careers.

All hell broke loose for Rooney and Ronaldo just after the hour mark in Gelsenkirchen when Wayne appeared to stamp on Ricardo Carvalho's groin. Referee Horacio Elizondo was standing next to him and was immediately harassed by a posse of Portugal players, including Ronaldo, who urged him to take action against Rooney for the challenge. Rooney shoved his Manchester United team-mate away and was red-carded. Ronaldo then winked to his coach Phil Scolari after Rooney's dismissal. It was a provocative action, a wink that would cause the young Portuguese months of aggravation in England. At the time, former England captain and now TV pundit Alan Shearer famously claimed that Ronaldo had deliberately set out to get his Man United team-mate dismissed, and added that he would not be surprised if, back at Manchester United, Rooney 'stuck one on' Ronaldo.

Ronaldo would claim to me he was unfairly castigated for his part in the sending off. He said, 'I complained about Rooney's tackle on Carvalho – but no way did I ask for the referee to show him a red card.'

In the aftermath of their confrontation, Ronaldo insisted he would have to leave Manchester United, and was linked with a move to Real Madrid. That would not happen – full credit due here to Alex Ferguson for refusing to entertain such a move. As with Cantona after the kung fu episode, the United boss simply would not allow his star man to walk away. I am told he was quickly on the phone to Rooney, telling him to forget the incident and to make up with Ronaldo, to tell him there were no hard feelings. The implication, as always with the United boss, was clear – Manchester United was more important than anything else in the world, certainly much more important than a squabble in an international match.

Ryan Giggs recognised that aspect of United – how the club would close ranks when one of its stars was on the receiving end of a public whipping – and spoke of a clear link between United's current number 7 and those previous wearers of the shirt, Cantona and Beckham. Giggs said, 'We are used to things like this. David Beckham had it and Eric Cantona had it. The players get around it by having a joke to make the person concerned feel a bit more relaxed about it. That is all you can do really. All it proves is that you are a good player. The opposition fans are trying to put you off your game because they realise you are a danger. That is what will happen to Cristiano. But he is a strong character and a talented player. All he can do is keep putting in the performances on the pitch and hope it all settles down after a while.'

Rooney did as he was told by Ferguson by texting Ronaldo and a peace was brokered. It is true to say that Rooney initially certainly did not want to make that peace – he was angry about the incident.

Rooney issued an official statement, saying, 'I was

disappointed by Ronny trying to get me carded and I gave him a bit of a push in the chest, but that was it. By protesting to the ref, Ronny was doing what he thought was good for his country. During that game, we were rivals, which was why I gave him a push when I thought he'd been out of order. But once it was all over, we were friends, club-mates again. It was all forgotten.

'In the tunnel, we wished each other good luck in the game, hoped it went well, which is what you say to a team-mate. OK, he wasn't in my team that day but you still wish a fellow professional a good game.'

The words had all the hallmarks of a solicitor's statement – can you really imagine Wayne Rooney saying 'I was disappointed' and 'you still wish a fellow professional a good game'?

Of the sending-off, Rooney would be quoted as saying, 'I will go to my grave and still maintain it was a complete accident. If you study the photographs you will see that I had my back to the player. I couldn't see him or where I was putting my foot. If it had been a definite stamp meant to harm him, the fellow would still be in hospital. But he was up on his feet in minutes, no worse for wear. It was the sort of thing that happens when you are fighting hard for the ball. However, the ref saw it differently. He saw it as violent play and I was off.'

England went out of the World Cup 3-1 on penalties after the match ended 0-0. Ronaldo would not return to United's Carrington training headquarters until August after being given an extended break. His country's final game was on 8 July; a defeat in the third-place play-off against hosts Germany.

I think the basic essential character differences between Rooney and Ronaldo need pointing out here. Rooney is a straight-down-the-line, what-you-see-is-what-you-get Scouser; Ronaldo is of an altogether more complex Latin nature. Rooney is a bullish battler with looks to match, while Ronaldo is a deeper-thinking, calculating Continental with the face of a matinée idol and the body of a male model. Ronaldo loves to tease and wind up his team-mates when the mood takes him; Rooney is much more the determined, mono-dimensional 'let's get down to work' player, moulded in the shape of, say, Alex Ferguson.

I am told that Ronaldo was winding him up in the tunnel and it took Rooney a lot of effort to ignore his taunts; he tried hard, apparently, to resist reacting to the idea that England were crap and that they would get the hiding their ugly mugs deserved. The World Cup incident does not reflect well on either player.

Referee Elizondo did not criticise Ronaldo after the match; instead, he turned his guns on Rooney, saying, 'Rooney was complaining all the time, always coming close to you and saying, "Referee this, referee that..." Protests and more protests. He reminded me of my kids.'

England's much celebrated midfield duo of Frank Lampard and Steven Gerrard were not as easygoing on Ronny. 'Sadly, a dark side stains Cristiano Ronaldo's game,' Gerrard writes in his autobiography. 'His part in Wayne Rooney's dismissal was a disgrace. What really [got to] all the England players was Ronaldo's wink to his bench. It was a wink which said "job done". How could he do that to his Manchester United team-mate?

'On the bus after the game, Wayne asked me, "What do you think about the wink?" I said, "Honestly, Wazza, if we were playing Spain and [Liverpool team-mates] Xabi Alonso or Luis Garcia winked at the referee or gave a signal for me to be sent off, I'd never speak to them again."'

Lampard was just as scathing, saying, 'He's supposed to be a team-mate of Wayne's at Manchester United and he does something like that.'

To his credit, Rooney tried to ease the pressure on Ronaldo by claiming that he was as guilty as him in terms of gamesmanship. Rooney said, 'I was trying to get him booked by the referee for diving in the first half but people probably haven't seen that.'

Despite attempts to calm the situation, the fallout threatened to engulf Ronaldo. His home in Woodford, near Macclesfield – a Manchester United-owned house that he shared with his mother Maria and sister Elma – would be attacked by vandals; he would receive death threats; and he even spoke about the possibility of moving to Real Madrid to escape the furore. The tabloids quickly dubbed him 'the most hated man in Britain' and even some United fans turned against him. Directly after the match, some gathered to protest outside Old Trafford, vowing to boo Ronaldo off the pitch. His neighbours in Chester Road also made it clear they were unhappy with his World Cup antics. One, Lee Evans, said, 'I was astonished, to be honest, but we don't know anything about him, really. I was just disgusted that he would do this.' Another, David McLeod, who lived across the road, said, 'We did see a couple of flags pinned to the fence, but there's luckily been no bother from angry fans. I can't imagine him coming back after this. He'll be sold – he doesn't want to stay anyway.'

Yet another resident, Keith Hampton, who was a football referee for 16 years, said, 'It's very simple – he had no reason to get involved in the incident because it was nothing to do with him. As far as I'm concerned, had it not been for his interventions, Rooney would not have been sent off.

'He will never be welcomed back into this country and he'll be out by Christmas. The fans will hound him out unless he comes back and apologises profusely to the whole country.' Vindictive websites also appeared, one of the most sickening featured pages of Ronaldo being shot and beheaded.

As is often the norm with heated issues like this in football, fans were generally split down the middle. Albert Katcher of Bromley in Kent said, 'As a long-standing Manchester United supporter (inherited from my father), I want Ronaldo to stay. He has matured as a player under Sir Alex Ferguson and I think he can only get better. He has a five-year contract to honour and I cannot see Sir Alex letting him go. I think he is mature enough to know that if he plays up to his potential, the demand for his services can only increase over the next few years. After all, United are usually in contention for domestic and international honours. So he has a chance to shine and I hope he does.'

And David Finch of Manchester backed that view, saying, 'I have been a Man Utd fan for 30 years and love having Ronaldo in the team. He has the talent to be regarded in the same light as Pelé, Maradona and Best, so it distresses me to see people (Scolari for one) excusing the amateur dramatics. Ronaldo needs a strong manager who will shield him from the inevitable vitriol and encourage him to develop his game in a positive direction; he will get that from Sir Alex, but I'm not so sure that he would get that sort of support in Spain.'

But Jason Tyldesley, also of Manchester, wanted United to kick him out. He said, 'I am a Manchester United fan and I believe Ronaldo should leave. The part he played in Wayne Rooney's sending off is indefensible. Yes, they were not team-mates in the game but the pair are allegedly friends off the field and he knew exactly the reaction he'd get when he approached the referee. Does any football fan honestly think Rooney will shake hands and forget everything? If he does, he is not the player (man) we all believe he is. If we can get £20 million, take the money.'

And Anne Bodman, of Chalfont St Peter, criticised Ronaldo for his lack of sportsmanship, saying, 'To me, it was obvious that Ronaldo urged the ref to send Rooney off. Of course, Ronaldo is very talented and good to watch. However, he is also shown to be mean-spirited and does his best to prevent others showing their footballing skills by foul tactics.'

Sir Alex Ferguson would see to it that Ronaldo did not pack his bags for Madrid, but United legend Sir Bobby Charlton warned the winger he would have to be strong when he returned to Manchester, that he would need to be to cope with some fierce barracking from fans across the country. Charlton said, 'I think he realises he's probably made a mistake, which he'll have to pay for. The fans will have a little go at him at the start of the season. But he is a great player, a marvellous young player. He's already spoken to Wayne Rooney and the other players. I don't see how he could have solved that problem in any other way than to come back to us.

'If he'd have wanted to go and forced us to send him off to Real Madrid or wherever, he would have had the same problem and it might never have gone away.'

United legend Eric Cantona chipped into the debate, urging Ronaldo not to quit Old Trafford, insisting he was already at 'the biggest club in the world'. Cantona said – and if anyone should know it was him – 'United is the perfect club to improve as a young player. United is the biggest club in the world and yet spend time working with young players, giving them a chance. Not many of the great clubs provide this opportunity – in fact, maybe United is the only one. My greatest moments in football were there.'

And even Chelsea boss José Mourinho got in on the act, advising his fellow countryman Ronaldo to stay. He said, 'If Ronaldo stays in England, I think he can turn things around. Footballers should play a lot and talk very little. He should keep quiet and do his job.'

Eventually, Ronaldo himself came out of hiding and told the world he would be staying at Old Trafford. He said, 'Manchester

United are the ideal club for me. It is true that I said one day I would like to play in Spain. But if that doesn't happen, it won't be a problem. I still feel very happy.'

His first match for United after the World Cup incident was in a 5-1 opening day of the new season thrashing of Fulham, in which he teamed up with Rooney again. Both scored and Ronaldo left the field with the cheers of the United faithful ringing in his ears. Inevitably, there were also some boos from the Fulham supporters who had made the long, fruitless journey north. Ronaldo said, 'Of course the whistles were a bit wearing. The away games are going to be complicated ... the one against Charlton will be the first, but I am going to take the chance to distance myself from it, and try to do my best. We will see what happens. I am thinking about just one thing – winning. We are confident, we are only thinking about three points, we need to be more consistent than last season and we will take the title. I believe that every year we can go further than the previous year, and so I hope that this year is our season and we can win the league.'

Sir Alex Ferguson simply smiled after the thrashing of Fulham and claimed, 'It was never going to be an issue between Wayne and Cristiano. Sometimes you have a training situation where players start arguing and then you see them in the dressing room ten minutes later and they're laughing.'

The away match at Charlton would finish 3-0 to United and Ronaldo was booed throughout, but did not let the catcalls get to him. Afterwards, he said, 'I knew I'd be whistled as soon as I put a foot on the pitch at Charlton, but I faced the game in a very calm way. I won't give any importance to the whistles or the insults.'

He also finally publicly defended his role in the Rooney sending off, saying, 'Throughout my career, I have always defended – in any circumstances – my country. It could be that my best friends play for other teams, but firstly I will defend my country and my shirt. Secondly, what happened was absolutely normal, and I think any player who was in the same situation would have done the same.'

Ronaldo claimed the incident had now been swept under the carpet at United and laughed off suggestions he was desperate for a move to Spain, adding, 'It's true I'm moving [from the house in Woodford], but I've moved house every year in Manchester.'

At the end of September, the Red Devils drew 1-1 at Reading and Ronaldo was in such fine form that a Royals player pleaded for his home fans not to have a go at Ronny next time United were in town, as the wind-ups seemed to have had the opposite effect – rather than putting him off his game, they helped him raise it to another level. Full-back Graeme Murty said, 'Leave him alone, for God's sake – you'll make him angry.'

Perhaps the most telling comment on Ronaldo and the aftermath of the World Cup incident with Rooney is this: by the start of 2007, there was little if any abuse being directed at Ronaldo. Sure, there were complaints about him diving, but there was nothing about the England game. Ronaldo must surely take a great deal of credit for that – he had dealt with it all so well that the issue had all but been forgotten. By refusing to rise to the bait in the early part of the season, he had taken the wind out of it all – and full credit to him, Ferguson and United for winning a tactical battle there.

Former United ace David Sadler also congratulated Ronaldo on beating his most persistent critics. He said, 'He has learned the right response, which is not to gesture to supporters or go into a sulk, but to laugh it off and put on a performance that shuts up the critics and the boo-boys.'

The careers of Rooney and Ronaldo appeared fated to

become intertwined on occasion as they developed into world-class stars. They had both made their names internationally with fine showings at Euro 2004, but it is an overlooked fact that both had also hogged the headlines at an international tournament two years earlier. In May 2002, the brilliant teenagers – Rooney then at Everton, Ronny at Sporting – played in the European U17 Championship in Denmark. They did not line up against each other in the event, but Rooney would steal the show, scoring five goals for England and being voted player of the tournament. Rooney, then 18, was England's key man as they reached the semi-finals, losing 3-0 to eventual winners Switzerland, while, at this particular juncture, it would be Ronaldo's turn to exit an international tournament in shame. Portugal crashed out in the group stages after Ronaldo, then 17, was sent off in a 2-0 defeat to France.

Ronaldo would make his senior international début on Wednesday, 20 August 2003, just five days after his United début against Bolton, in the friendly 1-0 home win over Kazakhstan. Ominously for Luis Figo, arguably Portugal's finest player since the great Eusebio, Ronaldo would replace him after the half-time interval, and made such an immediate impact with his swerving runs and dribbling that he had a previously mute 15,000 crowd in Chaves – who had jeered Portugal off at half-time – on their feet.

Afterwards, Ronaldo refused to swap his number 16 shirt with the opposition – he was desperate to keep it as a lifetime memento of his international début. He said, 'I wasn't going to swap my shirt with anybody else, and I'm never going to give it away. It was my first international, and I felt very proud to be making my début, so it's important to me that I keep that shirt. The game wasn't great, but it was a good exercise for what is to come. I had an OK game, and the fans were good to me. I hope very much to play against Spain in our next match. That will be up to the coach. But now that I have played, I want to become a regular player in the team.'

He would achieve that aim and even win over Scolari, who had also initially harboured doubts about his attitude right up to the start of the World Cup Finals in 2006. Two incidents in warm-up matches prior to the event had got the big Brazilian worrying. Ronaldo clashed with an opponent during the 4-1 win over the Cape Verde Islands in May 2006, and did so again in the 3-0 stroll against Luxembourg the following month. On both occasions he was booked and substituted and I am told Scolari 'gave him the biggest bollocking of his life' after the Luxembourg clash – although, in public, Big Phil would blank all questions on their relationship, smile infuriatingly and only say, 'He is a youngster who listens.'

As with Sven-Göran Eriksson and Wayne Rooney, Scolari realised the true importance of Ronaldo to his team. With Figo in decline, Ronaldo was rapidly becoming the main man. In fact, Scolari admitted he could see the day when Ronny would be skipper of Portugal, and that it was not that far away. Scolari said, 'During my time in Portugal, I think he will become one of the captains of our team, because he has the charisma for it, he has the potential. He is young, but he is learning how to lead a group.'

Sure enough, Cristiano was named the national team captain for the first time in a friendly match against Brazil on 6 February 2007, a day after his 22nd birthday. The decision by Scolari was in honour of Carlos Silva, the Portuguese Football Federation vice-president who had died two days before. Scolari explained, 'Mr Silva asked me to make him a captain as a gesture. He thought the English fans would give him a difficult time and this was a response.'

Like Rooney, Ronaldo was certainly the man for the big

stage. Ronaldo had scored Portugal's only goal in their 2-1 loss to Greece in the opening match of Euro 2004 and the first goal of the semi-final against the Netherlands, which Portugal won 2-1.

He also represented Portugal at the 2004 Summer Olympics, and was the second highest scorer in qualification for the World Cup in the European zone with seven goals. In September 2005, Rooney and Ronaldo's paths would cross again on the international stage when Rooney was voted the World Young Player of the Year by the players themselves at the FIFPro awards ceremony, and Ronaldo received the same honour, but from the worldwide fans' votes.

The 2006 World Cup would end in tears for Ronaldo after a Zinedine Zidane penalty earned France a 1-0 semi-final triumph over a disappointing Portugal. It seemed that the gladiatorial quarter-final against England had drained him and his team-mates of their physical and mental strength.

From that match on 5 July, Cristiano Ronaldo had just 25 days to recharge his batteries, then it was back to Old Trafford on 31 July and the inevitable barrage of questions about his run-in with Rooney, his future and a chorus of boos. It was testament to his strength of character that, by the start of 2007, he was still going strong in the face of continued adversity and that he would defiantly say, 'I want to leave my mark so the fans will say I was one of United's greats.'

Would George Best have been able to keep going under the mountain of negative pressure sustained by Ronaldo? Probably not ... George was a genius on the pitch but could not survive off it. He might well have run away from it all, saying he did not need the aggro.

What would Beckham have done? In 1998, he had been tough enough to battle on after his own World Cup low-point but, nine years later, he would probably have cried as he did when he was forced out of England's World Cup 2006 loss against Ronaldo's Portugal, believing – correctly, as it transpired – that his number was up for the national team.

That Ronaldo not only stayed in England but grew in stature as a player and a man after that torrid summer of 2006 is a remarkable testament to his character and inner strength. As Sir Alex Ferguson says, 'Cristiano Ronaldo is a leader, an absolute leader. He is a magnificent personality – intelligent, powerful, strong, courageous. He is a leader; him and Rooney are the leaders of the new team.'

15

The New King

'His strokes of artistry put paint on the canvas.'
SIR ALEX FERGUSON, MAY 2007

'He winks on the left, he winks on the right ... that boy Ronaldo, makes England look shite.'
MANCHESTER UNITED TERRACES CHANT, 2006/07

H is year of strife and tribulation would come full circle on the evening of Thursday 17 May 2007. That night, Cristiano Ronaldo would receive a standing ovation from some of those who had vilified him most at the World Cup 11 months previously. Ronny took it in his stride, wearing that innocent yet mischievous smile we have come to associate him with, as the UK's football writers followed in the footsteps of the players by naming him their Footballer of the Year. What a turnaround. Who, in all honesty, would have anticipated that outcome when Ronaldo had returned to Manchester for the 2006/07 season?

Most pundits had put their bets on him staying for the campaign and then shooting off to the warmer climes of Madrid or Barcelona. I don't know of any who predicted he would stay and become the undisputed new king of Old Trafford and British football. After Ronny collected his award at the scribes' dinner, Sir Alex Ferguson paid tribute to the boy by whom he has stood with that Cantona-esque quote about artistrty, paint and canvas. He also pointed to his boy's lionheart, guts and strength. Ronaldo himself would admit that his bulking up had helped take him to a new level, saying, 'I have worked hard this season, not only on football but physically as well, and it's helped me.'

The following Monday he would complete his clean sweep when Ferguson presented him with the Manchester United Player of the Year award at an Old Trafford dinner. Inevitably, that grin appeared yet again and his team-mates, led by Wayne Rooney who had won the award the previous season, burst into a rowdy rendition of the chant at the start of this chapter – only with some of the tired and emotional guests substituting the word England for Beckham, which only seemed to make the beaming Ronaldo and Ferguson beam even more. Naughty boys....

It had all become clear as Christmas 2006 turned into the usual bleak January in 2007. That winter, Cristiano Ronaldo had stepped up another gear; his searing performances of the first part of the new season were eclipsed by a series of world-class shows. In previous campaigns it had been Rooney who had dragged United upwards, but now Ronaldo would take over his mantle as the No 1 at Old Trafford. As the club headed towards that all-important title win, it was Ronaldo who earned the victories that made it all possible. He was a one-man express train determined to do what many had considered impossible: derail the Chelsea express.

By the end of the campaign, he had matched Rooney's 23 goals and earned £500 off Ferguson after the manager had earlier struck a bet that he would not make it to 15. In 2007 Cristiano Ronaldo was unstoppable: his power and skill left opponents bedevilled and, in some sick cases, angry and seeking vengeance. Michael Ball being a prime example as he left his studs imprinted on Ronny's chest after he was given an almighty runaround in the Manchester derby. In what appeared true karmic retribution, Ronaldo would convert a penalty to win the game for United – after he had been tripped by Ball. A stuttering run-up and he sent Andreas Isaksson the wrong way from the spot to score what was a landmark goal – his 50th for United.

It was clear how much of an impact Ronny had made during the season when motormouth and fellow Portuguese Jose Mourinho turned his guns on him. Mourinho had been a breath of fresh air in his first two seasons in the English game but by 2007 he was becoming a tiresome sideshow; a parody of himself as he commented on about everyone and everything else. Injuries, backroom unrest, United getting penalties they didn't deserve … Mourinho's scattergun moans became both dull and predictable.

Then, in a sign that he was clearly ruffled by United's renaissance, his comments also became personal. It showed how Ronaldo had got under his skin when he called him a 'liar' after the winger disputed his claim that penalties were never awarded against United. Then he would sneeeringly add a below-the-belt comment: 'Maybe it's about a difficult childhood, no education.' It was out of order: Mourinho, a product of a comfortable middle-class uprbinging in the Portuguese city of Setubal was having a dig at a boy who had had it tough; who had to battle from poverty to get where he was.

Sir Alex Ferguson would put Mourinho in his place with a perceptive, withering response, 'Just because you come from a poor, working-class background does not mean to say you are not educated. What Ronaldo has are principles, that is why he has not responded to it. Other people are educated but have no principles.'

Quite. The point beneath the point-scoring was that Ronaldo had irritated his countryman. His form had taken United to the top of the Premiership – a position they would then not abdicate for the rest of the season. It served to show how well Ronny had done that season but my sources tell me there was another element to the distasteful row.

Mourinho, in a season that would bring only the consolation prizes of the Carling and FA Cups, might end up looking for pastures new like Real Madrid. Once upon a time he had been an assistant to Bobby Robson at Barcelona, but the fans and suits had continually dubbed him 'the translator', belittling his achievements with the moniker even when he took Chelsea to two Premiership titles and beat them in the Champions League.

Any love between him and Barca had long gone: would he have the chance to take them on from Madrid and show them he was no longer a nobody by destroying their monopoly of Spanish football from a new position of strength in the Santiago Bernabeu?

Ronaldo – after weeks of speculation – signed a new deal at United on Friday 13 April 2007. Ronaldo's deal saw him agree terms on a new five-year contract at Old Trafford. The £119,000-a-week deal was set up to keep him at the club until at least June 2012 – when he would be 27. United were hopeful it would now put to bed the still constant rumours linking him with Real and Barcelona. United boss Sir Alex Ferguson breathed a sigh of relief as he said, 'It is fantastic news, it emphasises the point that Cristiano is happy here and that he is at the right club. At 22 he has the same skill factor as Maradona or Pele. He has a great relationship with the team, staff and the fans and he will go on to be one of Manchester United's great players.'

Days earlier it had been reported that the player's agent –

who is, intriguingly, Jorge Mendes, who also reprsents Mourinho – had held talks with Madrid. But Ronaldo said: 'I am delighted. I spoke with Sir Alex and [chief executive] David Gill about my future and everyone knew that I wanted to stay. I believe I am at the right club. The spirit is amazing and I am very happy at the club and I want to win trophies and hopefully we will do that this season.' Which , of course, they did – with the welcome return of the Premiership title. Although disappointed by the loss in the Champions League to Milan in the semis, and Chelsea in the FA Cup final, Ronny would later claim that it was the Premiership winner's medal he most craved. He said, 'It was the big priority. We worked so hard to get it … it was our main aim at the start of the season.'

Ronaldo was humble enough to admit that the title success was not down to him alone – that he owed a debt of gratitude to the men alongside him. He said: 'Every season I try to improve and I have learned a lot this season, but I think playing alongside great players like Giggsy, Scholesy and Wayne has made me a better player. This season I am more consistent and I understand the game a lot better, which comes with experience. I am only 22 but I feel much more mature now.'

The winger also paid tribute to Ferguson and his assistant Queiroz. Ronaldo said, 'The boss and Carlos have been great with me. It is good to have Carlos here because he speaks my language. But Sir Alex always supports me, too. I always want to express myself on the pitch and he gives me the opportunity and encouragement to do that.'

At the end of May 2007, I was told by a reliable source at Old Trafford that Queiroz had unexpectedly now jumped to the top of the queue as the man most likely to replace Ferguson when the Scot eventually moved aside. The board saw Roy Keane as eventually becoming the new Ferguson: the man who would build his own long-time managerial dynasty, but would only arrive after Queiroz had been given his chance. The reason for Quieroz's elevation in esteem was twofold: he was a nice bloke, someone the board could enjoy a pleasant chat with over a glass of port and some stilton but, more importantly, the suits saw him as the man who could keep Ronaldo at United.

Carlos would survive as long as he had the ear of the brilliant winger. And, luckily for him, Ronny adored him – many at United comment on the way Quieroz has become a surrogate father to the boy. So there you have it … Keano must await the departure of the new boy wonder before he can begin his own gloriously anticipated return to Old Trafford.

Ronaldo also admitted that the freedom given to him by Ferguson and Queiroz to express himself had been a vital facet in his development as a world-class player in 2007. But, like Cantona before him, he also stressed the need for long hours of practice to perfect the skills he had been given. He said, 'I was born with skills and tricks but I have to work very hard in training every day to try to improve. I try new things in training. I work on lots of things because that is the only way you can become the best, by working hard.'

Ten days after signing his new deal, Ronaldo became the first player in 30 years to pick up the two main PFA awards in London. He was voted Player of the Year and Young Player of the Year by his fellow professionals. No player had received both awards since Aston Villa and Scotland striker Andy Gray in 1977.

Ronny beat Chelsea striker Didier Drogba to the award, with United's former England midfielder Paul Scholes in third place. Ryan Giggs and the previous year's winner, Steven Gerrard, also made the shortlist, alongside 19-year-old Arsenal midfielder Cesc Fabregas.

Ronaldo said, 'It is a special night. It is amazing and a big honour for me to win trophies like this in the Premier League. I am very proud. My colleagues have voted for me and that is fantastic because the players know the qualities of players. I want to keep working hard and getting better because these trophies have given me more motivation.'

Sir Alex Ferguson was also honoured – with the PFA Special Merit Award – and he used his speech to pay yet another tribute to his winger, saying, 'I think he is the best player in the world and his season has been incredible.'

The tributes also flowed when Ronny subsequently won the Football Writers' Association Footballer of the Year award. 'Cristiano was a runaway winner, and deservedly so,' said Paul Hetherington, chairman of the FWA. His United team-mates Ryan Giggs and Paul Scholes were third and fourth respectively in the vote and Hetherington added, 'After the events of last summer at the World Cup, the vote of the Football Writers' Association shows that what we are all interested in is honouring the best player in the country. There has been no agendas carried over from last summer.'

Yet some writers would continue to belittle Ronaldo's achievements, arguing that he was 'a bottler' and that he could not hack it in the really big games. They would use the losses against AC Milan in the Champions League semi-final, and Chelsea in the FA Cup final as the basis of their arguments – although my view of it was that both matches came at a time when the boy was exhausted. Both were a match too far at the time. Also, in both games there is a fair argument that Ferguson got his tactics wrong. In both, United reverted to the dreaded 4-5-1 with Rooney upfront alone and Ronny suffocating in a congested midfield. Again and again in big games like this Ferguson was surely the man who should be accused of 'bottling it'? United are best when at their most expressive – when they press forwards with a passion.

When they play their own uninhibited brand of attacking football rather than trying to copy Chelsea and contain the opposition. When they worry about their own game rather than their opponents' they are usually unstoppable – as best exemplified in the 7-1 Champions League destruction of Roma. Then, Ferguson, gave his team free reign from a platform of 4-4-2 with Smith upfront and Ronaldo and Rooney swinging in from the holes behind him. So why the panic, and the more defensive approach in Milan and at the new Wembley?

The normally incisive James Lawton typified the chorus of disapproval against Ronaldo when writing in the *Belfast Telegraph* after the FA Cup disappointment. He wrote, 'Great players – and Ronaldo has already been categorised as such even to the point of being compared to Pele and George Best – embrace such games as Saturday's because they are the purpose of their lives. Cutting it against some of the Premiership's mediocrities is one thing; taking hold of the big stage, and the toughest opponents in the land, should be a progressively routine test of players who announce they are going to be remembered through the football ages.

'Now those who so enthusiastically announced that Ronaldo had already arrived on such a plane surely have enough evidence to think again; to think mostly, that is, of the criteria of performance which separates in the all-time ratings those of the outstanding natural gifts with which Ronaldo undoubtedly has been bombarded and the others who also have the nerve and the vision to make them work under the greatest pressure.

'It is in the second category that we find the Bests and the Peles. It is the first where Ronaldo remains anchored by his failure to confidently negotiate the end of a season in which he had received unprecedently lavish acclaim.'

It was harsh rhetoric. It came a few days after Eric Cantona had offered an altogether different view of the man who now wore his No 7 shirt at United. Eric had this to say about Ronaldo, 'Last season he did not score any goals. We had the impression he did not care. Something was missing. Now he scores and he is a new player. World class. One of the ten best players on the planet. In modern football, playing as a team is very important, but we always need that kind of player who is going to strike out, to provoke.'

After the FA Cup final 1-0 loss to Chelsea, Ronaldo was once again protected by his inner circle: his family. Mother Maria and brother Hugo were waiting for him back at the hotel and offered support and consolation. The boy was inconsolable after the defeat, crying in the dressing room. Ferguson and Queiroz told him there would be other occasions to put it right and then his mother and brother helped him over the anguish of defeat at the post-final dinner.

During 2007 more details began to emerge about his family, his upbringing and his early life – and also about the tragic early death of his father, Jose Dinis. It was revealed that Ronny still torments himself about his father's death, believing he could have done more to save him from the alcoholism that blighted his life. His father suffered a chronic liver condition due to heavy drinking and Ronaldo paid for him to have treatment – but to no avail.

Ronaldo also revealed more details about his fear of leaving home at such an early age for Lisbon. He said, 'It was very traumatic to leave my family. I had never been on an aeroplane before. When I saw my mother crying at the airport, it made me want to cry as well. There were a lot of tears in my first few weeks in Lisbon. Madeira is so small. I couldn't believe the traffic and noise of a capital city. About 10 of us lived in a room inside the Sporting Lisbon stadium.

'In the beginning, nobody could understand me because of my accent and I couldn't understand them. I used to call my family whenever I could. I remember buying phone cards and looking at the units go down as I spoke to my parents and brothers and sisters.'

Ronaldo, speaking in a TV documentary called *Planeta Ronaldo* that was aired in Portugal during FA Cup final week, also spoke about his debt to his family for their constant support. He said, 'My mother was a cook who worked hard all her life. The first thing I did after signing for United was to call her and say she didn't have to work ever again.'

In turn, his family adore him and are fiercely protective of him. His sister Katia revealed a little more about their lives, saying, 'He is an amazing brother. He calls his family every day and about 30 of us spend Christmas with him in Manchester. Growing up in Madeira, we had a comfortable home, but it wasn't big. Cristiano shared a bedroom with Hugo and the two girls shared another bedroom. Now there is plenty of room for everyone, sometimes too much room! Cristiano bought me a watch last Christmas but I find it difficult to buy him things because he has them already. He likes simple family presents really, so last time I got him a framed picture of my six-year-old son Rodrigo. He is a very proud uncle.'

While Katia is making a name for herself as a pop star in Portugal – under the name of Ronalda – elder sister Elma is cashing in on Ronny's name, much to his delight. She has opened a clothes shop in Madeira called CR7, a reference, of course, to the player's initials and shirt number at United. Brother Hugo, who is also close to Ronaldo, plays lower division football in Madeira but travels to Manchester as much as he can. He was instrumental in persuading Cristiano to stay at Old Trafford after the World Cup furore surrounding him and Rooney.

Hugo said, 'Me and the family always told him to stay in Manchester, that this would be a passing thing. He feels good in Manchester and it was too early to make the step to one of the Spanish clubs. At the beginning he was a little bit afraid of the situation but once the season started and he was playing he didn't think about it again. We told him, "When the people are whistling at you, that's a signal that you are the best player on the pitch, so it's better for you if they whistle – it's a compliment."'

Cristiano repaid his brother's love by helping him avoid a similarly early death like his father – this time from drugs . In an interview in April 2007, Cristiano's mother Maria said, 'Cristiano has seen what drink and drugs can do to people close to him and it's part of the reason why he has become who he is today. What has happened to our family explains why Cristiano doesn't smoke and he doesn't drink. His only addiction is football. His father drank himself into an early grave which left Cristiano devastated. He would have loved him to still be around to see the player he is today. It's very sad.

'I paid to send Hugo away to a specialist clinic for treatment. I was working as a cleaner then only earning £400 a month and I had to take out a loan.'

In the interview, Maria told the *Sunday Mirror* that Hugo failed to stay clean and two years later needed a second course of treatment. She said, 'Cristiano was 16 then. He was earning more and paid for his brother's treatment. There's no doubt his money helped to save Hugo.'

In May 2007 it was rumoured that his family were keeping a

close eye on him with his new girlfriend – 22-year-old *Hollyoaks* 'star' Gemma Atkinson. Of course, they would not talk about it – they will go to any lengths to protect his privacy, and Ronaldo himself declined to comment. It seems he and Gemma had been together in a four-month on-off relationship that was probably not helped (on Ronaldo's side anyway) by Gemma talking to *Loaded* magazine about him. She told the lads' mag that she had ways of keeping him happy. 'I trained as a stripper for *Hollyoaks* so I'm really good. I've got a couple of wicked moves up my sleeve.' She said she knew exactly what she would do if he cheated on her. 'I'd dump him immediately,' she said. 'The best revenge is getting on with life and showing what a good time you're having.'

Ronaldo had other things to think about. He took United to that Premiership title but was too knackered to also propel them to Champions League and FA Cup glory. At the same time, he would again show the caring side of his nature ... making an appeal for help in finding Madeleine McCann, the three-year-old English girl who had been snatched while on holiday with her parents in Portugal's Algarve. Clearly moved, Ronaldo went on Portuguese TV and said, 'I was very upset to hear of the abduction of Madeleine. I appeal to anyone with information to come forward. Please come forward.' It was typical of the boy who had become the new king at Old Trafford. As well as being the best player in Britain, and one of the three best in the world along with Kaka and Ronaldinho, he was a boy with a growing compassion and integrity – the exact opposite of how he had been portrayed after the winking episode following Rooney's sending off in the 2006 World Cup Finals. That boy Ronaldo, as United fans call him, had become a man.

He also had this to say about becoming a No 7 at Old Trafford, 'It is a sacred line – David Beckham, George Best. I am honoured to form part of this list. History will judge if I am worthy. Each one of them was a special player. And ooh, ah, Cantona – he is a great. I admire him. He was a super player and a strong character. When I first put on the red shirt with No 7, I could have been weighed down by this number after the men who wore it. But no, it didn't stop me.'

Ronaldo is the boy who took all the world could throw at him and managed to remain standing and smiling through it all. He is the man who will surely one day be granted the recognition he deserves – as Ronaldinho's successor; as *the* best player in the world in the modern era. As Sir Bobby Charlton said, 'He's a great player and potentially a phenomenally great player. He has the sort of ability, talent, pace and invention that people love. It's why people used to love Stanley Matthews and George Best – because of their footwork and the things they were capable of. Ronaldo's the same. He could be sensational for the next ten years.'

He was certainly sensational as he drove United on in their 2008 title battle with Chelsea and Arsenal – even beating Best's scoring record with another brace in their 2-0 win over Bolton on Wednesday 19 March. The two goals put United three points clear at the top of the Premiership – and took Ronaldo to 33 goals for the season, 24 in the league. That eclipsed the record 32 for a winger, set by Georgie boy back in the 1967-68 season.

But will he stay at United? That, as they say, is the $64,000 question. Will he go in 2012 when his new deal is up, or even earlier?

I do not believe he is as committed to the club's long-term cause in the same way as were, say, the Nevilles, Beckham or Butt. That is inevitable – he is not United born and bred. Despite his fantastic form during the 2006/07 season, he could still be tempted if Barca or Real Madrid came in. I would love to be proved wrong and watch him see out his career at United, but it is a big ask for a boy with no natural allegiance to the club, a boy who once admitted he would love to play at the Bernabeu.

Yet if he does stay at Old Trafford, and is allowed to play, to simply get on with his normal game, he has enough talent to be up there as the best of the lot – yes, the ultimate king of Manchester United's Magnificent Sevens....

Acknowledgements

George Best
Michael Parkinson
Brian Glanville
Arsène Wenger
Tommy Docherty
Sir Alex Ferguson
Ian Wooldridge, the *Daily Mail*
Sandy Best
Alex Best
Tommy Gemmell
Alex Butler and the *Sunday Times*
Angie Best
Blessed: The Autobiography, George Best (Ebury Press, 2002)
Bestie: A Portrait of a Legend, Joe Lovejoy (Pan books, 1999)
George Best: The Good, the Bad and the Bubbly,
Ross Benson (Pan, 1991)
Manchester Evening News
BBC Sport

Jimmy Greaves
Euan Ferguson, the *Observer*
Bill W, Dr Bob, Alcoholics Anonymous

Bryan Robson
Bryan Robson
Arnold Mühren
James Lawton
My Memories of Manchester United, Norman Whiteside
    (Britespot Publishing, 2003)
Ooh! Aah! Paul McGrath: The Black Pearl of Inchicore,
    Paul McGrath (Mainstream Publishing, 1994)
Robbo: My Autobiography, Bryan Robson
    (Hodder & Stoughton, 2006)
Dave Morgan
Nick Chapman
Hugh Sleight, Editor of *FourFourTwo* magazine
Mike Tuck

Eric Cantona
Eric Cantona
Michel Platini
Eric Cantona, FourFourTwo Great Footballers, Rob Wightman
    (Virgin Books, 2004)
Hughsie, Mark Hughes (Mainstream Publishing, 1994)
Howard Wilkinson
Dave and www.mightyleeds.co.uk
Brian Oliver
Jimmy Greaves
Alan Wilkie
The *Guardian*
The *Observer*

ACKNOWLEDGEMENTS

Richard Williams
Red Issue
Alan Smith
Kevin Bowring
Iain Dowie
Alex Paylor
Duleep Allirajah
The University of Stirling
TF1 France
Cantona on Cantona by Eric Cantona and Alex Finn
  (Andre Deutsch, 1996)
Zinedine Zidane
Tony Parsons, *Daily Mirror*
Cantona Speaks (video)
Rolland Courbis
Guy Roux
Steve Curry
The *Daily Mail*
Cantona: The Red and the Black, Ian Ridley (Gollancz, 1995)
Glenn Hoddle
Matthew Norman
Dylan Jones
The *Mail on Sunday*

David Beckham
David and Victoria Beckham
Eric Harrison
Ted Beckham
Nick Chapman
Lee Clayton and the *Daily Mail*
Steve McClaren
Chris Casper

Gary Peters

Glenn Hoddle

Ian McGarry

My Side – The Autobiography, David Beckham
(HarperCollinsWillow, 2004)

My World, David Beckham (Hodder & Stoughton, 2001)

Cristiano Ronaldo

Cristiano and Maria Ronaldo

'Big Phil' Scolari

Sir Bobby Robson

Sir Alex Ferguson

Arsène Wenger

Antonio Mendosa

Luis Figo

Octavio Machado

Roy Keane

Wayne Rooney

My Story So Far, Wayne Rooney (HarperSport, 2006)

Rooney: Wayne's World, Frank Worrall
  (Mainstream Publishing, 2006)

Ian Dovaston and Sky News

José Mourinho

Cristiano Ronaldo, Michael O'Connell (Artnik, 2006)

Henry Winter, the *Daily Telegraph*

Jeff Powell, the